THE SUCCESSFUL
INVESTOR

Robin Duthy

THE SUCCESSFUL INVESTOR

A Guide to
Art, Gold, Wine, Antiques
and
Other Growth Markets

COLLINS
8 Grafton Street · London W1

TO MY FAMILY

William Collins Sons & Co. Ltd
London · Glasgow · Sydney · Auckland · Toronto
Johannesburg

ISBN 0 00 217534 7

First published in 1986

Design and typography by Tony Fahy

Duthy, Robin
  The successful investor: a guide to art,
  gold, wine, antiques and other growth
  markets.
  1. Investments
  I. Title
  332.6   HG4521

Typeset by Ace Filmsetting Ltd, Frome
Origination by Gilchrist Bros. Ltd, Leeds
Printed in Great Britain by
Butler & Tanner Ltd, Frome and London

CONTENTS

ACKNOWLEDGEMENTS

I AM GRATEFUL to Christie's and Sotheby's for providing the great majority of the illustrations for this book. I am also indebted to many Christie's experts for their views of the market and for their help in arriving at estimates of value over a number of years. My thanks are also due to Phillips, Glendining's and Bonham's for similar help.

The illustrations on pages 39 and 40 are reproduced by permission of the Trustees of the Wallace Collection.

I acknowledge my debt to the annual series Art Sales Index edited by Richard Hislop which provided the raw material for the art indexes, and to Gerald Reitlinger's trilogy *The Economics of Taste* which provided useful information on art prices and fashions prior to 1970; also to the Martin Gordon Print Price Annual from which the print indexes were compiled; to the Diamond High Council in Antwerp for permission to reproduce their diamond index (adapted); to *The Coin Dealer Newsletter*, Hollywood, California, for the prices from which the US Coin Index is compiled; and to *Linn's Stamp News*, Sidney, Ohio, for permission to reproduce their US Stamp Index (adapted).

I am also grateful to Judith Banister, Rosemary George, Robson Lowe, Martyn Marriott, Peter Mitchell and Anthony Rota for reading parts of the manuscript and for their helpful suggestions. I would also like to record my thanks to the many authors whose works are listed in each section under Further Reading for their stimulating ideas.

INTRODUCTION

PAINTINGS, FURNITURE, silver, wine and most other investments covered in this book have been rising in value fast. But how fast? Will the growth rates of recent years be sustained? Or will they accelerate? What are the market forces at work in each field? And what are the hazards facing first-time buyers? These are some of the questions this book sets out to answer.

Many people have a large part of their wealth tied up in assets they do not think of as investments. Yet over the last twenty years these assets have mostly risen faster than the world's stock markets. Their potential for continued growth is clearly recognized and, increasingly, investors are switching money into these more promising areas.

None of the investments considered here produces income, so any change in their monetary value comes about through a change in the market's view of their aesthetic, historic, functional or some other value. Buyers are influenced too by the marketability of the objects themselves. They are affected by what critics and art historians write, by exhibitions they see and by what dealers choose to stock. They are also impressed by the track record of each investment field and by their own and other people's expectations of its future performance.

Their attitudes have been altered too by the widening acceptance of art objects as a field for investment. They recognize that to admire and enjoy a painting is quite compatible with buying it because it promises to be a sound investment. Though buying art in Britain is still felt by many to be an elitist activity, things are changing. Increased television coverage of the arts and a growing number of publications and exhibitions have enabled more people to work out their feelings towards art and encouraged many of them to go out and buy something for themselves.

The text of each chapter assesses the status and stability of one particular market, and the indexes that follow monitor the changes in value since 1975. The same criteria that are used to evaluate conventional investments – namely, liquidity, security and return – can be used for paintings, antiques and so on.

All the investments discussed here, with the exception of gold, are less liquid than ordinary shares and gilts which can be turned into cash in a matter of days. Works of art can, of course, be sold to a dealer for cash, though in the nature of things, owners prefer to sound out several buyers before agreeing a price – a process that can take several weeks.

To attract business, salerooms will now usually pay, if requested, 50% of the agreed reserve price to sellers as soon as the object is consigned, the balance becoming payable within four weeks of sale in the ordinary way. Furthermore, banks are often willing nowadays to accept works of art as collateral for loans, and, under a scheme pioneered by Sotheby's, part of their value may be counted as personal wealth for the purposes of Lloyds membership.

Security in the context of works of art is to do with authenticity. In other words, is the Picasso painting I propose to buy really by Picasso? Although journalists always seize upon stories of forgery in the art world, 95% of the deals done in the art and related markets involve objects about whose genuineness there need be no doubt. Investors should steer clear of the more controversial areas of painting, though with the growing publication of definitive listings of individual artist's work – usually by the leading authority on the subject – buying is becoming safer all the time.

If security in the context of investment has anything to do with stability, it is worth noting that an Old Master painting cannot cut its dividend, nor can it overtrade and go bankrupt. Equities and indeed all income-bearing investments share an inherent instability based on the possibility that they may one day cease to produce income.

The return from an investment is defined as income or capital gain or both. Readers may compare the performance of each sector of the art and other markets with the *FT* 30 Share Index and the Dow Jones Industrial Average (page 238) and also with the former index recalculated to show its performance as if net income had been reinvested. To enable readers to measure the performance of an investment field against inflation, the UK Consumer Price Index (rebased at 1000 in 1975) appears in the form of a narrow bar alongside each index. The figures from which the in-

dexes are calculated are auction-room 'hammer' prices and therefore ignore the costs of buying and selling. At most auction houses selling commission is 10% and a premium of 10% is payable by the buyer. Charges for illustration in a catalogue and insurance over the selling period plus VAT bring the in-and-out expenses of a saleroom investment to around 30%.

All successful investment depends on paying and receiving a fair market price. But the true market value of a unique object such as a painting is not easy to establish. A watercolour by Turner may change hands unrecognized at a flea market for £50; for £5000 at a provincial auction, and perhaps for £25,000 at a major London auction. It all depends on who recognizes its authorship and value. And though it is potentially tough on the seller, using expertise to buy advantageously in the saleroom is regarded as fair dealing.

At its best the public auction provides the fairest way of determining a market price. Regrettably though, malpractices in certain salerooms are rife. There are signs of a crackdown both in Britain and in the United States, but illegal bidding rings are proving hard to stamp out. Auctioneers have been known to collude with ring members – or at least fail to establish a high enough reserve to protect the sellers for whom they claim to act. For all that, investors should aim to buy at auction even if it means paying a 10% commission to a dealer to do the bidding for them. For dealers still tend to look upon the salerooms as their wholesale suppliers and retail mark-ups of 100% and more are common.

Dealers for their part argue that auctioneers put over-flattering descriptions on the objects they sell; that they ignore restoration and damage; that they shelter behind the general disclaimer on authenticity printed at the front of most catalogues, and that they manipulate prices by taking bids from phantom bidders even after the reserve has been reached.

A lot of mud has been slung at auctioneers by dealers and *vice versa* and outsiders sometimes imagine the art world to be one great minefield. There will always be dealers and auctioneers who don't run quite straight but at the same time there is no shortage of sound professional firms to deal with.

Taxation

The investments analysed here enjoy two major advantages over conventional investments under the present tax system. First, thanks to the so-called 'chattels exemption', any object disposed of for less than £3000 (after expenses) is free of Capital Gains Tax, regardless of the size of the gain. Furthermore, there is no limit to the number of tax-free disposals a taxpayer may make in any one year. Thus, if you were to realise £30,000 worth of silver, furniture and wine in the course of a tax year and your total net gain was £25,000, there would be no tax to pay provided each individual item fetched less than £3000. Under current rules anyone realising a £25,000 gain on ordinary shares would be liable – ignoring indexation allowances – to pay Gains Tax of £5600, that is, 30% of the £25,000 gain after deducting allowable gains of £6300.

The full value of all assets discussed in this book is assessable for Inheritance Tax purposes. What is the full value? In practice, market values cannot be precisely determined. A painting that carries an auction estimate of £2000 to £3000 could well make £5000 on a good day. Since a wide range of valuations for each object is tenable tax inspectors will be inclined, or at least think it fairer, to accept a valuation for probate or lifetime transfer towards the lower end of the range. This can result in a considerable tax saving for the donor. The value of quoted securities on the other hand is easily ascertained from the Stock Exchange Official List and taxation on their full value is always payable.

Insurance

Insurance is an additional cost investors in these assets have to bear. The premiums to cover full replacement value vary according to the location and circumstances in which the assets are held. Premiums for diamonds, silver and gold will normally be higher than for paintings, furniture and ordinary household effects. Rates vary too between town and country, between one town and another and between one insurance company and another. So investors must shop around for quotations but should expect to pay a rate, depending on circumstances, of between 0.2% and 0.5% for cover against fire and theft.

Illustrations

Most of the illustrations are of objects that have been sold at auction over the last two years. In these cases the hammer price is given in the caption; in other cases their auction market value is estimated.

The Indexes

The indexes are shown on a logarithmic scale. Details of the components

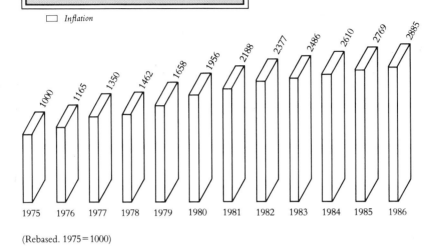

UK CONSUMER PRICE INDEX

□ Inflation

1000 · 1165 · 1350 · 1462 · 1658 · 1956 · 2188 · 2377 · 2486 · 2610 · 2769 · 2885

1975 1976 1977 1978 1979 1980 1981 1982 1983 1984 1985 1986

(Rebased. 1975 = 1000)

are given below each index. Where the base period is 1973–7, 'sleeper' bars of 1000 are given for 1976 and 1977, as well as for 1975, for stylistic reasons.

Paintings

The 1975 base figure for each artist is the average price of the central 80% of the paintings and watercolours by that artist sold during the 1973/4, 1974/5 and 1975/6 auction seasons, as reported in the annual Art Sales Index. The exclusion of the top and bottom deciles removes from the sample exceptional prices for exceptional works and other potentially distorting factors.

Certain artists are grouped together into schools of painting and their collective performance is shown in the form of a bar chart. The figures are based on the mid-market price calculated as above for each artist in each year up to 1985. The artists in each index are given equal weighting in the base year. Where too few examples of an artist's work were sold

in any one year, the calculations have been based on a series of overlapping pairs of years. Though the base as calculated includes sales that occurred in 1976, a figure for 1976, based on an assumption of steady change between 1975 and 1977, has been interpolated for stylistic reasons.

The performance figures for individual artists are based on sales occurring during the 1984/5 auction season. The 1986 figure given in the bar charts for groups of artists and for furniture, silver and all other sectors is a forecast for the year, taking into account, where possible, market prices recorded up to the end of April 1986. The method, worked out with the help of the late Professor Sir Roy Allen, is the most accurate and reliable index of the art market yet published.

Prints

The central 80% of all prints by each artist listed as sold in the Martin Gordon Print Price Annual from 1977 to 1985 forms the basis of the print indexes. No splicing of Martin

Gordon with the less comprehensive listing of print sales in 1975 and 1976 that appeared in Meyer's International Auction Records has proved possible. However, after careful study of both sources for the overlapping years, an annual growth rate of 10% in dollar terms between 1975 and 1977 for each artist has been assumed.

Porcelain, furniture and silver

The indexes for these sectors are all based on the so-called basket method whereby a selection of actual objects sold at auction in 1975 forms the basis of the index and estimates of their values in subsequent years are made in the light of prices being paid for comparable material passing through the salerooms. A number of experts from Christie's have kindly helped me in the preparation of these figures. Their estimates have in some cases been reconciled with the evolution of prices suggested by a careful analysis of the annual price-lists published by the Antique Collectors Club. The final figures are a sound indicator of movements in each market but should be regarded as more tentative than those given for other sectors.

Gold

The average annual price of gold in US dollars per ounce from 1975 to 1986 is shown in list form. A further index, taking the average price of gold over the 1974–6 period – $148.3 – as its base, is shown as a bar chart.

Stamps

The GB stamp index is based on a 'basket' of stamps sold at auction in 1975. Estimates of auction values in subsequent years have been given by Harmers of London Stamp Auctioneers. The US stamp index is based on the figures used by Linn's Stamp News in their monthly index, rebased at 1000 in 1975 and converted into sterling at the yearly average exchange rates.

Coins

The ancient Greek and Roman coin index is based on a selection of coins sold in 1975. Estimates of auction values in subsequent years have been arrived at with the help of Christie's. The English coin index is based on values given in Seaby's Standard Catalogue of British Coins, modified by evidence from auctions.

The American coin index is based on values given in The Coin Dealer Newsletter, the leading price-guide in its field, converted into sterling at the yearly average exchange rates.

Wine

The Bordeaux, champagne and port indexes are based on the middle prices of the range of prices recorded at auction in the course of the year for a number of wines in each category.

Diamonds

The index of investment diamond prices is adapted from the index compiled by the Diamond High Council in Antwerp, published monthly in L'Echo de la Bourse, and is based on dealer-to-dealer prices for the twenty-five highest-graded 1 carat stones. The index is based in dollars – that being the currency in which diamonds are primarily traded.

RIGHT *Jan Josefsz. van Goyen (1596–1665)*: '*Fishermen raising lobster pots in an estuary*' *(1654), £110,000.*

PICTORIAL AND
GRAPHIC ART

17th Century Dutch and Flemish Painting

The 17th century has been recognized as the golden age of Dutch and Flemish painting for over two hundred years. Market prices have broadly reflected that view since the 18th century, although it took longer for the worth of certain artists – including Rembrandt and Vermeer – to be appreciated. Jan Steen and David Teniers the Younger, for example, were among the most expensive of all artists in the late 18th century. Prices for Dutch School paintings reached a new peak in the 1910s but dropped sharply in the 1930s. Between 1950 and 1975 prices rose 1500% or nearly 12% a year. Since 1975 the increase has been 270%, suggesting a slight acceleration to an annual $12\frac{1}{2}$%.

Comparing value for money between schools of painting is a personal business, though many buyers now recognize that £10,000 spent on a fine van Goyen or Teniers is a better buy than a trifling and even hamfisted sketch by Renoir at £20,000.

Much of the money being spent on art goes into early 20th century and contemporary painting, and young collectors are inclined to go after something new rather than buy the works that were in vogue ten generations ago. Paintings by many of the

ABOVE *Jan Steen (1623–79): 'A country inn with skittle players, onlookers and travellers', £10,000*

BELOW LEFT *Adriaen Jansz. van Ostade (1610–84): 'A woman seated holding a child on her lap' (1652), £60,000.*

BELOW RIGHT *Joost Cornelisz. Droochsloot (1586–1666): 'A village with beggars receiving alms outside a church' (1654), £20,000.*

BOTTOM *Pieter Brueghel the Younger (1564–1637): 'St John the Baptist preaching in the Wilderness', £55,000.*

OPPOSITE *Adam Willaerts (1577–1669): 'A coastal scene with fishermen and huntsmen on the shore', £24,000.*

greatest Dutch and Flemish artists are in any case unobtainable. Yet, even if works by Rembrandt, Hobbema, Steen, de Hooch and Vermeer are seldom seen in the market, there are dozens of second division artists whose paintings are both affordable and available. The surge in prices over 1985 and 1986 may not be sustained but at least the intrinsic excellence of the painting should underwrite steady growth in the future.

The great flowering of art in the Netherlands in the 17th century occurred during a period of unprecedented prosperity. The connection at one level is natural: artists can expect to sell their work more easily when there is more money around. Yet increased prosperity does not explain the dramatic rise in the quality of the painting. The spirit of innovation in the field of art no doubt draws strength from the greater confidence that is felt at a national level. Several factors combined to create the right conditions for this change, though the precise origin and cause are buried in the character of the people.

Within the Dutch-Flemish index, the six artists specializing in scenes of carousing peasants have risen by an average of 225% since 1975 – slightly more than the index has as a whole. They are Pieter Brueghel the Younger (+370%), Jan Miense Molenaer (+80%), Egbert van Heemskerk (+140%), Joost Cornelis Droochsloot (+50%), Adriaen van Ostade (+280%) and David Teniers the Younger (+430%). The exceptional rise in Teniers can be explained as part of a long-delayed catching-up process. Teniers, who said he covered three leagues of canvas in his lifetime, died a very rich man in 1690. There has never been a shortage of his work on the market and prices hovered between £1000 and £2000 during the 150 years to 1960. The mid-market price for Teniers has now risen to over £15,000, putting him among the highest-rated Dutch artists in the index. In the case of van Ostade too, some element of catching up is present – the going rate for his work having barely moved between 1860 and 1960.

The disappointing record of the Dutch-Flemish School between 1975 and 1984 is all the more surprising considering the remarkable technical quality of the paintings. A guild system operated in the Netherlands in the 17th century whereby an apprentice was required to serve four to six years with an established master. At the end of that period he would submit a painting (his masterpiece) to the guild. If this was approved the apprentice might then call himself a master and sell paintings signed with his own name.

It was a time when the love of paintings extended right across the social spectrum. An English traveller to Amsterdam in 1640 noted that everyone liked to adorn their houses with paintings. Butchers and bakers had them in their shops and '. . . yea many tymes blacksmithes, Coblers etts., will have some picture or other by their Forge and in their stalle. Such is the generall Notion, enclination and delight that these Countrie Native[s] have to Paintings'.

Many of the buyers would have been exacting clients. Those who bought marine paintings, for instance, might well have had a professional interest in the sea. For the Dutch dominated the corn-carrying trade round Europe and were in business everywhere through their East India Company and its counterpart in the West. Apart from providing a livelihood for those who sailed on it in the course of trade, the sea supplied the herring which was the Dutchman's staple diet. For these reasons marine paintings had a special importance for the Dutch. Those with first-hand knowledge of the sea would have been quick to spot any mistake in the painting of the rigging or ordnance and they would have been looking at the movement of the

waves, the strength of the wind and sun and the colour of the sky.

Dutch marine artists therefore painted with great precision. Though this sometimes results in a virtuoso performance, it never interferes with the overall balance and effect of the composition. Surprisingly, the group of marine artists in the index have managed a rise of only 170% since 1975. Jan van Goyen, the most expensive of them with a mid-market price of £26,700, is up just 150%; Abraham Storck has risen 330%, while Ludolf Bakhuyzen is up only 25%.

The excellence of Dutch and Flemish flower and still-life painting and its popularity today explains the 300% rise in the five artists forming this part of the index. Frans Snyders has risen 350%; Pieter Casteels is up 100%; Jan van Kessel 210%; Roelandt Savery 460%; and Cornelisz. de Heem 360%.

The landscape painters in the index have put up a mixed performance. Most of Philips Wouwerman's work, which was fetching £500 to £2000 even in Regency times, now sells for between £2000 and £10,000 and put on 100% since 1975. Thomas Heeremans is up 140%, Jan Frans van Bloemen up 130% and Abraham Begeyn up 130%. Of the two great Ruysdaels, Salomon has risen 500%, while his nephew Jacob has put on 210%.

Over the next ten years the Dutch-

OPPOSITE *Frans Snyders (1579–1657): 'Fruit in a basket, with game on a table', £6400.*

ABOVE *Salomon Jacobsz. van Ruysdael (1600–70): 'A wooded river landscape with a peasant couple in a rowing boat', £230,000.*

RIGHT *Joos de Momper (1564–1635): 'A winter landscape with figures on a road by a village', £50,000.*

BELOW RIGHT *Philips Wouwerman (1619–68): 'Labourers loading peat on to a waggon', £22,000.*

BELOW *Jacob van Ruysdael (1628–82): 'A wooded landscape with a waterfall', £230,000.*

BOTTOM RIGHT *Salomon van Ruysdael (1600–70): 'A wooded river landscape with a ferry' (1665), £175,000.*

ABOVE *Jan Griffier the Elder (17th–18th century):* *'Extensive mountainous river landscape with peasants merrymaking outside the inn', £48,000.*

BELOW *Jan Brueghel the Elder (1568–1625): 'A coastal landscape with fishermen unloading their catch' (1607), £240,000.*

BOTTOM LEFT *Abraham Jansz. van Beyeren (1620–75): 'An estuary with fishermen in a rowing boat and smalschips tacking out to sea', £14,000.*

BELOW RIGHT *Abraham Jansz. Storck (1635–1710): 'The River Ij, Amsterdam, in breezy weather', £21,000.*

BOTTOM RIGHT *Philips Wouwerman (1619–68): 'A Market Scene', £35,000.*

Flemish School is unlikely to grow at less than 10% annually. Performances will continue to be mixed; some artists that have underperformed significantly since 1975 may catch up, but the highest rates of growth will be achieved by the leading artists in each field.

TOP LEFT *David Teniers the Younger (1610–90):* '*A peasant smoking in an inn*', £15,000.

ABOVE LEFT *Jan van Kessel (1626–79):* '*An allegory of water: a sea nymph by a reedy shore with fish, shells, etc.*', £10,000.

ABOVE RIGHT *Nicolaes Maes (1632–93):* '*Boy in a landscape with a finch and a spaniel*', £15,000.

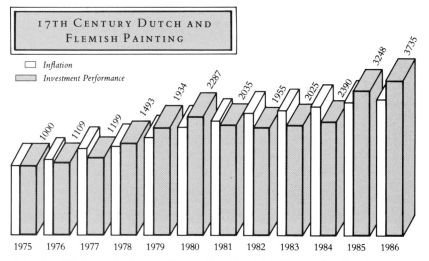

17TH CENTURY DUTCH AND FLEMISH PAINTING

☐ Inflation
▨ Investment Performance

1000 1109 1199 1493 1934 2287 2035 1955 2025 2390 3248 3735

1975 1976 1977 1978 1979 1980 1981 1982 1983 1984 1985 1986

Artists: Ludolf Bakhuyzen, Jan Frans van Bloemen, Pieter Brueghel the Younger, Joost Cornelisz. Droochsloot, Frans Francken II, Jan van Goyen, Egbert van Heemskerk, Thomas Heeremans, Jan van Kessel, Nicolaes Maes, Jan Miensze Molenaer, Aert van der Neer, Adriaen van Ostade, Salomon van Ruysdael, Abraham Storck, David Teniers the Younger

Artist	Mid-market price £	Change since 1975 %
Ludolf Bakhuyzen (1631–1708)	3500	+25
Abraham van Beyeren (1620–75)	10,100	+190
Jan Frans van Bloemen (1662–1749)	5100	+130
Jan Brueghel the Younger (1610–78)	36,800	+220
Pieter Brueghel the Younger (1564–1637)	117,000	+370
Pieter Casteels (1684–1749)	5700	+100
Joost Cornelisz. Droochsloot (1586–1666)	7600	+50
Frans Francken II (1581–1642)	2700	+40
Jan van Goyen (1595–1665)	26,700	+150
Egbert van Heemskerk (1634–1704)	1800	+140
Thomas Heeremans (fl. 1660–97)	10,900	+140
Jan van Kessel (1626–79)	14,600	+210
Nicolaes Maes (1632–93)	8600	+430
Jan Miensze Molenaer (1610–68)	4000	+80
Pieter Molyn (1595–1661)	4800	+140
Joos de Momper (1564–1635)	15,000	+140
Aert van der Neer (1603–77)	11,600	+100
Adriaen van Ostade (1610–84)	14,300	+280
Jacob van Ruysdael (1628–82)	38,700	+210
Salomon van Ruysdael (1600–70)	102,600	+500
Roelandt Savery (1576–1639)	34,900	+460
Frans Snyders (1579–1657)	16,700	+350
Abraham Storck (1635–1710)	15,800	+330
David Teniers the Younger (1610–90)	15,400	+430
Philips Wouwerman (1619–68)	15,500	+100

Further Reading

Bob Haak, *The Golden Age. Dutch Painting of the 17th Century* (London, 1984)

L. Pyvelde, *Flemish Painting of the 17th Century*: various monographs

Jean Leymarie, *Dutch Painting* (London, 1956)

Walther Bernt, *The Netherlandish Painters of the Seventeenth Century* (London, 1970)

Svetlana Alpers, *The Art of Describing. Dutch Art in the Seventeeth Century* (London, 1973)

Gerrit van Honthorst (1590–1656): 'An Arcadian double portrait of two ladies as shepherdesses', £24,000.

18th Century English School

Until the 19th century Englishmen were, on the whole, willing to buy paintings by their compatriots of themselves, their wives and families, their horses, perhaps their houses, and occasionally shipping scenes. For classical and religious works, landscapes and still lifes, they looked overseas to the Italians, the Dutch and the French.

The great portrait painters of the 18th and 19th centuries have recently proved an excellent investment. Made up of Romney, Reynolds, Gainsborough, Beechey and Hoppner, the index is up 520% since 1975. There have been swings in the market's estimation of these artists, though the revaluation in the last decade looks soundly based.

Between 1910 and 1940 the market was elaborately hyped by Duveen. His American millionaire clients were easily persuaded that these portraits of English aristocrats should be ranked with the greatest of Old Masters and parted with sums that make hardboiled dealers wince even today. Henry Huntington is said to have paid £148,000 in 1921 (equivalent to £2.2 million today) for Gainsborough's *The Blue Boy*, and many a portrait was sold for over £50,000. The Second World War, however, brought the market down with a jolt. Duveen was reputed to have sold Hoppner's *The Tambourine Girl* for £72,000 in 1914, but when the painting appeared at auction in 1944 it fetched only £2500.

The individual performances reveal how each artist is now estimated by the market. One of the fastest rises since 1975 has been registered by Sir Joshua Reynolds with 520%. As President of the Royal Academy, Reynolds had been able to charge 100 to 200 guineas for a portrait in the 1770s and, with Gainsborough, he was rated the best portraitist of his time. Prices for his work rocketed between the wars, then climbed slowly during the 1950s and 1960s. Next come Hoppner with 450% and Raeburn with 490%. Hoppner was the leading English portrait painter after Reynolds died and was able to charge even more than Lawrence, who is now considered the better painter. The collapse of Raeburn's prices in the 1930s was the most dramatic of all and a major revaluation now seems logical. Lawrence had never been considered the equal of Reynolds and Gainsborough, until Andrew Mellon's buying in the 1920s put him theoretically on level terms. With a rise of 590% since 1975 the momentum behind the revaluation is being maintained.

Of the rest, Beechey has added 500% Gainsborough 650% and Romney 210%. Beechey was never quite in the same league as the rest and

Sir Joshua Reynolds (1723–92): 'Miss Theophila Gwatkin', £220,000.

was hardly affected by the hysteria of the 1920s. The comparatively small increase in Romney suggests that he is beginning to be rated about as modestly as he was in the 19th century and even in his own day.

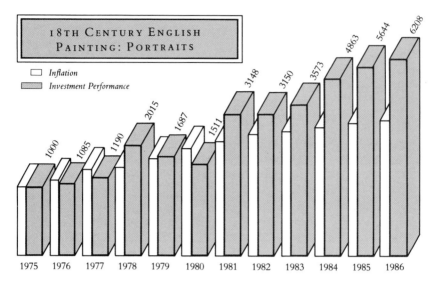

18TH CENTURY ENGLISH PAINTING: PORTRAITS

☐ Inflation
▨ Investment Performance

1000 · 1085 · 1190 · 2015 · 1687 · 1511 · 3148 · 3150 · 3573 · 4863 · 5644 · 6208

1975 1976 1977 1978 1979 1980 1981 1982 1983 1984 1985 1986

Artists: Sir William Beechey, Thomas Gainsborough, John Hoppner, Sir Joshua Reynolds, George Romney

Artist	Mid-market price £	Change since 1975 %
18th Century English Portrait Painters		
Sir William Beechey (*1753–1839*)	2800	+500
Thomas Gainsborough (*1727–88*)	41,000	+650
John Hoppner (*1758–1810*)	6600	+450
Sir Joshua Reynolds (*1723–92*)	13,900	+520
George Romney (*1734–1802*)	7600	+210
Other 18th Century Artists		
William Anderson (*1757–1837*)	2900	+430
John Downman (*1750–1824*)	1800	+460
John Glover (*1767–1849*)	4100	+260
Julius Caesar Ibbetson (*1759–1817*)	2700	+300
William James (*18th century*)	13,900	+220
Sir Thomas Lawrence (*1769–1830*)	15,500	+590
Thomas Luny (*1759–1837*)	3100	+290
Peter Monamy (*1689–1749*)	4900	+220
Alexander Nasmyth (*1758–1840*)	3600	+250
Sir Henry Raeburn (*1756–1823*)	6500	+490
Allan Ramsay (*1713–84*)	2900	+210
John Russell (*1745–1806*)	1500	+360
Charles Towne (*1781–1854*)	6700	+680
Thomas Whitcombe (*1760–1824*)	7200	+170

ABOVE *Julius Caesar Ibbetson (1759–1817): 'A View of the Market at Richmond'*, £4000.

RIGHT *William Anderson (1757–1837): 'Men of War at Spithead' (1794)*, £820.

CENTRE RIGHT *Peter Monamy (1689–1749): 'The Evening Gun, a ketch-rigged royal yacht and other vessels offshore'*, £900.

BELOW LEFT *Thomas Luny (1759–1837): 'The Battle of San Domingo' (1818)*, £7000.

BELOW RIGHT *Thomas Whitcombe (1769–?) 1824): 'An Extensive View of Blackett's Wharf, Limehouse Reach' (1811)*, £13,000.

ABOVE *Julius Caesar Ibbetson (1759–1817): 'A Lake District View', £3400.*

RIGHT *William James (18th century): 'A view of the Grand Canal', £10,500.*

BELOW RIGHT *George Morland (1763–1804): 'A Breezy Day, Freshwater, Isle of Wight', £2600.*

BELOW LEFT *William Hannan (?–1775): 'A View of the Temple of Venus at Stowe', £6600.*

English Sporting Painting

The index of English sporting artists has risen by 440% since 1975. Works by the two highest-rated artists of this school, George Stubbs and Ben Marshall, are sold too seldom to be indexed. Of those in the index John Frederick Herring (Sr), John Nott Sartorius and John Wootton have all risen by 540%; James Ward by 80% and John Ferneley (Sr) by 230%. Subject matter has an important bearing on price. Whereas in 1960 a Herring fox-hunting scene and a Herring racing scene were each worth £1000

to £2000, the racing picture will now be worth twice as much as the other at between £50,000 and £100,000.

The major salerooms now hold specialist sales of sporting paintings in the United States where demand is at least as strong as in the United Kingdom. Museums in America will compete for exceptional works but on both sides of the Atlantic the market is supported by the sportsman-collector.

Throughout the 18th and 19th centuries horse-racing and fox-hunting were the commonest subjects for sporting painters, though paintings of every sport from cricket to cockfighting are known. As prices are now linked to demand from sporting collectors the future popularity of each sport may well determine the course of prices. Any shift in public opinion against a sport will affect demand.

In the United States animal welfare organizations now believe the hunting ethic is on the decline, though 150 packs of hounds still hunt coyote, foxes, hares and rabbits. Cock-fighting and dog-fighting, though illegal, are still common in parts of Texas, New Mexico and Southern California. In the United Kingdom too, blood sports are under attack, but if hunting is in decline, interest in racing is growing.

The first Arab horses were brought to England in the 17th century, Most stood no more than fourteen hands

TOP *John Frederick Herring (Sr) (1795–1865): 'Preparing to start for the Doncaster Gold Cup, 1825' (1827), £320,000.*

CENTRE *John Frederick Herring (Sr) (1795–1865): 'Partridge Shooting at Six Mile Bottom' (1833), £140,000.*

ABOVE *Ben Marshall (1767–1835): 'Mr Wastall with his jockey, Frank Buckle, and his trainer and a groom', £10,000.*

high though their proud owners did not object if artists chose to add a few few inches. Foreign blood accounted for the excellence of English sporting art as well as of English horses. The tradition went back to Dutch and Flemish hunting scenes and was largely established in England by foreigners. The Sartorius family came from Bavaria, the Alken family from Denmark and the Herrings from Holland via America.

Properly organized horse races took place during Charles I's reign and later gatherings in Hyde Park and at Newmarket are shown by Wootton as elegant affairs. Historic wagers of a thousand pounds and more were struck between rival owners and it wasn't long before betting turned the racecourse into the spiritual home of the riffraff.

Owners felt passionately about their horses and the competition between them was intense. Sporting artists were well paid and Ben Marshall was not the only one who found he could make more money painting horses than people. Explaining to a friend why he had moved to Newmarket, he said, 'I discover many a man who will pay me fifty guineas for painting his horse, who thinks ten too much for painting his wife.'

In spite of the high prices now paid for paintings by Ferneley, Herring and Pollard, their work is not regarded as great art. On the other hand, experts refer to George Stubbs as being 'more than a sporting artist' and any important work by him would surely fetch half a million pounds. Yet as recently as the 1910s he was out of fashion. Fine equestrian portraits sold for £300 – no more than Stubbs had charged his patrons 150 years earlier. By the 1960s they had reached £20,000; by 1970 the record was £220,000.

TOP *George Stubbs (1724–1806): 'A Bay Arab' (1779), £56,000.*

ABOVE *Henry Alken (Sr) (1785–1851): 'The Finish of the St Leger, 1848', one of a pair, £45,000.*

Sporting paintings should keep rising at least in line with the market, but there are important points investors should bear in mind. There were several painters in each of the Alken, Sartorius, Herring and Ferneley families. Henry Alken (Sr), for example, was a more accomplished artist than his son and commands higher prices. But similarities of style within each family can make firm attributions difficult. Buyers should therefore seek a second opinion. Furthermore, the best sporting artists were widely imitated during their lifetimes. Works by would-be clones are usually sold as 'Style of Henry Alken (Sr)' though some dealers persuade themselves too easily that they are offering the real thing. Since works by the leading artists now fetch £10,000 and more, semi-primitive and provincial artists may appreciate more quickly.

Racing pictures should continue to rise faster than those showing hunting scenes. Paintings of shooting, fishing, archery, boxing and other rare subjects could well rise fastest of all, while those of cock-fighting, and other sports for which there is a growing distaste, are likely to do least well.

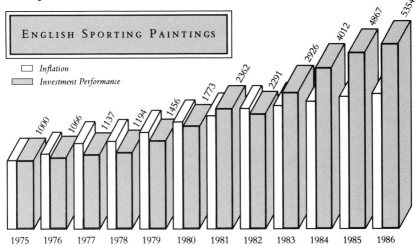

ENGLISH SPORTING PAINTINGS

☐ Inflation
▨ Investment Performance

1000 1066 1137 1194 1456 1773 2362 2291 2926 4012 4867 5354

1975 1976 1977 1978 1979 1980 1981 1982 1983 1984 1985 1986

Artists: John Ferneley (Sr), John Frederick Herring (Sr), John Nott Sartorius, James Ward, John Wootton

Artist	Mid-market price £	Change since 1975 %
English Sporting Paintings		
John Ferneley (Sr) (*1781–1860*)	20,900	+230
John Frederick Herring (Sr) (*1795–1865*)	26,500	+540
John Nott Sartorius (*1759–1828*)	7200	+540
James Ward (*1769–1859*)	1800	+80
John Wootton (*1686–1765*)	21,500	+540
Other Sporting Artists		
Henry Alken (Sr) (*1785–1851*)	3400	+50
Harry Hall (*19th century*)	4600	+710

James Ward (1769–1859): 'Dr Syntax, a bay racehorse, standing in a coastal landscape' (1820), £16,000.

John Nott Sartorius (1759–1828): 'Sir H. T. Vane's "Hambletonian" beating Mr Cookson's "Diamond" at Newmarket' (1799), £12,500.

English Watercolours

The English watercolour index is up 450% since 1975. There is plenty of momentum in the market even though there are few buyers outside the United Kingdom to keep prices moving.

Paul Mellon was among the first to recognize the undervaluation of English watercolours back in the 1950s and the results of a massive buying programme can be seen today at the Yale Center for British Art at New Haven, Connecticut. Although Mellon certainly pushed the market up during the 1950s and 1960s, he was only paying between 5% and 10% of the prices ruling today.

Three reasons explain the market's strength. First, English watercolours are inexpensive seen alongside oil paintings of comparable quality; works by most of the twenty artists in the index still fall in the £1000 to £3000 range. Second, watercolours have benefited from the revaluation of 19th century art; and thirdly, the art-form lends itself to restrained, subtle and highly personal interpretations that have simply become more widely appreciated.

In the early 19th century the impact of these paintings was considered feeble compared to oil paintings, and for a time watercolourists tried to compete by using richer colours and heavy gold frames. But the attempt

LEFT *Peter de Wint (1784–1849): 'The Square of the Elephant', £620.*

BELOW *Joseph Mallord William Turner (1775–1851): 'Stirling', £22,000.*

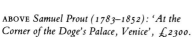

ABOVE *Samuel Prout (1783–1852): 'At the Corner of the Doge's Palace, Venice', £2300.*

ABOVE RIGHT *John Robert Cozens (1752–99): 'Between Salerno and Eboli', £32,000.*

RIGHT *David Cox (1783–1859): 'View on the Usk above Brecknock' (1825), £1150.*

CENTRE RIGHT *Thomas Rowlandson (1756–1827): 'Undergraduates leaving for London', £1500.*

BELOW *John Varley (1778–1842): 'View at Nine Elms' (1830), £520.*

was misconceived, rather like trying to make a string quartet sound like a full orchestra, and watercolours soon returned to their natural idiom.

Some famous English artists, including Constable and Turner, worked in watercolour as well as oil, but many more – Girtin, Cozens, Cotman, Varley and de Wint – are celebrated entirely for their watercolours. They were not innovators as such. The medium had been used by Albrecht Dürer in the 15th century and by Dutch artists such as Cuyp, Avercamp and Bol in the 17th century. These Englishmen developed the art-form to its highest point and used it to represent the mellow colours of the English countryside. The medium and the subject matter were in perfect harmony and landscapes had never been painted with greater feeling.

The golden age of watercolours runs from 1794 to 1815. The period coincides roughly with that of the Napoleonic Wars and for much of it English artists, who had earlier travelled extensively in Europe, were more or less obliged to stay at home and paint scenes of their native land.

It was the new technique first adopted by Girtin and Turner that transformed the quality of water-

TOP *Myles Birket Foster (1825–99): 'Haymakers', £14,000.*

ABOVE *Paul Sandby (1725–1809): 'Windsor Park and Castle from Snow Hill' (1792), £2300.*

colour painting in the 1790s. Instead of using washes of grey to indicate shadows and forms before painting over the whole with the appropriate colour, they set to work with colour straightaway. The process was more difficult; it called for the closest study of the way light was modified by the object it struck and, as one art historian put it, opened the way for the subject of the picture to become light itself. It was the highly accomplished use of local colour by Girtin and Turner that raised the status of these so-called stained or tinted drawings to that of paintings in watercolour. No more delicate effects of weather and light have ever been achieved, which gives watercolours of this period their investment credentials.

Turner's work has risen by 260% over the period. Together with Constable and perhaps Bonington, Turner is really in a class by himself. Girtin, who died in 1802 at the age of twenty-seven, was more admired in his day than Turner. Indeed Turner himself said he would give a little finger to be able to make one of Girtin's 'golden drawings'.

Towards the end of the 18th century drawing lessons became a standard part of the education of children in every well-heeled family. Drawing masters were suddenly to be found all over England making ends meet by giving lessons and selling their work. During the next hundred years literally millions of watercolours were produced by amateurs, several of whom are considered important today.

Approximately fifty thousand watercolours are sold at auction in Britain every year – three-quarters of them for less than £200. Many are signed, though experienced auctioneers are often able to identify the artist when they are not. Cast-iron attributions are never easy unless the painting is well documented from the moment of its creation. In the case of important artists such evidence is often available and acts as protection for the investor. Appraising watercolours is a highly personal business and experts regularly disagree on the importance and value of a watercolourist. Dealers, collectors and, to some extent, art historians are continually causing adjustments within the market, particularly in the middle price-range.

One result of the sudden popularity of watercolours in the first half of the 19th century was that some artists began to overpopularize their subjects. After 1840 those with a romantic disposition went too far and a sickly sentimentality creeps into their work. Myles Birket Foster was an outstanding draughtsman but falls into this category. Yet, with a 370% rise in the value of his work since 1975, his style is more admired than ever.

The rich industrialists of the Midlands formed a new and important clientele for watercolours after 1830. They were attracted to idealized scenes of rural England – children skipping down country lanes between banks of primroses, misty mountain lakes and so on. Provided the artist's technique is first class, such subjects still fetch enormous prices.

One of the strongest areas of the watercolour market today is the 1880–1910 period when such artists as Henry Sylvester Stannard, Albert Goodwin, Hercules Brabazon Brabazon, George Goodwin Kilburne and Helen Allingham were at their peak. In the cases of Goodwin and Brabazon, one dealer has affected prices by buying much of their work appearing at auction over a long period and subsequently holding a major exhibition for each artist. Higher price-levels have now been established and it remains to be seen whether the new wave of enthusiasm for these artists will sustain prices in the salerooms.

One conspicuous trend in the watercolour market is the shift away from figure-subjects towards more decorative material. Demand seems to be swinging towards drawings with greater 'wall power' – brightly painted scenes with flowers and figures, and indeed anything that offers plenty for the eye to take in.

Seeing watercolours on view in public galleries protected from the light by cloth curtains has deterred many would-be buyers. Direct sunlight can indeed ruin a watercolour by fading the colours. First to go are

the blues, which can quickly turn to brown – the freshness of a sky can be lost forever in a matter of days, and with it perhaps half the drawing's value. Yellow is the next to suffer. Nearly all colours can be affected to some extent but, alarming as this may sound, nearly all rooms have walls where watercolours can be safely hung and the precautions taken in many public galleries are not essential.

Another feature of this market which may lead to adjustments in due course is that those watercolourists who were most admired ten and twenty years ago, such as Cotman, Sandby, David Cox (Sr), Peter de Wint and John Varley, are being overtaken in price by the late 19th century 'Foxglove Cottage' School.

Many collectors have concluded that this is one field where they can still hope to acquire really fine material for £2000–£3000. It is moreover a broadly based market, attracting new collectors all the time, and likely to keep up a 12% to 15% annual growth rate.

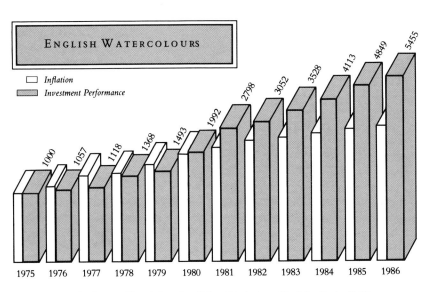

ENGLISH WATERCOLOURS

☐ Inflation
▨ Investment Performance

1975	1976	1977	1978	1979	1980	1981	1982	1983	1984	1985	1986
1000	1057	1118	1368	1493	1992	2798	3052	3528	4113	4849	5455

Artists: Hellen Allingham, William Callow, David Cox (Sr), Anthony Vandyke, Copley Fielding, Myles Birket Foster, Albert Goodwin, Thomas Bush Hardy, Augustus Osborne Lamplough, David Roberts, Peter de Wint

Artist	Mid-market price £	Change since 1975 %
Helen Allingham (1848–1926)	3600	+1150
William Callow (1812–1908)	1600	+310
David Cox (Sr) (1783–1859)	1200	+220
Anthony Vandyke Copley Fielding (1787–1855)	1000	+230
Myles Birket Foster (1825–99)	1700	+370
Albert Goodwin (1845–1932)	1300	+490
Thomas Bush Hardy (1842–97)	600	+190
Augustus Osborne Lamplough (1877–1930)	1000	+410
David Roberts (1796–1864)	3200	+320
Peter de Wint (1784–1849)	1300	+160

Other English Watercolour Artists

Artist		
Hercules Brabazon Brabazon (1821–1906)	1200	+500
George Chinnery (1748–1847)	1600	+40
John Sell Cotman (1782–1842)	1400	+70
Charles Dixon (1872–1934)	1000	+360
Thomas Girtin (1775–1802)	4500	+200
George Goodwin Kilburne (1839–1924)	1100	+360
Walter Langley (1852–1922)	1000	+220
Edward Lear (1812–88)	3000	+480
George Edward Lodge (1860–1954)	1000	+120
Samuel Prout (1783–1852)	800	+340
Thomas Miles Richardson (1813–90)	700	+310
Thomas Rowlandson (1756–1827)	1500	+190
John Ruskin (1819–1900)	2200	+480
Paul Sandby (1725–1809)	1200	+90
Archibald Thorburn (1860–1935)	2100	+150
Joseph Mallord William Turner (1775–1851)	15,200	+260
John Varley (1778–1842)	1000	+200
William Lionel Wyllie (1851–1931)	1000	+210

OPPOSITE LEFT *John Glover (1767–1849): 'Mill in Bonsall Dale, Derbyshire', £2100.*

OPPOSITE RIGHT *Thomas Jones (1742–1803): 'Larici (Ariccia) from the Convent of the Galoro' (1777), £21,000.*

RIGHT *Charles Towne (1781–1854): 'A View near Snowdon' (1815), £450.*

John Glover (1767–1849): 'Travellers approaching a town in a valley', £24,000.

Edward Dayes (1763–1804): 'Thorshaven, Faroe Isles', £650.

Further Reading

Martin Hardie, *Watercolour Painting in Britain*, 3 vols. (London, 1966–8)

Michael Clarke, *The Tempting Prospect: a Social History of English Watercolours* (London, 1981)

Graham Reynolds, *A Concise History of Watercolours* (London, 1971)

Judy Egerton, *English Watercolour Painting* (Oxford, 1979)

Victorian Painting

Victorian painting as a whole has undergone a revaluation that would have been unimaginable twenty years ago. The index of 19th century English painting, comprising ten of the most prolific artists, has risen by 270% since 1975. The rate of appreciation over the previous decade was slightly faster.

The Pre-Raphaelites were by far the most influential group of the century and their message, championed by Ruskin, was to affect whole areas of English art. Critics are still divided as to their worth. Most agree that they helped to raise the art of Victorian England from the shallow grave in which Landseer, Etty and others had all but buried it. Yet, on the other hand, their pictorial language included the kind of moralistic cant that rings hollow today. A creepy piety pervades much of their painting, giving it more the character of a homily than a work of art. Outside Britain their work arouses polite rather than serious interest, while prices on their home ground suggest that their standing is higher than ever.

The Pre-Raphaelite Brotherhood was formed in 1848. It had seven members, of whom only three – William Holman Hunt, John Everett Millais and Dante Gabriel Rossetti –

Thomas Smythe (1825–1906): 'A Suffolk Morning', £1500.

were to become major artists. Most important Pre-Raphaelite works are now in public collections, so few get auctioned these days. On the modest saleroom evidence available values seem to have risen by 300% or more since 1975. Members of the Pre-Raphaelite circle have led the revaluation of 19th century art, but their record as investments is chequered and their status could be vulnerable even now.

The record for a Pre-Raphaelite work stands at £780,000, paid for Millais's *The Proscribed Royalist* at Christie's in 1983. The same painting had sold in 1897 for £2300 before the Pre-Raphaelites had gone out of fashion. The art world applies the test of time on a continuous basis, so will the 19th century idols hold their own, or will they, as happened before, get knocked off their pedestals and their places taken by others? Though the craftsmanship of the Pre-Raphaelites is not in doubt, the basis of their artistic principles may be less secure.

In 1848 Millais and Hunt were two young students who saw that the cloistered world of art was ripe for change. They were sick of the rigidities imposed at the Royal Academy Schools. Teachers laid down how figures should be grouped and what gestures they might make. They decided what range of colours was acceptable as well as the relationship between light and shade. The students also objected to the trivial or lascivious subjects chosen by such established artists as Landseer and Etty. They resented too the mandatory coat of toning varnish that choked the life out of the bright colours in which they liked to work.

The Pre-Raphaelites took their inspiration from Keats, Tennyson and Byron, from the novels of Sir Walter Scott, the social idealism of Carlyle, from Dante and the early Italian poets, and from the Oxford Movement, an Anglican High Church revival with a distinctly Romish tinge. Lastly, and most importantly, they were inspired by the Italian primitive painters of the 14th and 15th centuries. It was a recipe with promising ingredients, yet, by the standards the Brotherhood set itself, the resulting creation was a failure.

The term 'Pre-Raphaelite' was suggested one evening by Holman Hunt when he and his friends were studying engravings of the frescoes in the Campo Santo in Pisa by Orcagna, Benozzo Gozzoli and other Tuscan painters. They were impressed by the power and simplicity of these 14th century images.

The name the students gave themselves led to a mistaken impression that they were actually anti-Raphael, and this belief was given some substance when Holman Hunt explained to fellow students at the Academy Schools that the decay of art might be seen in the 'unspiritual attitudinizing of the Saviour in Raphael's *Transfiguration*'. Far from being anathema, Raphael actually appeared on the students' 'List of Immortals', albeit in the fourth rank. At the head of the list came Jesus Christ with four stars. Next, with three, came Shakespeare and Job; a third group included Dante, Leonardo da Vinci and George Washington. Raphael appeared in the fourth group with Longfellow.

To start with the Pre-Raphaelites aroused considerable hostility. Dickens attacked Millais for his *Christ in the House of His Parents*, describing the figure of Christ as 'a hideous, blubbering red-haired boy'. Other ferocious reviews followed and Queen Victoria had the painting brought to her for a special viewing. But rescue was at hand. John Ruskin, already established as Britain's oracle on matters of taste, wrote to *The Times* in the Brotherhood's defence and the tide of opinion turned. Suddenly the minutely observed realism and heavy symbolism of Pre-Raphaelite work was being hailed as the dawn of a new artistic era. Holman Hunt's *The Light of the World* set the seal on their popular success when it appeared in 1854 and began to be reproduced by the million in bibles and prayer books.

The third major figure in the Brotherhood, Dante Gabriel Rossetti, is now rated a better poet than painter. Yet his paintings of dreamy, heavy-jawed and slightly androgynous women are immensely admired. He created an image of brooding female beauty which he seems to have adapted to fit every model he painted. For all that, his work has an enjoyable extravagance that sets it apart from the rest and should better enable it to withstand the test of time.

The 1860–1900 period was in many ways a golden age for the artist – provided he supplied what the public wanted. Millais trimmed his sails to the wind as early as 1853. He could and did paint like Frans Hals, Gainsborough, Reynolds and even the early Renoir. As an old man he was moved to tears on seeing an exhibition of his early work. However, he got a good price for his soul. By 1868 he was earning £20,000 a year and said he could make £100 a day doing watercolour copies of his popular works.

Prices paid to artists were enormously boosted by various rights dealers could exploit. Holman Hunt sold his *The Finding of Christ in the Temple* to a dealer for £5775 including reproduction rights. The dealer made £4000 in one-shilling exhibition fees, £5000 in profits on the engraving and still sold the painting to a Leeds stockbroker for £3000.

The backing of Ruskin and the wide availability of their work in the form of prints meant that the Pre-Raphaelites and their followers were rather foisted on the public as the approved art. The neoclassicists Alma-Tadema, Leighton, Poynter and Long also enjoyed great success. Whereas in the 18th century aristocratic Englishmen returned from the grand tour with a pronounced taste for Italian, Dutch and Flemish masters, the big buyers in the 19th century were mostly rich industrialists who made no pretence to good taste and bought what the dealers told them.

During the first twenty years of the 20th century prices for the Pre-Raphaelites and their circle began to collapse. The market for Old Masters, meanwhile, could hardly have been stronger – J. Pierpont Morgan gave £100,000 in 1901 for Raphael's *Colonna Altarpiece* – and even the Impressionists were beginning to advance. Furthermore, contemporary art in the form of the Expressionism, Cubism and Futurism was turning the world on its head. Amid all this, the Pre-Raphaelites lacked both the status of Old Masters and the excitement of the Moderns.

In 1891 Edwin Long turned down an offer of £5250 for his *The Parable of the Sower*; seventeen years later his widow sold it for £130. Alma-Tadema's *The Finding of Moses*, sold in 1904 for £5250, made £250 in 1960. Hardest hit of all was Burne-Jones. His *Love and the Pilgrim*, sixteen feet long, sold for £5775 in 1898; the highest bid in 1942 was £21.

With hindsight, the market for Victoriana – particularly the technically accomplished works – was bound to recover. Someone who bought for practical rather than speculative reasons in the 1950s was Billy

ABOVE LEFT *Eloise Harriet Stannard (19th century):
'Fruit painted from Nature' (1857), £4800.*

TOP *William Shayer (Sr) (1788–1879):
'Fisherfolk on the Quay at Hastings' (1846),
£3600.*

ABOVE *Charles Cooper Henderson (1803–77):
'The London to York Mail', £11,000.*

BELOW *Sir Lawrence Alma-Tadema (1836–
1912): 'Caracalla and Geta, Bear Fight in the
Coliseum, 203 AD', £145,000.*

Butlin, the founder of Britain's low-budget holiday camps. Wishing to acquire Victorian religious paintings to hang in the camp chapels, he would leave a bid of £50 for anything measuring over fifty square feet. This simple strategy netted some very bad paintings but a few fine ones too – among them *The Lamentation of Christ* by William Dyce which sold for £125,000 in 1983.

Idealisation in art produces the kind of falsity that collectors seemed to have rumbled when they down-graded the Pre-Raphaelite circle early this century. The majority of collectors, however, now find Victorian painting, with all its short-comings, extremely attractive and their buying power should keep prices rising annually by at least 10%.

TOP *James Webb (?1825–95): 'The Pont Neuf,
Paris, with Notre Dame beyond', £10,000.*

ABOVE *Benjamin Williams Leader (1831–1923):
'The Last Gleam' (1879), £6000.*

TOP *Edward Williams (1807–81): 'A Wooded
Norfolk Landscape', one of a pair, £15,000.*

ABOVE *William Turner of Oxford (1789–1862):
'Travellers on a path, with a distant view of
Oxford', £1900.*

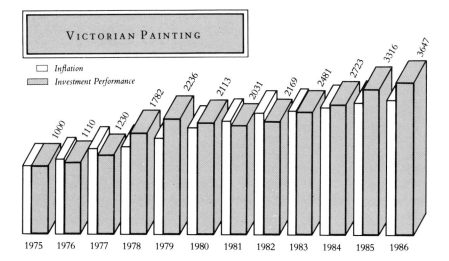

VICTORIAN PAINTING

☐ Inflation
▨ Investment Performance

| 1000 | 1110 | 1230 | 1782 | 2236 | 2113 | 2031 | 2169 | 2481 | 2723 | 3316 | 3647 |

| 1975 | 1976 | 1977 | 1978 | 1979 | 1980 | 1981 | 1982 | 1983 | 1984 | 1985 | 1986 |

Artists: Atkinson Grimshaw, Benjamin Leader, Edmund Niemann, Sidney Richard Percy, Henry
Redmore, William Shayer, George Smith, George Turner, Frederick William Watts, James Webb

Artist	Mid-market price £	Change since 1975 %
John Atkinson Grimshaw (*1836–93*)	7100	+340
Benjamin Leader (*1831–1923*)	3000	+200
Edmund Niemann (Sr) (*1813–76*)	1200	+110
Sidney Richard Percy (*1821–86*)	2900	+220
Henry Redmore (*1820–87*)	4400	+440
William Shayer (Sr) (*1788–1879*)	3700	+280
George Smith (*1829–1910*)	1100	+140
George Turner (*1843–1910*)	1100	+170
Frederick William Watts (*1800–62*)	4300	+190
James Webb (*?1825–95*)	2800	+220
Other Victorian Artists		
Richard Ansdell (*1815–85*)	5500	+550
George Armfield (*1840–75*)	1200	+280
Thomas Baker of Leamington (*1809–69*)	1000	+60

RIGHT *Frederick William Watts (1800–62): 'The Watermill', £18,000.*

BELOW *Henry H. Parker (1858–1930): 'Cattle watering in a river landscape', £1600.*

ABOVE *Frederick Goodall (1822–1904), 'Leading the Flock, Early Morning, Cairo', £1500.*

LEFT *Henry Bight (1814): 'Wolf's Crag, Dumbarton Castle', £3500.*

CENTRE LEFT *Thomas Sidney Cooper (1803–1902): 'On a Dairy Farm' (1871), £7700.*

BOTTOM LEFT *John Atkinson Grimshaw (1836–93): 'Three Hundred Years Ago' (1892), £3400.*

BELOW *John Frederick Lewis (1805–76): The Houri: an Eastern lady with a hookah', £3800.*

Artist	Mid-market price £	Change since 1975 %
Charles Thomas Bale (*19th century*)	800	+190
Alfred de Breanski (Sr) (*19th century*)	2200	+330
Sir Edward Coley Burne-Jones (*1833–98*)	4500	+110
Thomas Blinks (*19th century*)	2600	+450
Henry Bright (*1814–73*)	1700	+90
Edmund Bristow (*1787–1876*)	3400	+320
Edgar Bundy (*1862–1922*)	1000	+120
John Wilson Carmichael (*1800–68*)	1800	+90
Oliver Clare (*19th century*)	1200	+270
Vincent Clare (c. *1855–1930*)	800	+150
Thomas Sidney Cooper (*1803–1902*)	1800	+200
William Etty (*1787–1849*)	1300	+260
David Farquharson (*1839–1907*)	1700	+280
Robert Gallon (*1845–1925*)	1500	+220
Alfred Augustus Glendening (*19th century*)	2000	+250
Charles Cooper Henderson (*1803–77*)	3700	+500
Frederick Goodall (*1822–1904*)	1300	+400
Edwin Hayes (*1820–1904*)	800	+130
Charles Hunt (*1803–77*)	2500	+260
Walter Hunt (*19th century*)	4800	+300
Robert Gemmel Hutchinson (*1855–1936*)	1600	+250
David James (*fl. 1881–98*)	1400	+250
John Yeend King (*1855–1924*)	900	+120
William Callcott Knell (*19th century*)	1100	+160
Edward Ladell (*1821–86*)	5700	+240
Sir Edwin Landseer (*1802–73*)	11,200	+580
Frederick Lord Leighton (*1830–96*)	11,300	+640
John Frederick Lewis (*1805–76*)	3800	+980
William McTaggart (*1835–1910*)	1400	+130
John Charles Maggs (*1819–96*)	2300	+230
Arthur Joseph Meadows (*1843–1907*)	1700	+210
William Mellor (*1851–1931*)	900	+230
William James Muller (*1812–45*)	1100	+80
Henry Parker (*1858–1930*)	2000	+230
Sidney Richard Percy (*1821–86*)	2900	+220
Edward Pritchett (*19th century*)	2800	170
James Baker Pyne (*1800–70*)	1200	200
Thomas Sewell Robins (*1814–80*)	1000	+250
Edward Robert Smythe (*1810–99*)	900	+60
Thomas Smythe (*1825–1906*)	1500	+40
Eloise Harriet Stannard (*19th century*)	2200	+180

ABOVE *Edward Robert Smythe (1810–99):*
'Countryfolk with cattle watering outside a cottage',
£3500.

RIGHT *Thomas Smythe (1825–1906): 'View of*
Ipswich', £3000.

BELOW *John Berney Crome (1794–1842): 'A*
View of Rouen', £15,000.

Artist	Mid-market price £	Change. since 1975 %
William Thornley (*19th century*)	1000	+170
Joseph Thors (*19th century*)	900	+80
James Jacques Joseph Tissot (*1836–1902*)	101,000	+1900
Ernest Walbourn (*19th–20th century*)	1200	+340
John Arnold Wheeler (*1821–77*)	1400	+240

Late 19th and 20th Century English Painting

A new low point in the taste of the Royal Academy, as shown by the artists chosen or invited to exhibit, was reached in the 1870s and 1880s. It was only a matter of time before artists formed themselves into break-away groups. The first exhibition of the New English Art Club took place in 1886 with Walter Sickert, Philip Wilson Steer and members of the Newlyn School, including Stanhope Forbes, Henry Scott Tuke and Frank Bramley.

The break with the styles and conventions of the Academy was important though much Newlyn School painting is marked by the oppressive *Weltschmerz* that had tainted Victorian painting for so long. Such titles as *A Hopeless Dawn* and *But Men Must Work and Women Must Weep* indicate the mood. All the same the Newlyn artists had mostly studied abroad and each was feeling his way towards an individual response to French Impressionism. Though by no means a watershed in the history of English art, 1886 serves well enough as a starting point for the modern period.

The ten artists taken to represent 20th century English art are anything but homogenous. Yet within the index it is possible to see how differently artists have grown in public estimation. As a whole, the index has risen by 330% since 1975, though the Newlyn School artists are showing a rise of 420% and others have performed equally impressively.

The two members of the London Impressionists group whose work is regularly sold at auction have fared quite differently. The paintings of Wilson Steer, which were often and not unflatteringly compared to those of Monet, have actually fallen in value by a few per cent since 1975. Sickert, with a rise of 120%, has also moved out of line with the index. Of the Glasgow School artists, only Sir John Lavery is available in any quantity and his work has risen by 1080% over the same period.

In the early years of the century a growing number of groups were formed and disbanded. The Society of Twelve included George Clausen, Gordon Craig, William Strang, Charles Shannon and D. Y. Cameron who organized exhibitions from 1904 to 1915. Of these, Clausen's work has risen by 550%; Cameron's 80%.

The Camden Town group was made up of Sickert and his friends Harold Gilman, Charles Ginner, Robert Bevan and Spencer Gore. There was the Bloomsbury group, the Fitzroy Street group and many more. These were on the whole loose associations whose members did not formulate nor adhere to specific artistic principles. The Vorticists, however, were an exception. This was a group of revolutionary artists, writers and sculptors, inspired by Wyndham Lewis, which included Ezra Pound, C. R. W. Nevinson, Edward Wadsworth, William Roberts and Gaudier-Brzeska. The first issue of the group's magazine *Blast*, published in June 1914, contained a fierce attack on English art, deriving much from the wild style and shock tactics of the Italian Futurist Manifesto of 1909. A high-voltage current was running through the London art circuit at the time but the horrors of the First World War succeeded in blowing the fuse. The Vorticist's postwar work was more subdued and by 1920 the group had broken up.

While the war was on, many leading artists were appointed official war artists. Henry Lamb, Nevinson, Paul and John Nash, Roberts, Wyndham Lewis, Augustus John, Munnings and Orpen were all at the front. When the war was over, no glorious battle scenes in the 19th century fashion were commissioned. So heavy and futile had been the carnage, and so suspect the leadership, it would have seemed in bad taste to commemorate the atrocity of trench warfare.

English artists returned to their traditional subject matter. Styles were tempered by their reactions to van Gogh, Gauguin, Cézanne and Matisse but were apparently unaffected by the recent cataclysm. The old debate was renewed during the 1920s about the role of the artist in society. The 'Art for Art's Sake' movement of the 19th century had asserted that the artist had no specific obligation to society and that each of his works should be considered by and for itself. As Whistler had put it in 1878, 'Art should be independent of all claptrap – should stand alone and appeal to the artistic sense of eye or ear, without confound-

ing this with emotions entirely foreign to it, as devotion, love, patriotism and the like.'

This was in sharp contrast to the view of William Morris who had sought to break down the barrier separating the fine from the applied arts. The doctrine that art should be placed at the service of the crafts had succeeded in raising the standard of English industrial design to a high level in the late 19th century and this collaboration between the arts and crafts was sustained in the Omega Workshops founded by Roger Fry in 1913. But most English artists had in any case seized their right to paint as they pleased. This freedom had been complemented by a more practical measure when in 1908 the critic Frank Rutter had proposed that any artist should be free to show his work at the annual exhibitions of the Allied Artists Association without first submitting it to a selecting jury. If it seems that a better deal had by then been won for artists, it is worth recalling that only in 1914 did the London group see fit to lift their ban on female artists. For all the liberal talk in the art world, the groundswell of opinion in the art schools, and even more among the British public, was firmly opposed to the newfangled ideas flowing across the Channel.

In 1920 the Seven and Five Society declared that there had of late been 'too much pioneering along too many lines in altogether too much of a hurry'. They wished to pursue their calling without confusion and conflict. The London group too lost much of its innovatory spirit in the 1920s and English art of the interwar period stayed well out of the mainstream of European development.

There were exceptions. Ben Nicholson was developing an abstract style that eventually won him more acclaim than any other 20th century English artist. Prices for his work reach up to £100,000 and have risen by just 70% since 1975. Stanley Spencer's work is auctioned too seldom to be indexed but cannot have climbed less than 250%.

During the 1950s and 1960s the art world was continuously dazzled by a galaxy of French and American artists. During the 1970s each country began to re-examine its own artists and invariably discovered work of real value. So far the revaluation of 20th century English artists, though substantial, has lagged behind French, German and American.

Prices for the leaders of the postwar generation of artists are as affected as any by their subject matter. After Nicholson, the artists with the highest mid-market prices are Sir Alfred Munnings and Montague Dawson at £11,100 and £11,600. Owners of racehorses and yachts are clearly attracted by their work and often have the means to buy it. Though no one would deny the brilliance of Munnings's technique, few would claim that he brought to his work any profound or original vision of the world. In judging an artist's investment potential the characteristics of the likely buyers are important. In these cases it may be assumed that horse- and yacht-owners have helped to drive up prices for Munnings by 270% and Dawson by 460%.

Explanations can also be given for some disappointing performances. The simplistic semiprimitive townscapes of L. S. Lowry which have delighted the British public for the last forty years have climbed by just 20% since 1975. The spate of fakes that reached the market in 1980 rather undermined buyers' confidence, but the decline must also reflect a downgrading of his status. Graham Sutherland is another case of an artist who at one level enjoyed loyal if uncritical support in England for several decades. But the major Tate Gallery exhibition in 1982 emphasized the stone-cold relationships he had with his sitters. Through his eyes nature itself took on a menacing disagreeable quality. People began to see why Lady Churchill burnt his portrait of Sir Winston. Sutherland prices have fallen by 20% since 1975 and no recovery seems likely.

The outlook for 20th century English art as a whole is bright. There are more affluent collectors in this field in Britain than ever before and prices still look low alongside comparable European and American art. A 15% growth rate looks sustainable in the medium term.

C. R. W. Nevinson (1889–1949): 'River Scene with Barges' (c. 1917), £4000.

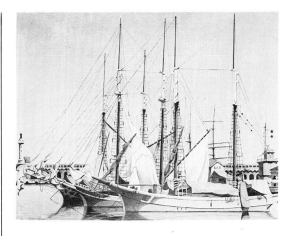

Edward Wadsworth (1889–1949): 'L'Avant Port, Marseilles' (1924), £10,000.

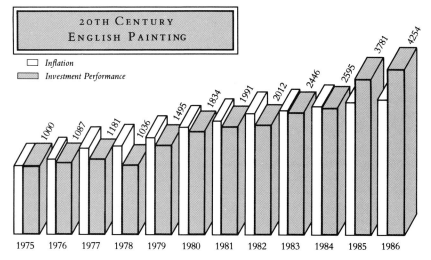

20TH CENTURY ENGLISH PAINTING

☐ Inflation
▨ Investment Performance

1000   1087   1181   1036   1495   1834   1991   2012   2446   2595   3781   4254

1975   1976   1977   1978   1979   1980   1981   1982   1983   1984   1985   1986

Artists: Montague Dawson, Sir William Russell Flint, David Hockney, Augustus John, Dame Laura Knight, Henry Moore, Sir Alfred Munnings, John Piper, Graham Sutherland

Artist	Mid-market price £	Change since 1975 %
20th Century English Painting		
Montague Dawson (*1895–1973*)	11,600	+460
Sir William Russell Flint (*1880–1969*)	2900	+170
David Hockney (*b. 1937*)	35,000	+630
Augustus John (*1878–1961*)	1100	+150
Dame Laura Knight (*1877–1970*)	3400	+760
Laurence Stephen Lowry (*1887–1976*)	2400	+10
Sir Alfred Munnings (*1878–1959*)	11,100	+270
Henry Moore (*b. 1898*)	15,400	+420
John Piper (*b. 1903*)	1000	+260
Graham Sutherland (*1903–80*)	2500	+20

Artist	Mid-market price £	Change since 1975 %
Other Late 19th and 20th Century English Painters		
Sir John William Ashton (*1881–1963*)	1700	+380
Vanessa Bell (*1879–1961*)	1600	+450
Frank Moss Bennett (*20th century*)	1100	+40
Samuel John Lamorna Birch (*1869–1955*)	900	+290
David Bomberg (*1890–1957*)	1800	+220
Sir Frank Brangwyn (*1867–1943*)	1100	+200
Francis Cadell (*1883–1937*)	2400	+300
Sir David Young Cameron (*1865–1945*)	800	+80
Sir George Clausen (*1852–1944*)	3000	+550
Charles Conder (*1868–1909*)	1900	+100
Stanhope Forbes (*1857–1947*)	2700	+630
Mark Gertler (*1892–1939*)	5700	+960
Dundan Grant (*1885–1978*)	1000	+220
Trevor Haddon (*1864–1941*)	1500	+310
Heywood Hardy (*1843–1933*)	8000	+630
Harold Harvey (*1874–1941*)	7700	+2100
Ivon Hitchens (*1893–1979*)	3500	+250
Edward Atkinson Hornel (*1864–1933*)	5900	+200
George Houston (*1869–1947*)	560	+90
Edgar Hunt (*1876–1953*)	6200	+220
Cecil Kennedy (*b. 1905*)	2900	+270
Sir John Lavery (*1856–1941*)	4500	+1080
John MacLaughlan Milne (*1885–1957*)	800	+170
Paul Nash (*1889–1946*)	2000	+100
Ben Nicholson (*1894–1982*)	11,600	+70
Roderick O'Conor (*1860–1940*)	2400	+440
Sir William Orpen (*1878–1931*)	1700	+330
Samuel John Peploe (*1871–1935*)	8800	+500
Anne Redpath (*1895–1965*)	1600	+250
William Roberts (*1895–1980*)	4900	+330
William Scott (*b. 1913*)	2900	+440
Edward Seago (*1910–74*)	2600	+170
Dorothea Sharp (*fl. 1920s; d. 1955*)	1800	+550
Walter Sickert (*1860–1942*)	2100	+120
Sir Matthew Smith (*1879–1959*)	2900	+140
Charles Spencelayh (*1865–1958*)	2800	+340
Philip Wilson Steer (*1860–1942*)	700	no change
Henry Scott Tuke (*1858–1929*)	800	+300
Keith Vaughan (*1912–77*)	1100	+300
Alfred Wallis (*1855–1942*)	1100	+400
Arthur Wardle (*1864–1947*)	2700	+600
Jack Butler Yeats (*1871–1957*)	4500	+90

ABOVE *Philip Wilson Steer (1860–1942): 'Boulogne Sands. Children Shrimping' (1891), £13,500*
LEFT *Paul Nash (1889–1946): 'Sunset below Wittenham' (1913), £3300.*
BOTTOM LEFT *Sir George Clausen (1852–1944): 'A Dutch girl with flowers (1878), £1800.*
BELOW *Stanhope Forbes (1857–1947): 'The Wanderers' Return' (1929), £3600.*
BOTTOM *Ben Nicholson: 'Still Life' (1945), £62,000.*

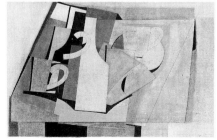

ABOVE *Sir John Lavery (1856–1941): 'The Artist's Distraction' (1884), £48,000.*

CENTRE RIGHT *William Lee Hankey (1869–1952): 'Girls with a vegetable cart in a village street' (1899), £2500.*

BELOW LEFT *Emily Court (20th century): 'A walk across the rocks', £3800.*

BOTTOM LEFT *Sir Alfred Munnings (1878–1959): 'Miss Etherington driving a dog cart', £70,000.*

BELOW RIGHT *Edward Seago (1910–74): 'Barges by the Pont Neuf, Paris', £4000.*

BOTTOM RIGHT *Harold Harvey (1874–1941): 'Cottages in a landscape' (1921), £350.*

Harold Harvey (1874–1941): 'Whiffling for mackerel, Newlyn Harbour' (1908), £1900.

Further Reading

Joseph Burke, *English Art, 1714–1800* (Oxford, 1976)

Michael Rosenthal, *English Landscape Painting* (Oxford, 1982)

Luke Herrman, *British Landscape Painting of the Eighteenth Century* (London, 1973)

William Gaunt, *The Great Century of British Painting: Hogarth to Turner* (London, 1971)

Ellis Waterhouse, *The Dictionary of British 18th Century Painters* (Woodbridge, 1981)

Christopher Wood, *The Dictionary of Victorian Painters* (Woodbridge, 1971)

John Rothenstein, *British Art since 1900. An Anthology* (London, 1962)

R. Ironside, *Pre-Raphaelite Painters* (London, 1948)

18th Century French Painting

The art market may be rising strongly in the long term, yet the swings in demand for certain schools of painting can be surprisingly wide. French 18th-century painters have been especially vulnerable to changes in fashion. Watteau, Lancret, Boucher and Fragonard have all been denigrated at times for being merely decorative painters though their reputations have been substantially rebuilt over the years. Others, including Jean-Baptiste Greuze (1725–1805), have not been so lucky. His portraits of soulful girls, usually close to tears, were immensely admired in his day. His style was in tune too with Victorian sentimentality and by 1860 collectors were paying £3000 to £4000 for his work. Very little of it would fetch that sum today.

Just to keep pace with inflation a Greuze bought in 1860 for £4000 would now need to be worth £125,000. On the other hand, £4000 spent on one of the many Rembrandts for sale in the mid-19th century would now be worth several million. Such variations in performance are not uncommon and investors should not regard the art market as a magic escalator that they can get on and off at will. For even now the prospects of a full revaluation of French 18th century painting back to its 19th century rating are remote.

'Naughty, but nice' might well be an apt description of the supremely pretty and sensuous dishes served up by Boucher, Fragonard and other sirens of 18th century French art. People somehow knew that art should be concerning itself with more serious matters, but could not help being seduced all the same.

The puritanical backlash of Victorian England ensured that these alluring works were considered a licentious aberration which could only have been committed by the French. There was more than a touch of hypocrisy in this, for naked ladies continued to adorn a good deal of Victorian painting even if their thoughts usually seemed fixed on something more sublime than a frolic.

Boucher's sensuous ladies and pudgy cupids have always been taken as the paradigm of 18th century French art yet there is a more serious side to the period to which art historians have recently called attention.

FROM TOP *Alexandre-François Desportes (1661–1743): 'A Dog with flowers and dead game', Wallace Collection.*

Jean Baptiste Oudry (1686–1755): 'A Hawk attacking partridges' (1747), Wallace Collection

Jean Honoré Fragonard (1732–1806): 'Cupids at Play', Wallace Collection.

ABOVE *François Boucher (1703–70), 'Shepherd watching a sleeping shepherdess' (1745), Wallace Collection.*

OPPOSITE *Hubert Robert (1733–1808): 'The Tomb of Jean-Jacques Rousseau at Ermenonville' (1802), £100,000.*

Four main types of painting flourished in France at this time, each with a recognized status based on the skills each was believed to require. First came history painting. Vast canvases depicting religious, mythological or historical scenes were commissioned for the royal palaces and called for an artist proficient in composition, perspective, portraiture and landscape.

Next in status came portraits. The century had opened with a great ceremonial portrait of Louis XIV, his face pinched and puffy, but his legs, if the artist Rigaud is to be believed, still elegant and strong. Instead of sending the portrait to his grandson in Spain as planned, Louis liked it so much he kept it and sent a copy instead.

The official style of portraiture barely changed even after the Revolution, though more intimate interpretations were used for family portraits. Sometimes every detail of a portrait could be taken as a clue to the sitter's personality, interests and achievements. Portraits by Rigaud, Largillière, Nattier, Tocqué, Drouais and the two great woman portraitists – Elisabèthe Vigée-Lebrun and Adélaide Labille-Guiard – can still be bought at auction. Prices run from £5000 to £30,000, depending not only on the artist but on the attractiveness and importance of the sitter. Investors should bear in mind that the demand for portraits was so great that Rigaud, like many others, had a large workshop of assistants. In 1735 he was charging 600 livres for portraits where he worked only on the face and hands and up to 3000 livres for something that was nearly all his own work.

From 1750 onwards the auction market for Old Masters as well as contemporary works was well organized. Many Parisian investors had

been roasted in the collapse of John Law's financial system in 1720. That episode created a widespread distrust of paper securities that was to last for generations. Land, houses and other tangibles resumed their place as the only prudent investments, and among the other tangibles it was noticed that paintings were doing well.

Throughout the century the nobility was being joined by a whole new class of rich bourgeois merchants. These parvenus were busy buying titles and estates, which gave them exemption from tax, and paintings and furniture to adorn their new houses. They eagerly commissioned portraits to reflect their families' new status, but even more popular with them and the old nobility were the light-hearted compositions of nymphs, satyrs and bacchantes disporting themselves on clouds, waves or silky sheets. For this was also an age of astonishing though well-managed promiscuity.

The English traveller Philip Thicknesse noted in 1777 that, having once seen the sights, 'Paris could become a melancholy residence for a stranger who neither plays at cards, dice or deals in the principal manufacture of the city, i.e., ready-made love'. Jealousy, he went on to remark, was scarcely known in France. 'After a year or so of marriage the husband and wife have their separate acquaintances and pursue their separate amusements undisturbed by domestic squabbles.'

No wonder then that Boucher's almost orgiastic compositions were in such demand. The female body was by no means a new subject for artists; it was simply that no artist had previously dared, or perhaps thought it fitting, to represent it so invitingly.

A third type of painting known as *genre* painting included scenes and subjects of simple everyday life often of an anecdotal nature. The 17th century Dutch painters were much admired and bought by French connoisseurs during the 18th century and several French artists – Leprince, Lépicié and Aubry – embarked on rather refined versions of Dutch *genre* painting but failed to capture its earthy simplicity.

Sometimes included with *genre* painting are the *fêtes galantes* originated by Watteau. In these, groups of costumed figures are seen strolling in idyllic parkland. The idea was inspired by the players of the Italian Comedy and developed by Pater and Lancret later in the 18th century. These strange parades of dreamers were especially popular with the French nobility, perhaps because they idealized in art their own somewhat unreal lives. Few Watteaus, Lancrets and Paters pass through the saleroom today. When they do the best fetch only £75,000 to £150,000 – about a tenth of what will be paid for a first-class Monet or Renoir.

The final category consists of still-lifes. The French nobility loved the hunting scenes of Desportes and Oudry and paid highly for them. Over the last twenty years the market for paintings of dead game has been subdued. There can be no doubt that the changed attitudes to the organized slaughter of animals has affected the market. Prices for 'still-deaths' have hardly changed since 1975 and it would be surprising if the market were to pick up.

The increases in value since 1975 for Boucher and Fragonard are tentatively put at 320% to 420%, while Hubert Robert, many of whose classical landscapes and ruins pass through the market every year, has climbed by 270%.

There have been two great surges in price for 18th century French painting. The first was in the mid-19th century when two English collectors – the Marquess of Hertford and Lord Dudley – and a number of Rothschilds began to buy heavily; the second was in the 1900–10 period when Pierpont Morgan, Frick and other great American collectors entered the field. At present though, parts of this market are clearly somewhere near the bottom of a cyclical trough. Anyone who believes the wheel of fashion will turn again might be wise to start buying now.

The Barbizon School

Even by the art world's fickle standards the Barbizon painters have had a difficult time. After years of rejection by the French academic elite a few won acceptance in 1850. Prices for their work soared only after they died and remained high until the Impressionists took over the limelight early this century. During the Depression demand for their work collapsed and for the last fifty years they have drifted in a kind of cultural limbo.

Since 1975 their work overall has climbed in value by just 170% – well below the art market average and equivalent to just 70% in dollar terms.

Some artists are selling at close on 1975 prices and bargain-hunters may scent a recovery situation. A fast turnaround usually brings a good profit but neither in the stock market nor in the art market do prices catch up without good reason. Sad to say,

the case for buying the Barbizon painters is weak even now. Their palette is heavy, their message dated and the market awash with fakes.

Artists discovered the hamlet of Barbizon on the edge of the Fontainebleau forest in the 1840s. Though just thirty miles from Paris, it was a pastoral backwater where time seemed to stand still. Peasants scattered seed as they had in biblical times; gleaners followed in the steps of the reapers; old women gathered faggots of wood; shepherd girls called their sheep by name and knitted as they led them to the fold. And the backdrop to all this was an eerie, magnificent forest.

Over the next fifty years artists from London, New York and from all over France gathered at Barbizon every summer. The leading figures of the group were Corot, Millet, Rousseau and Daubigny. They rejected the pretentious classical, Romantic and historical compositions of the French Academic School and took their inspiration from the great Dutch landscapists Hobbema and Ruysdael. They admired and drew on Constable whose work they saw at the Salon of 1824, and they borrowed the ordered tranquillity of Claude and Poussin.

Although their work is generally Romantic in conception – amounting mainly to variations on the theme of natural beauty – their scrupulous observation of nature and light led them towards a more atmospheric rendering of landscape. Corot and Daubigny in particular saw light as the counterpart of matter and in this they were the forerunners of Impressionism.

The Barbizon artists had to fight as hard as anyone to get their work accepted, for they had a political as well as an artistic battle on their hands. Their pastoral subject matter was at odds with the mood of Imperial France. They were briefly in favour during the Republican period from 1848 to 1851 but were back under a cloud with the advent of the Second Empire.

Millet's *The Winnower* of 1848 shows a gnarled peasant at work,

OPPOSITE *Jean Baptiste Camille Corot (1796–1875): 'Le Soir dans la Campagne' (c. 1870),* £15,500.

RIGHT *Constant Troyon (1810–65): 'Return from the Fields',* £3500.

BELOW LEFT *Théodore Rousseau (1812–67): 'An Extensive River Landscape',* £18,000.

BELOW RIGHT *Charles François Daubigny (1817–78): 'L'Attelage des Boeufs',* £2000.

dressed in red cap, white shirt and blue apron. It was a defiantly Republican statement that might have been calculated to send shivers down every bourgeois spine.

By 1870, even if for some the struggle was not over, Barbizon art had become respectable and by the turn of the century it was all the rage. But collectors gradually fell under the spell of the Impressionists and Barbizon art began to look cold and drab. Since then they have been treated, as one art historian put it, with that cool respect that amounts almost to disrespect.

The best-known of the School, Jean-Baptiste Camille Corot, has always posed problems. A prodigious worker, he painted three thousand canvases in fifty years. 'Of that number,' the old chestnut goes, 'some five thousand are believed to be in the United States.' This joke was first cracked before the turn of the century. Knoedler had introduced Corot to New York collectors and, in the ensuing scramble to buy, many a dubious Corot changed hands.

For every genuine Corot sold at auction today at least ten are rejected as copies or fakes. The authenticity question, however, is easily settled. If a painting purporting to be by Corot neither appears in Alfred Robaut's definitive catalogue of 1905 nor has a certificate from Jean Dieterle, the leading authority on Corot, then no investor should touch it.

Corot himself did not help matters by touching up his students' work and adding his signature. But his style in any case lent itself perfectly to faking. The soft-green willow groves were painted in broad imprecise strokes, and these were scenes Corot himself repeated with little variation over the years.

Corot's work has climbed in value by only 160% since 1975 and the mid-market price for his work now stands at £33,400. The reaction that set in over the years against the big 'Bond Street' Corots that were fetching £5000 to £10,000 at the turn of the century now looks irreversible. The works that arouse more interest today are the small sketchy landscapes of the Campagna around Rome done during his visits of the 1820s and 1830s. These have the freshness and strength that was emulated by the Italian Macchiaioli in the 1860s. The market's judgement of Corot has been harsh. Exceptional works can fetch over a million dollars but admiration for what Oscar Wilde called his 'silver twilights and rose-pink dawns' is waning.

Of all the Barbizon artists, Millet is the one who makes most impact today. He endured hardship in his Norman peasant family and as a struggling artist in Paris did pastiches of Boucher's naked ladies. But these made him feel a traitor to his pious family and after his move to Barbizon in 1849 he applied himself to his beloved peasant subjects.

'At bottom it always comes to this,' he wrote. 'A man must be moved himself in order to move others, and all that is done from theory, however clever, can never attain this end, for it is impossible that it should have the breath of life.' Artists of Brueghel's time usually showed peasants skating or carousing. Millet saw them differently. He believed deeply in the nobility of a peasant's work and was the first to represent it in that light. In this more cynical age it might seem impossible to convey such an idea without sentimentality. Yet if Millet's message seems heavy and moralistic, the forceful style and obvious sincerity come to his rescue.

Millet sold his best-known painting *L'Angelus* for £72 in 1859. Thirty years later when it came up at auction in Paris, Cornelius Vanderbilt instructed a dealer to bid up to $100,000, but the Louvre outbid him. Later in 1889, $250,000 was reputedly paid for *La Bergère* – a price that stood as the highest paid for a modern painting for forty years.

Prices for Millet, along with the rest of the Barbizon painters, was high at the turn of the century but slumped after 1920 as competition for the Impressionists gathered pace. Since 1975 his work has climbed by 290%. Though not as widely faked as Corot, there are problems with Millet too. His nephew was convicted for selling works painted in his uncle's style complete with a fake atelier stamp and no definitive catalogue has yet been published.

Daubigny prices also took a hammering between the wars. In 1919 £8200 was paid for his *Retour du Troupeau*, yet in 1935 an eight-foot canvas, admittedly of a flock of sheep at midnight, was knocked down for 3 guineas. Like Corot, Daubigny repeated himself too often, but in spite of this he is the most attractive of the Barbizon School. Obsessed by the play of light on water, he had the idea, taken up by his friend Monet, of using a studio-boat from which he could paint the river. In this he moved around the Marne, the Seine and the Oise painting glorious views of the banks and water meadows. Corot had persuaded Daubigny to forego detail in the interest of natural effects and whatever he showed at the annual Salon was savaged by critics for its slapdash handling. Though his work was often sombre it missed the sentimental trap that caught many of his fellow artists. If any Barbizon painter deserves to be revalued Daubigny must be the frontrunner.

The work Théodore Rousseau submitted to the Paris Salon was rejected every year from 1836 to 1848. The Louvre finally bought *La Clairière* for £160 though that mark of official acceptance hardly made life easier. Rousseau's personal spectrum seemed to run from emerald green to mossy green and his ruminating landscapes, like Daubigny's, are a little heavy for modern tastes and have risen only 70% since 1975.

The market for middle-range Barbizon pictures looks set to stay weak. Top-flight works on the other hand – and this means just the twenty or so best paintings of each artist – should still prove a sound buy. For fifteen years Japanese demand for the Barbizon School has been a key factor in the market. Of all European cultures the Japanese feel greatest affinity with the French and since Japan was until this century basically a peasant economy, they find Millet's paintings irresistible. Their buying though has become more selective and they can no longer be sold run-of-the-mill work.

Sooner or later, perhaps in Japan, a major exhibition of Barbizon artists is sure to be held. Critics will commend their nobility of purpose and the market may splutter into life. People will remind themselves how worthy these artists could be – but also how dull – and apathy will set in again. It may be a shameful way to treat good artists, but if you are born a generation ahead of Monet, Degas and Renoir the going is certain to be tough.

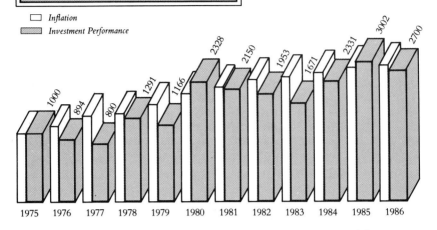

THE BARBIZON SCHOOL

☐ Inflation
▨ Investment Performance

1975 1976 1977 1978 1979 1980 1981 1982 1983 1984 1985 1986

Artists: Jean-Baptiste Camille Corot, Charles François Daubigny, Jean-François Millet, Théodore Rousseau, Constant Troyon

Artist	Mid-market price £	Change since 1975 %
The Barbizon School		
Jean-Baptiste Camille Corot (*1796–1875*)	33,400	+160
Charles François Daubigny (*1812–78*)	4000	+140
Jean-François Millet (*1814–75*)	27,300	+290
Théodore Rousseau (*1812–67*)	2300	+70
Constant Troyon (*1810–65*)	2300	+330
Other Artists of the School		
Narcisse-Virgile Diaz de la Pena (*1807–76*)	2300	+130
Jules Dupré (*1811–89*)	1400	+100
Henri Harpignies (*1819–1916*)	1300	+80
Charles Emile Jacques (*1813–94*)	2500	+260
Léon Richet (*1847–1907*)	2800	+360

The French Impressionists

The time to buy Impressionist paintings was at the auction arranged by the artists themselves in 1874. Seventy or so works by Renoir, Monet, Sisley and Berthe Morisot fetched the pitifully low average price of £6 each. Prices in the early years of this century had gone over £1000 for all the leading figures in the group and have never really looked cheap since.

Leaving aside the early years, the growth rate reached a peak over the 1955–65 period when prices rose by 370%. Between 1965 and 1975 there was a slowdown to 120% but between 1975 and 1985 growth has accelerated to 370% – the increase between 1983 and 1985 alone amounting to 60%. That rate is not sustainable and has much to do with the weakness of sterling against the dollar. A rate of 10% to 15% for the mainstream of the market should be sustainable *in dollar terms* over the next decade.

Competition for the greatest works has been made worse by the new kind of ratings war that leading museum curators are now engaged in. Their buying power is formidable and since they are intent on acquiring crowd-pullers they are certain to drive prices for the very best works ever higher. The theory that newly established or less well-endowed provincial galleries around the world will need to have a holding of Impressionist work, and therefore create steady demand for medium-quality works, may well prove correct. And in any case prices in the art market are fixed by reference to works of comparable quality. The moment a new record is set, the owner of a slightly less important work by the same artist will revalue it in the light of the record price just paid and the whole complex price-structure will be ratcheted up.

Performances within the index vary though in general the Impressionists are still riding high on a wave of admiration unmatched by any other school of painting. Many potential buyers of the French Impressionists have had to settle for other modern schools of painting where prices are more reasonable and they would be back in the market if prices were ever to fall.

Some collectors admittedly see themselves as having developed beyond the Impressionists. They prefer paintings in which the artist is more

ABOVE *Edgar Degas (1834–1917): 'Trois Danseuses' (c. 1880), £750,000.*

BELOW *Henri Fantin-Latour (1863–1904): 'Vase de fleurs, melon, raisins et poires' (1869), £50,600.*

ABOVE *Camille Pissarro (1830–1903): 'Rue de la citadelle' (1873),* £600,000.

LEFT *Alfred Sisley (1839–99): 'La Seine à Argenteuil',* £320,000.

BELOW *Claude Monet (1840–1926): 'Chemin dans les vignes, Argenteuil' (c. 1872),* £150,000.

OPPOSITE *Pierre-Auguste Renoir (1841–1919): 'Au Théâtre; La Loge' (1894),* £605,000.

involved; paintings that make some kind of statement about their subject rather than passively record its existence. For however revolutionary the Impressionists may have seemed in their day, it was soon objected that their approach was too lyrical and too neutral. Impressionism did not concern itself with the search for a definition of the role of art or the artist in society, not at any rate of the kind that preoccupied later movements. These collectors may have a point but for the time being they are an insignificant force in the market ranged against the admiring hordes.

Within the index Renoir has risen 430% since 1975; Degas 50%; Monet 730%; Pissaro 120% and Sisley 310%. Outside the index but associated with the group are Fantin-Latour, who is up 320%, and Boudin, up 210%.

About a thousand Renoirs have been sold at auction over the last ten years; the highest-priced quintile advancing appreciably faster than the lowest. Too many collectors are determined to own a Renoir at any cost and pay silly prices for scraps from the great man's studio. Renoir himself said, 'If I sold only good paintings I should starve', and collectors should take seriously the implications of that statement. He once left a stack of sketches with his brother-in-law in Champagne but, on returning to collect them, found that they had been used to roof some rabbit hutches. When asked why he had treated the canvases in such a way, the brother-in-law explained that he could not see how anything produced so quickly could have any value.

Buyers must therefore be selective, treating Renoir as dealers and collectors did from the very first, like a vineyard whose produce varied in quality from year to year. In 1910

the dealer Vollard suggested to Count Isaac de Camondo that he might buy a Renoir. 'Perhaps,' replied the Count, 'but none of your 1900s, nor your 1896s either.' Vollard proposed a magnificent portrait of 1889. 'I don't want any of your '89s either, for that is the middle of the dry period. . . But I have decided to have some Renoirs, so find me some good '70s, even '65s – women of course. Watch out for the hands. None of those kitchen-wench hands of his. . . Bear in mind that the pictures will go to the Louvre some day.'

With the mid-market price for a Renoir now standing at £80,900, buyers are getting more and more cautious. For the better paintings the outlook is good; buyers considering paying £30,000 for one of Renoir's dashed-off sketches should not expect to do well.

The mid-market price for a Monet is up from £41,000 in 1975 to £344,000 today – the highest figure for any artist of the last two hundred years. Monet's life spanned an artistic era running from Impressionism to abstraction and even now about twenty of his works are sold at auction every year. Throughout his life he retained the individual, sensuous style he first braved in the 1860s and travelled widely through France and the rest of Europe applying it to a great variety of landscapes. But it is his handling of water and his relationship with it that developed through-

ABOVE *Claude Monet (1840–1926): 'Antibes vue de la Salis' (1888), £1,000,000.*

LEFT *Camille Pissaro (1830–1903): 'Vue de Pontoise' (1871), £62,000.*

BELOW *Vincent Van Gogh (1853–90): 'Paysage au soleil levant', £7,200,000.*

OPPOSITE *Gustave Caillebotte (1840–94): 'La Maison dans les arbres' (1880), £50,600.*

out his life that produced the most astonishing work. At first he painted water in a side-by-side relationship to the land – earth to sea, river bank to river, and so on. Later the water-earth theme changes into a vertical configuration in which the mirroring effect makes the earth seem to enclose the water from below as well as from above. In the final studies of water there is no land at all. As an old man, when he was not painting from the studio-boat he had made, Monet liked to surround himself with his studies of water as though he had sought to immerse himself in it all his life.

These are among the great artistic achievements of all time and as secure as any investment can be. But prices have trebled in the last four years and must be expected to settle back to an annual rate of 15% to 20%.

Up 50% to a mid-market price of £79,000, Degas's work is instantly identifiable. It is not only his style but his recurring themes – race horses, the ballet, nudes and milliners – that make immediate recognition possible. His work sold for £50 to £500 until 1900. In 1912 an exceptional £20,000 was paid for *Danseuses à la Barre*, now in the Louvre, but for most of the first fifty years of this century his paintings fell in the £2000 to £15,000 range.

Degas was as solidly bourgeois an artist as it is possible to be. He was also, in the eyes of those who knew him best, cantankerous and caustic. The dealer Durand-Ruel described him as a 'dreadful man' and for the last thirty years of his life found it nearly impossible to prise anything from his studio.

For an artist who achieved such recognition during his lifetime it is surprising that in 1960 Degas was valued well below Renoir and only began to rise swiftly during the late 1960s and early 1970s. Degas has now caught up the ground he seems to have lost over the 1910–50 period. His most creative years were from 1878 to 1883, yet some of his later works, executed when his eyesight was failing, fetch surprisingly large sums.

Subject matter always plays a big part in the value of any painting. The highest-rated Degas works are ballet scenes and nude figures; next come racing scenes and portraits; lastly, milliners and washerwomen. Untypical works usually underperform those for which an artist is best known. Buyers of Degas should do best by sticking to the subjects that made him famous.

Sisley's work has risen by 310% since 1975. Though about a thousand paintings have survived, only ten or fifteen pass through the salerooms each year. Sisley was the only Impressionist to devote himself entirely to landscape. He painted in a mild, contemplative idiom that makes it difficult to believe that his work was so little appreciated at the notorious auction of 1874. The few brave collectors who bought at that time paid between £2 and £12 a canvas.

Although Sisley was unappreciated throughout his life – he lay dying of cancer and was too poor to call a doctor – prices for his work took off the moment he was dead. He is still the least known of the Impressionists

but the mid-market price for his work at £145,000 is second only to Monet. Throughout the long years of failure Sisley never budged from the style he believed in. It was as though he waited for the rest of the world to fall into line. To a great extent that has now happened. Several national museums – including the National Gallery in London – have poor holdings of Sisley. The Japanese too are keenly interested in Sisley – perhaps for his remarkable evocations of weather – and prices for his paintings may well grow faster than for other French Impressionists.

Pissarro has lagged behind the other Impressionists with a rise of just 120% since 1975. He was nonetheless the archetypal Impressionist, painting lyrical country scenes with a magical portrayal of light. Under his hand even factories became idyllic havens of work, puffing pure white smoke and nestling harmoniously into the landscape. Even if his work lacks the force of Cézanne, Pissarro is surely one of the greatest landscape painters.

It was not until he was sixty-eight

TOP LEFT *Eugène Boudin (1824–98): 'La Plage à Trouville à l'Heure du Bain' (1868)*, £120,000.

TOP RIGHT *Camille Pissarro (1830–1903): 'Le Bassin des Tuileries; Après-midi (1900)*, £121,000.

ABOVE LEFT *Paul Cézanne (1839–1906): 'La Mer à l'Estaque' (1876)*, £704,000.

ABOVE RIGHT *Armand Guillaumin (1841–1927): 'La Côte du Val André (Bretagne)'*, £11,000.

BELOW *Armand Guillaumin (1841–1927): 'Côte d'Esterel' (c. 1905)*, £15,000.

that his paintings began to command reasonably high prices. A group of businessmen got together in 1899 to push his work and the same year several paintings sold for £200 to £300. By 1903 though, the year of his death, he wrote to his son Lucien saying that his fortunes were at their lowest ebb. His work was now selling for £40 at auction and he had failed to sell a single painting at the two exhibitions to which he had sent work. In line with the macabre work-ings of the art market, Durand-Ruel organized an exhibition six months after he died and prices jumped to between £400 and £600.

The mid-market price for Pissarro stands at just £33,000. Though he was more prolific than most of the Impressionists, and about sixty of his canvases are sold every year, there is no reason why the growth rate for his work should not at least match that of the group.

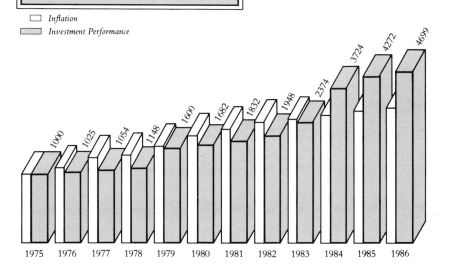

THE FRENCH IMPRESSIONISTS

☐ *Inflation*
▨ *Investment Performance*

1975	1976	1977	1978	1979	1980	1981	1982	1983	1984	1985	1986
1000	1025	1054	1148	1600	1682	1832	1948	2374	3724	4272	4699

Artists: Edgar Degas, Claude Monet, Camille Pissarro, Pierre-Auguste Renoir, Alfred Sisley

Artist	Mid-market price £	Change since 1975 %
French Impressionists		
Edgar Degas (*1843–1917*)	36,600	+ 50
Claude Monet (*1840–1926*)	344,000	+ 730

Artist	Mid-market price £	Change since 1975 %
Camille Pissarro (1830–1903)	33,000	+120
Pierre-Auguste Renoir (1841–1919)	80,900	+430
Alfred Sisley (1839–99)	145,100	+310
Other Artists Related to Impressionism		
Eugène Boudin (1824–98)	27,700	+210
Gustave Caillebotte (1840–1894)	137,000	+3700
Paul Cézanne (1839–1906)	121,300	+240
Henri Edmond Cross (1856–1910)	16,300	+1020
Henri Fantin-Latour (1836–1904)	30,100	+320
Armand Guillaumin (1841–1927)	10,200	+210
Stanislas Lépine (1835–92)	9100	+400

Artist	Mid-market price £	Change since 1975 %
Selected 18th and 19th Century French Artists		
Louis Léopold Boilly (1761–1845)	8400	+590
Rosa Bonheur (1822–99)	1200	−20
François Boucher (1707–70)	18,100	+320
William Adolphe Bouguereau (1825–1905)	27,900	+1280
Gustave Courbet (1819–77)	27,100	+340
Karl Daubigny (1846–86)	1900	+180
Alexandre Defaux (1826–1900)	1300	+150
Eugène Delacroix (1798–1863)	14,700	+60
Hippolyte Camille Delpy (1842–1910)	2500	+300
Gustave Doré (1832–83)	2900	+510
Alfred de Dreux (1810–60)	33,900	+1370
Jean-Honoré Fragonard (1732–1806)	26,500	+420
Eugène Fromentin (1820–76)	3100	+520
Eugène Galien-Lalou (1854–1954)	4000	+360
Jean Léon Gérôme (1824–1904)	c. 50,000	+2500
Jean-Baptiste Greuze (1725–1805)	10,200	+270
Constantin Guys (1802–92)	900	+90
Paul-César Helleu (1859–1927)	4500	+970
Jean-Jacques Henner (1829–1905)	2000	+150
Eugène Isabey (1803–86)	1900	+160
Charles Euphrasie Kuwasseg (1838–1904)	3000	+320
Nicolas de Largillière (1656–1746)	15,200	+350

ABOVE *Claude Monet (1840–1926): 'Pins, Cap d'Antibes' (1888), £374,500.*

RIGHT *Henri de Toulouse-Lautrec (1864–1901): 'The Female Clown – Cha-u-Kao', £3,200,000.*

Artist	Mid-market price £	Change since 1975 %
Maurice Levis (*1860–1902*)	2500	+450
Léon Lhermitte (*1844–1925*)	6200	+270
Paul Madeline (*1863–1920*)	2900	+480
Adolphe Monticelli (*1824–86*)	2100	no change
Henry Moret (*1856–1913*)	11,700	+440
Alfred Arthur Brunel de Neuville (*19th century*)	1400	+290
Edmond Petitjean (*1844–1925*)	2600	+310
Jean Pillement (*1728–1808*)	2900	+50
Jean François Raffaelli (*1850–1924*)	5900	+240
Hubert Robert (*1733–1808*)	2300	+70
Henri de Toulouse-Lautrec (*1864–1901*)	16,100	+50
Paul Désiré Trouillebert (*1829–1900*)	4600	+200
Emmanuel de la Villéon (*1858–1944*)	2000	+80

Edmond Petitjean (1844–1925): 'Un Village au bord d'une rivière', £4500.

Emile Othon Friesz (1879–1949): 'Déchargeurs dans le port, Anvers' (1906), £26,000.

Artist	Mid-market price £	Change since 1975 %
The School of Paris		
Pierre Bonnard (1867–1947)	59,100	+260
Georges Braque (1882–1963)	43,000	+140
Marc Chagall (1887–1985)	44,400	+140
Kees van Dongen (1877–1968)	18,000	+280
Moïse Kisling (1891–1953)	13,600	+130
Marie Laurençin (1885–1956)	14,800	+450
Pablo Picasso (1881–1974)	40,800	+90
Georges Rouault (1871–1958)	21,300	+60
Maurice Utrillo (1883–1955)	30,100	+200
Edouard Vuillard (1868–1940)	30,300	+610
Other School of Paris: French Artists		
Jean Atlan (1913–60)	6200	+120
André Bauchant (1873–1958)	5000	+510
André Beaudin (1895–?)	1600	+280
Emile Bernard (1868–1941)	4300	+460
Camille Bombois (1883–1970)	5700	+90
Yves Brayer (b. 1907)	1300	+190
Maurice Brianchon (1899–1979)	8700	+1000
Bernard Buffet (b. 1928)	7600	+90
Charles Camoin (1879–1965)	4400	+210
Roger Chapelin-Midy (b. 1904)	1600	+180
Jean Crotti (1878–1958)	2100	+470
Olivier Debré (b. 1920)	1300	+180
Sonia Delaunay (1885–1979)	2700	+320
Maurice Denis (1870–1943)	8100	+460
André Dérain (1880–1954)	4100	+140
François Desnoyer (1894–1972)	800	+60
André Dignimont (1891–1965)	600	+200
Jean Dubuffet (1901–85)	21,600	+250
Charles Dufresne (1876–1934)	2300	+290
Raoul Dufy (1877–1953)	20,000	+310
André Dunoyer de Segonzac (1884–1974)	3600	+90
Georges d'Espagnat (1870–1950)	3500	+160
Henri le Fauconnier (1881–1946)	700	+120

Henri Manguin (1874–1949): 'Nature Morte aux Cyclamens' (1912), £60,000.

Artist	Mid-market price £	Change since 1975 %
Jean Fautrier (1852–1931)	6000	+140
Jean Louis Forain (1852–1931)	2000	+80
Emile Othon Friesz (1879–1949)	2400	+60
Gen-Paul (1895–?)	1000	−30
Paul Elie Gernez (1888–1948)	2400	+340
Albert Gleizes (1881–1953)	9600	+370
Edouard Goerg (1893–1969)	2500	−20
Marcel Gromaire (1892–1971)	2600	+130
André Hambourg (b. 1909)	1900	+180
Hans Hartung (b. 1904)	5800	+30
Auguste Herbin (1882–1960)	3500	+80
Camille Hilaire (b. 1916)	700	+100
Felix Labisse (b. 1905)	2000	+30
André Lanskoy (1902–76)	1700	+10
Charles Lapicque (1898–?)	2700	+170
Pierre Laprade (1875–1932)	1500	+150
Louis Latapie (1891–?)	400	+10
Fernand Léger (1881–1955)	13,700	+60
Marcel Leprin (1891–1933)	2300	+130
André Lhote (1885–1962)	3000	+180
Bernard Lorjou (b. 1908)	1800	+60
Jean Lurcat (1892–1966)	1100	+140
Mané-Katz (1894–1962)	3000	+40
Henri Manguin (1874–1949)	11,300	+560
Louis Marcoussis (1883–1941)	5100	+10
Albert Marquet (1875–1947)	16,200	+200
Georges Mathieu (b. 1921)	2400	−20
Henri Matisse (1869–1954)	23,400	+20
Jean Metzinger (1883–1956)	8400	+130
Anders Osterlind (1887–1960)	600	+80
Roland Oudot (b. 1897)	1400	+160
Jules Pascin (1885–1930)	1190	−30
André Planson (b. 1898)	800	+160
Jean Pougny (1894–1956)	1200	+200
Jean Puy (1876–1959)	3200	+410
Alphonse Quizet (1885–1955)	1200	+60

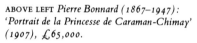

ABOVE LEFT *Pierre Bonnard (1867–1947):
'Portrait de la Princesse de Caraman-Chimay'
(1907), £65,000.*

ABOVE RIGHT *Auguste Herbin (1882–1960):
'Fleurs' (c. 1926), £10,000.*

LEFT *Roland Oudot (b. 1897): 'La Ferme
Normande', £2800.*

BELOW LEFT *Natalia Gontcharova (1881–1962):
'The Ice Cutters', £59,000.*

BELOW RIGHT *Paul Elie Gernez (1888–1948):
'Le Port d'Honfleur' (1927), £1200.*

ABOVE LEFT *Maurice Denis (1870–1943): 'Scène Bretonne' (1893), £40,000.*

ABOVE RIGHT *Maurice Denis (1870–1943): 'Dans les bras de sa soeur' (1914), £18,000.*

RIGHT *Maurice Utrillo (1883–1955): 'Le Pavillon Sévigné à Vichy' (1934), £34,000.*

Artist	Mid-market price £	Change since 1975 %
Raffy-Le-Persan (*20th century*)	600	+50
Alfred Reth (*1884–1966*)	1100	+50
Ker Xavier Roussel (*1867–1944*)	2300	+260
Paul Sérusier (*1863–1927*)	12,500	+430
Paul Signac (*1863–1935*)	7300	+180
Pierre Soulages (*b. 1919*)	11,300	+140
Chaim Soutine (*1893–1943*)	42,800	+60
Léopold Survage (*1879–1968*)	1600	+120
Suzanne Valadon (*1865–1938*)	8400	+330
Georges Valmier (*1885–1937*)	8000	+520
Jacques Villon (*1875–1963*)	8200	+290
Maurice de Vlaminck (*1876–1958*)	18,900	+90
Henry de Waroquier (*1881–1970*)	800	+140

ABOVE LEFT *Frank-Boggs (1855–1926): 'Le Quai des Grands Augustins', £18,000.*

ABOVE RIGHT *Marcel Leprin (1891–1933): 'Le Port de Caen' (1930), £1600.*

Artist	Mid-market price £	Change since 1975 %
The School of Paris: Non-French Artists		
Pierre Alechinsky (*b. 1927*)	6900	+250
Karel Appel (*b. 1921*)	2500	+40
Francisco Bores (*1898–1972*)	1100	+20
Massimo Campigli (*1895–1971*)	16,500	+100
Carlo Carra (*1881–1966*)	13,500	+130
Serge Charchoune (*1888–?*)	1300	+160
Antoni Clave (*b. 1913*)	5900	+290
Nils Dardel (*1888–1942*)	10,700	+600
Oscar Dominguez (*1906–1958*)	1900	+30
Leonor Fini (*b. 1908*)	1900	+60
Tsuguharu Foujita (*1886–1968*)	15,400	+410
Alberto Giacometti (*1901–1966*)	7300	+230
Natalia Gontcharova (*1881–1962*)	1100	+160
Emile Grau-Sala (*b. 1911*)	1400	+120
Michel Kikoine (*1892–1968*)	1500	+50
Pinchus Kremegne (*1890–?*)	1200	+10
Frank Kupka (*1871–1957*)	1800	+80
Alberto Magnelli (*1888–1971*)	2600	−50
Amedeo Modigliani (*1884–1920*)	34,100	+30
Piet Mondrian (*1872–1944*)	10,500	+220
Filippo de Pisis (*1896–1956*)	4000	+80
Serge Poliakoff (*1906–1969*)	15,200	+290
Jean-Claude Riopelle (*b. 1922*)	8100	+90
Diego Rivera (*1886–1957*)	13,500	+560
Gino Severini (*1883–1966*)	7300	+50
Nicolas de Staël (*1914–55*)	24,800	+20
Felix Vallotton (*1865–1925*)	8500	+130

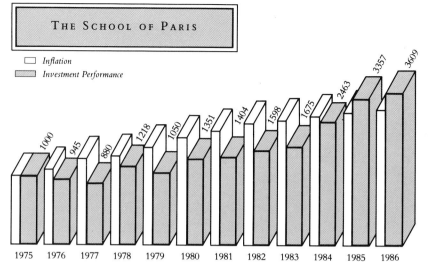

THE SCHOOL OF PARIS

☐ Inflation
▨ Investment Performance

1000 / 945 / 880 / 1218 / 1050 / 1351 / 1404 / 1598 / 1675 / 2463 / 3357 / 3609

| 1975 | 1976 | 1977 | 1978 | 1979 | 1980 | 1981 | 1982 | 1983 | 1984 | 1985 | 1986 |

Artists: Pierre Bonnard, Georges Braque, Marc Chagall, Kees van Dongen, Moïse Kisling, Marie Laurençin, Pablo Picasso, Georges Rouault, Maurice Utrillo, Edouard Vuillard

Artist	Mid-market price £	Change since 1975 %
Other 20th Century French Artists		
Pierre de Belay (*1890–1947*)	1700	+ 320
Jacques Emile Blanche (*1861–1942*)	2100	+ 320
Antoine Bouvard (*?–1956*)	1700	+ 170
Victor Charreton (*1864–1937*)	3200	+ 310
Edouard Cortes (*1882–1969*)	4400	+ 330
Jean Gabriel Domergue (*1889–1962*)	2100	+ 260
Jean Dufy (*1888–1964*)	2700	+ 180
Marcel Dyf (*b. 1899*)	1700	+ 290
Frank-Boggs (*1855–1926*)	1500	+ 230
François Gall (*1912–1945*)	1400	+ 310
Henri Hayden (*1883–1970*)	700	− 10
Jean Jansem (*b. 1920*)	1300	+ 110
Abel Lauvray (*1870–1950*)	2100	+ 290
Henri Lebasque (*1865–1937*)	9700	+ 690
Albert Lebourg (*1849–1928*)	6800	+ 280
Gustave Loiseau (*1865–1935*)	16,800	+ 320
Maximilien Luce (*1858–1941*)	3400	+ 150
Elisee Maclet (*1881–1962*)	1600	+ 180
Aristide Maillol (*1861–1944*)	3200	+ 330
Henri Martin (*1860–1943*)	9300	+ 590
Maxime Maufra (*1861–1918*)	6000	+ 340
Pierre Eugène Montezin (*1874–1946*)	2700	+ 150
Henri le Sidaner (*1862–1939*)	9900	+ 310

ABOVE LEFT *Henri Lebasque (1865–1937)*: 'Bord de Rivière' (c. 1925), £28,000.

ABOVE RIGHT *Henri le Sidaner (1826–1939)*: 'La Nappe Blanche' (1930), £10,500.

LEFT *Gustave Loiseau*: 'Le Cathédrale de Rouen', £13,000.

OPPOSITE *Jasper Cropsey (1823–1900)*: 'Lake George' (1871), £15,000.

Further Reading

Edmond and Jules de Goncourt, *French Eighteenth-century Painters* (London, 1981)

Joseph C. Sloane, *French Painting. Artists, Critics and Traditions from 1848–1870* (Princeton, 1951)

Philip Conisbee, *Painting in Eighteenth-century France* (Oxford, 1981)

David Wakefield, *French Eighteenth-century Painting* (London, 1984)

John Rewald, *The History of Impressionism* (New York, 1946)

William Gaunt, *The Impressionists* (London, 1970)

Phoebe Pool, *Impressionism* (London, 1967)

Germain Bazin, *L'Epoque Impressioniste* (Paris, 1947)

Raymond Cogniat, *The Century of the Impressionists* (London, 1985)

John Rewald, *Post-Impressionism from Van Gogh to Gauguin* (New York, 1956)

Wend Graf Kalnein and Michael Levey, *Art and Architecture of the Eighteenth Century in France* (London, 1972)

American Painting

American painting of all periods has risen strongly since 1975 and looks set for further growth. Now that market prices have advanced so far it is time to reconsider the real artistic status of each field and size up its prospects.

Special forces are at work in the market for American art. Compared with most European countries there is a large volume of money in the United States chasing a relatively small body of work. One effect is that the less important paintings command more than their counterparts elsewhere.

The number of American paintings extant varies from one period to another though rarity does not necessarily indicate a high price. Only a few hundred 17th century paintings can be firmly attributed to American artists. Most of these are now in museums and the few that have passed through the market have been of greater curiosity than artistic value.

By the beginning of the 18th century the concept of a professional painter had at least become recognized, though people generally wanted portraits. John Singleton Copley complained that painting was regarded as no more than a useful trade. Even in the later part of the century established artists were still expected to paint sign-boards, emblems on

carriages and do other humdrum work. Artists had to paint what people would pay for and not many were willing to part with good money for a landscape. The severely practical lives led by colonial Americans left them with little time for cultural pursuits, and if any painting was to be done at all their puritanical disposition dictated that the style should be rigidly factual.

Is there such a thing as an American style? American painters have always felt ambivalent about European culture and Copley's vacillation over whether to join Benjamin West in London in the 1770s was not only to do with political problems at home and his doubts about succeeding in London. It was the feeling of most American artists who during the 18th and 19th centuries went to study in London, Rome, Paris and Munich. They would have preferred to stay put and 'make it' at home. That after all was what America was all about. The pioneer farmers who fought their battles with nature did not return to Europe for seed corn and building materials; they succeeded by using what was to hand. But for the American painter the right growing conditions were only to be found in Europe. In America, at least during the 18th century, there was no teaching, no example and no market.

Many Americans had even expressed misgivings about culture, at least as it manifested itself in Europe. Benjamin Franklin, for example, had written, '. . . with countries as with young men, you must curb their fancy to strengthen their judgement . . . thus poetry, painting and music are all necessary and proper gratifications of a refined state of society, but objectionable at an earlier period since their cultivation would make a taste for their enjoyment precede its means.' In other words, first things first. The arts were not on most people's list of first things and the artist's battle for recognition in America was as hard as anywhere.

The earliest American painters painted what they saw and in so doing laid the foundation of the American style. That realism is the thread that links those first portraits to America's greatest artist, Thomas Eakins, who in pursuit of realism used trigonometry to work out his perspectives.

Early American Portraits

Early American portraits usually seem austere and forthright but, along with other American folk art that has come to the fore as a field for serious collectors, are often attractive.

Many portraits are unsigned and this makes the field difficult to monitor. Prices since 1975 would seem to have risen by at least 250%. The work of the earliest known artists such as Smibert and Feke seldom reach the salerooms and the last recorded prices are in the low thousands. Several sectors of 18th century art are now swinging back into fashion and no matter how provincial and unaccomplished these early portraits may be, they should benefit from this trend.

The work of the later portraitists such as J. S. Copley, Gilbert Stuart and the Peales has always been considered more interesting. Benjamin West's long residence in London, where he became president of the Royal Academy and where he was host and mentor to every visiting American painter, puts him outside the mainstream of American painting. His style became so totally European that many Americans see him as an English painter. Copley's early work before he left for England will always be highly rated for it shows best the realism he cast off to fit in with the superficial conventions of portraiture in London. Not often seen at auction today, Copley portraits fetch up to £100,000.

Prices for Gilbert Stuart's work have risen strongly and it now sells mainly in the £3000 to £20,000 range. He painted three main versions of the portrait of George Washington but sold so many copies he came to refer to them as his 'hundred dollar bills'. Investors should be careful not to overpay for one of these for the quality is variable and the later versions quite mechanical.

Most works by America's leading portrait painters, such as Inman, Sully, Morse, the Peales and Neagle, still fall in the £2000 to £10,000 range. Those by unknown artists can be bought for under £500. At worst these are wooden and lifeless; occasionally they can be appealing. As with all portraits, prices depend less on technical competence than on inspired interpretation and an attractive subject.

The Hudson River School

The decade of the 1830s was a turning point in American painting. Political independence in 1776 had created the desire for cultural independence but in the field of painting at least this had not been achieved.

The whole tenor of American painting both in subject matter and execution continued to reflect the grand tour of Europe that many American painters made. Classical landscapes were still in the style of Claude and Poussin, the few *genre* paintings there were bore the stamp of Jan Steen, portraits showed the influence of Lely, Gainsborough and Reynolds, while the great historical set-pieces were largely indistinguishable from their European counterparts.

American society was still fervently religious and this, as elsewhere, precluded the proper study and representation of the human body. The occasional nude appeared in the guise of a Greek slave or classical nymph but there were difficulties in getting models and the whole issue was allowed to remain in abeyance.

Surprisingly, American painters had largely ignored the landscapes in which they lived. Several important studies of the new continent had been, or were being, completed by Catlin of the Red Indian tribes and by Audubon of the birds of America, for instance. Emerson tried to sever the umbilical cord by which American artists were still being nourished from Europe. His Phi Beta Kappa address of 1837 asserted, 'Our day of dependence, our long apprenticeship to the learning of other lands, draws to a close. The millions that around us are rushing into life cannot always be fed on the sere remains of foreign harvests. Events, actions arise, that must be sung, that will sing themselves.'

Artists set off to celebrate the natural beauty of the Catskills, the Adirondacks and other virgin tracts in a spirit of reverence and discovery. Their idea was no less than that through such beauty God's presence itself would be revealed.

Although the Hudson River School is not regarded as an indigenous art movement, its leading exponents, in spite of their European connections, covered new ground in American painting. Prices have risen strongly since 1975. Jasper Cropsey's work is up 490%; Worthington Whittredge's by 320%. Paintings by Jervis McEntee, Thomas Cole and Asher Durand are not often sold at auction but are estimated to have climbed 300% over the same period. With a rise of just 170% Thomas Kensett's work looks set to catch up. The status of all these painters is firmly established. Demand for the Hudson River School is still concentrated in the United States, though their record could prompt further investment buying in Europe.

The Luminists

The Luminist School has usually been hailed as the first genuinely American school of painting though it developed quite naturally from the Hudson River School. And though the Luminists are sometimes described as

imaginative realists, the thread of realism running through American painting is stretched to its limit at this point.

During the 1970s the Luminists began to appeal ever more strongly to American collectors and £1.15 million was paid for Frederick Church's *Icebergs*. Since 1975 prices have risen by 410% for works by Sanford Gifford, 240% for Thomas Moran and 500% for Martin Johnson Heade. Mid-market prices are well up in five figures and the finest works are now hard to find.

Whereas the Hudson River School, as its name implies, drew its inspiration from American territory, the Luminists travelled widely outside the United States. Church, for example, travelled to the Arctic, to South America and to the ancient ruins of Greece and the Middle East.

John Wilmerding has described as the philosophical headwater of the movement Emerson's statement: 'Standing on the bare ground – my head bathed by the blithe air and uplifted into infinite space – all mean egotism vanishes. I became a transparent eyeball; I am nothing; I see all; the currents of the Universal Being circulate through me; I am part and parcel of God.'

Many of the Luminists had been impressed by Ruskin's conception of art, nature and morality being linked together. They even sought to link

OPPOSITE LEFT *Worthington Whittredge (1820–1910): 'Landscape near Minden, Germany' (1855), £100,000.*

OPPOSITE RIGHT *Jasper Cropsey (1823–1900): 'Indian Summer', £14,000.*

OPPOSITE BELOW *Thomas Moran (1837–1926): 'Near Fort Wingate, New Mexico', £55,000.*

RIGHT *John George Brown (1831–1913): 'At Home', £20,000.*

BELOW RIGHT *Joshua Shaw (1776–1861): 'View in the Pennsylvania Countryside', £16,000.*

up these three with the destiny of America, and where this message is evident the paintings seem to suffer for it. While the Luminists were ascending the peaks that afforded the most dramatic views, down on the ground the horror and tragedy of the Civil War was being recorded by Winslow Homer. Elsewhere and also at ground level, it was fortunate that the last thought in Cézanne's mind as he painted the sea at l'Estaque was the destiny of France. It was to be some time before painting was purged of its supposed powers of moral therapy.

The Luminists discovered a new and impressive way of representing all the shades and qualities of light. In this they were helped to some extent by the introduction of new cadmium pigments. But they also discovered the dramatic positioning of the landscape in such a way as to open up a vast expanse of sky, but using the water and vapour below and even the trees as a source or as reflectors of light.

But Luminism was not entirely an American phenomenon. The influence of the German Romantic painters is especially evident in the work of Albert Bierstadt, himself a German who studied at Düsseldorf. His work has risen 440% since 1975; the mid-market price now stands at £18,400 though his major works fetch up to £150,000.

Whatever its origins, the Luminist School is now clearly perceived as *the* American school. The 1980 Luminist exhibition placed it more firmly than ever on the map and the outlook for market prices is good.

The Physical Realists

Winslow Homer and Thomas Eakins – perhaps America's two greatest artists – certainly manifest that powerful realism that is the most constant element in the elusive American style. Homer has for years been a national institution. During the Civil War he was sent by *Harper's Weekly* to the front where he made sketches that were used as illustrations for the magazine. His work revealed a gift for quickly observing and recording a scene with extraordinary intensity.

In his later years he lived on the coast of Maine studying every storm from a shelter he had specially built on a promontory. A collector who had hung a Homer sea study in his rather small library once said it gave him the feeling he might be washed out of his house at any moment. Homer's great stature has always been recognized. £700,000 was paid for *The Signal of Distress* in 1980 but even the small watercolours, measuring, say, ten by fourteen inches, can fetch well over £50,000.

Thomas Eakins ranks as America's most intellectual artist. Deeply committed to the accurate representation of what he saw, he used not only trigonometry to work out his perspectives but also studied the mathematics of the reflection and refraction of light.

Although he studied in France and was well aware of the activities of the

Alfred Thomson Bricher (1837–1908): 'Breaking Surf', £6700.

French Impressionists, he took little interest in their attempts to tackle the problem of light that he himself was facing. His insistence on realism led him into trouble with the prudish society of Philadelphia. At Pennsylvania Academy he insisted that his pupils draw from the female nude but in the ensuing furore was forced to resign his professorship. William Rush had also shocked these guardians of the nation's morals when he used a nude model while sculpting the allegorical figure of the Schuylkill River. Eakins painted the scene in which the sculptor is at work, his naked model and her chaperone sitting knitting at her side.

Any important work by Eakins would fetch over a million pounds today. Even the few small drawings that have recently been sold fetch around £5000 but should prove excellent investments.

Lying third behind Eakins and Homer is Eastman Johnson. The only artist of the three whose market trend can be reasonably monitored, his work has climbed 260% since 1975. Though an uneven artist this seems an unduly slow climb and prices for his better work may be expected to accelerate.

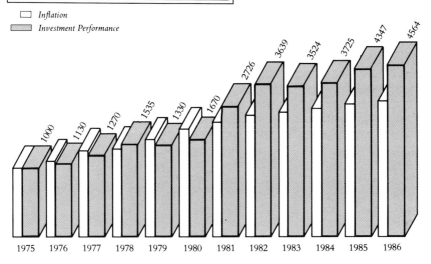

19TH CENTURY AMERICAN PAINTING

☐ Inflation
▨ Investment Performance

1000 1130 1270 1535 1330 1670 2726 3639 3524 3725 4347 4564

1975 1976 1977 1978 1979 1980 1981 1982 1983 1984 1985 1986

Artists: Albert Bierstadt, Alfred Thomson Bricher, John George Brown, Jasper Francis Cropsey, Sanford Gifford, James MacDougal Hart, Martin Johnson Heade, Thomas Hill, George Inness, Antonio Jacobsen, Eastman Johnson, John Frederick Kensett, Daniel Ridgway Knight, Thomas Moran, Robert Salmon, Thomas Sully, Arthur Fitzwilliam Tait, William Aiken Walker, Worthington Whittredge, William L. Sonntag

Artist	Mid-market price £	Change since 1975 %
19th Century American Painting		
Albert Bierstadt (*1830–1902*)	18,400	+440
Alfred Thomas Bricher (*1837–1908*)	3500	+200
John George Brown (*1831–1913*)	8100	+430

Artist	Mid-market price £	Change since 1975 %
Jasper Francis Cropsey (*1823–1900*)	11,900	+490
Sanford Gifford (*1823–80*)	10,500	+410
James MacDougal Hart (*1828–1901*)	4700	+290
Martin Johnson Heade (*1819–1904*)	24,600	+500
Thomas Hill (*1829–1908*)	5900	+580
George Inness (*1825–94*)	4400	+40
Antonio Jacobsen (*1850–1921*)	3500	+340
Eastman Johnson (*1824–1906*)	11,800	+260
John Frederick Kensett (*1818–72*)	5500	+170
Daniel Ridgway Knight (*1839–1924*)	11,700	+680
Thomas Moran (*1837–1926*)	32,800	+240
Robert Salmon (*1775–1842*)	26,600	+580
Thomas Sully (*1783–1872*)	3000	+90
Arthur Fitzwilliam Tait (*1819–1905*)	5100	+170
William Aiken Walker (*1839–1921*)	5100	+260
Worthington Whittredge (*1820–1910*)	6300	+320
William L. Sonntag (*1822–1900*)	3300	+210

The American Impressionists

Of all styles and periods of American painting, the Impressionists have been rising fastest. The index is up by 620% since 1975 – a rather better performance than that of the French group. The principal figures of the movement were Theodore Robinson (who was an informal pupil of Monet), Childe Hassam, Maurice Prendergast and William Merritt Chase. Mary Cassatt should be included too, though, along with Sargent and Whistler, she formed the great trio of expatriate American artists. Not only was she arguably the best of the American Impressionists, her role as midwife at the birth of Impressionism in the United States and in working for its subsequent acceptance was crucial.

The group that broke away from the Society of American Artists in 1897 and banded themselves together as 'The Ten' were mostly established artists. They decided to hold their own exhibitions and show whatever they liked without first submitting work to a jury. Their shows ran for twenty years and became a high spot of the New York season.

The Ten

John Henry Twachtman (*1853–1903*)
Thomas Dewing (*1851–1938*)
Willard Metcalf (*1859–1925*)
Robert Reid (*1862–1929*)
Childe Hassam (*1859–1935*)
J. Alden Weir (*1852–1919*)
Frank Benson (*1862–1951*)
Joseph De Camp (*1852–1923*)
Edmund Tarbell (*1862–1938*)
Edward Simmons (*1852–1932*)

OPPOSITE *Mary Cassatt (1844–1926): 'Sarah Coiffée d'un Bonnet' (c. 1901), £75,000.*

ABOVE *Williams Glackens (1870–1938): 'Curving Beach, New England', £110,000.*

RIGHT *William Merritt Chase (1849–1916): 'Playing Horse', £240,000.*

But the success of Impressionism in the United States was by no means automatic. From the early days in France the debate over its status and validity had rumbled on. George Inness had called it 'the original pancake of visual imbecility' and even J. Alden Weir, later to become one of The Ten, wrote after attending an Impressionist exhibition in Paris in 1877, 'I never in my life saw more horrible things.'

By the early 20th century the critical stance had shifted to a condemnation of Impressionism's genteel, pretty qualities and its refusal to confront the harsh realities of urban life. A group of artists who had grown up under the influence of Impression-

ism, but who rejected the overdecorative style to which it had sunk, began to paint with noticeable rigour and vitality. Forming themselves into 'The Eight' in 1908 – also known as the Ash Can School – they built in their different ways and worked for a time in the American Impressionist idiom.

The Eight

William Glackens (*1870–1938*)
John Sloan (*1871–1951*)
Robert Henri (*1865–1929*)
Maurice Prendergast (*1861–1924*)
Ernest Lawson (*1873–1939*)
Everett Shinn (*1876–1953*)
George Luks (*1867–1933*)
Arthur Davies (*1862–1928*)

The French Impressionists still command far higher prices than the American but the gap is closing as collectors in the United States rediscover the major talents in their own backyard. No one doubts that the innovative geniuses of Impressionism were all French – Manet, Degas, Renoir, Pissarro, Monet and Sisley – nor that their American followers, most of whom had studied in Paris, were indelibly influenced by them. But how should the American painters be rated?

The market usually values most highly those artists who have broken new ground; artists who have discovered some truth about themselves or about the world around them and have found an original means of communicating it. That particular quality may be hard to define but it isn't hard to recognize. The French Impressionists had it all right. Yet however original their style may be, it did not materialize out of the blue. Each artist in turn had come under a sequence of influences including Courbet, the Barbizon School, Bastien-Lepage, photography, Japanese prints and, not least, the great English proto-Impressionists, Constable and Turner.

One injustice of the art world is that if a painter makes it to the top people say he has brilliantly assimilated the influences that worked upon him. If on the other hand he lacks the originality and expressive power that might have carried him to the top, people will tend to call him derivative. That is the main distinction critics have made between the French and American schools.

Yet the art market is beginning to see this as no more than an art historian's quibble. Until recently collectors rated the American Impressionists much as their forebears in the 1890s, namely, a poor shadow of their French teachers. Just as rich New Yorkers in those days went to great lengths to buy clothes from Parisian *couturiers* – sometimes assisted by Mary Cassatt – so it became fashionable to buy art in Paris too.

As John Henry Twachtman told students at the Art Institute of Chicago in 1893, '. . . some day some of you will become painters, and a few of you will do distinguished work, and then the American public will turn you down for second- and third-rate French painters'. Almost a century later these artists are the subject of a massive re-evaluation – long overdue and still with some way to go.

Though the current boom will certainly flush out more sellers, there is a serious shortage of American impressionists on the market. Whereas eighty or so Renoirs and sixty Pissarros pass through the salerooms every year, the total for the ten leading American Impressionists was little more than a hundred. Private and institutional collectors in the United States are

ABOVE *William Merritt Chase (1849–1916):*
'Long Island Pier', £10,000.

RIGHT *Maurice Prendergast (1861–1924): 'A*
Grey Day – Boston Harbour', £11,000.

BELOW *Ernest Lawson (1873–1939): 'Country*
Village', £16,500.

aware of the scarcity and will surely keep prices on the boil. The overwhelming preference among collectors seems to be for decorative paintings with the result that works by Frank Benson, Edward Potthast, Frederick Frieseke and Richard Miller, which have an obvious lollipop quality, have rocketed in price.

In the long run, prices for the leading artists of the group should perform best. The market for Cassatt, unlike the others, has always been international. Deeply respected by the French Impressionists with whom she was invited to exhibit in 1877, she painted mother and child studies of great beauty and without a trace of sentimentality. Prices have risen by 340% since 1975. As an artist Cassatt matured slowly and her early work up to 1873 is of secondary importance. Investors should also beware the work executed after 1910 when her eyesight began to fail. Prices of portraits, whether of men or women, depend on the looks of the sitter.

Mary Cassatt (1844–1926): 'Jules being dried after his bath', £85,000.

Prendergast was the most innovative of the group and might better be described as the first American post-Impressionist. Prices have risen 390% since 1975. Watercolours that sold for $500 in the early 1960s now make $50,000. Work dating from after 1900 is in greatest demand. Influenced by such diverse artists as Carpaccio, Whistler and Cézanne, Prendergast developed his own powerful and original style which places him among the top rank of American painters.

Childe Hassam was the most lyrical of the American Impressionists and was among the first to be revalued, though even since 1975 his work has risen 420%. No major museum exhibition of his work has yet taken place and plenty of research remains to be done. His best work is currently considered to date from his stay in France

– the Parisian streetscapes being especially attractive. Leaving aside the somewhat problematic late works, Hassam is by no means overvalued and prices should maintain an annual growth of 15% from now on.

With a rise of 1230% since 1975, William Merrit Chase's reputation just keeps on growing. His flamboyant personality and brilliance as an artist made him a celebrated figure in New York even in the 1880s. The scenes in greatest demand are set in the Shinnecock Hills or Central Park; these now fetch up to £125,000 and are still climbing.

Theodore Robinson's work rarely appears at auction. His technique was fully mature by the 1880s and the paintings done in France, particularly at Giverny and in Normandy, are his most highly regarded. The use he made of photography is sometimes a little obvious but the strong and beneficial influence of Monet makes his work most desirable. Works re-sold privately in recent years suggest an annual growth rate of 15%.

In the early 1960s, most museums that possessed American Impression-ists had them stacked in the basement. Curators however responded quickly to the revival of interest and the paintings are mostly back on view. Even so, in art-historical terms this is a comparatively new field and much work remains to be done.

Despite its aesthetic and investment appeal this is by no means a simple field to enter. Not only were all American Impressionists uneven in terms of quality, many painted at different times in styles that are likely to remain less popular. The market as a whole is surely set for further growth but investors would do well to go for the style and subject matter that made each artist famous.

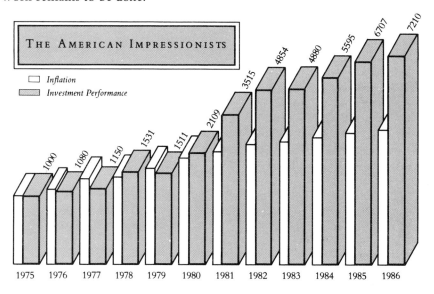

THE AMERICAN IMPRESSIONISTS

☐ Inflation
▨ Investment Performance

1000 1080 1150 1531 1511 2109 3515 4854 4880 5595 6707 7210

1975 1976 1977 1978 1979 1980 1981 1982 1983 1984 1985 1986

Artists: Mary Cassatt, William Merritt Chase, John Enneking, Childe Hassam, Ernest Lawson, Willard Metcalf, Edward Henry Potthast, Maurice Prendergast, John Henry Twachtman, J. Alden Weir

Artist	Mid-market price £	Change since 1975 %
American Impressionists		
Mary Cassatt (*1844–1926*)	36,800	+340
William Merritt Chase (*1849–1916*)	30,100	+1230
John Enneking (*1840–1916*)	1500	+120
Childe Hassam (*1859–1935*)	26,400	+420
Ernest Lawson (*1873–1939*)	9800	+210
Willard Leroy Metcalf (*1859–1925*)	7500	+200
Edward Henry Potthast (*1857–1927*)	13,800	+1490
Maurice Prendergast (*1862–1924*)	26,600	+390
John Henry Twachtman (*1853–1902*)	5000	+170
J. Alden Weir (*1852–1919*)	5300	+390

American Painting (1910–40)

The American art world sustained two major shocks over the 1910–40 period. The first was psychological and came in the form of the Armory Show of 1913. This was a rude awakening to the daring and brilliance of modern European painting, and one that jolted every American artist into a painful reconsideration of his work. The second was the Depression. Those who lived through it saw how quickly material security could vanish. But the problem was not only one of being cold or hungry or unemployed; disillusion set in for a whole generation. The American dream had turned sour and artists were not alone in their search for more lasting values.

The Federal Art Project got under way in 1935 and supported 5000 artists, enabling them to work in their studios all over America rather than be drawn to New York in search of a market. The new social consciousness of artists in the thirties, often expressed in their work, caused Americans at large to recognize that art could be a meaningful occupation concerned with real-life problems. This was a major advance, for, prior to the Armory Show, art was, as Meyer Schapiro pointed out, looked upon as a rare cultural commodity, usually created in Europe, that existed only in museums or as ornaments in the homes of the rich.

It was these experiences that made possible the flowering in the 1940s and 1950s of the New York School – the first school of American painting to catch the eye of the world. But the lengthy gestation period of the 1920s and 1930s also yielded important painting. It also produced a large body of respectable work as well as a few cartloads of rubbish. The index of eight key artists working in the 1910–40 period shows a rise of 420% since 1975, a performance that falls short of the Impressionists but is ahead of the New York School.

At the beginning of this century American art was at a low ebb. The two greatest painters of the 19th century, Winslow Homer and Thomas Eakins, were still working, though their finest painting, and that of the American Impressionists too, had already been done. Fashionable collectors were buying Old Masters and the Barbizon School. The market was dominated by the great Italian specialist, Bernard Berenson, who claimed to admire the drawing of Degas but regretted that it was wasted on laundresses. But such attitudes hardly mattered, for the modern bandwagon was beginning to roll. In 1908, under the influence of Robert Henri, the group who banded themselves together as 'The Eight' (see page 72), soon to be known as the Ash Can School, still painted in traditional styles yet created an impact through their exploration of seedy urban subject matter. In the same year Alfred Stieglitz began to exhibit *avant garde* American and European artists, including Matisse and Braque, but their work was received with blank incomprehension.

But these were faint stirrings compared to the Armory Show. This was a watershed, catalyst and bombshell. Though most of the 1500 exhibits at the Sixty-ninth Regiment Armory on Lexington Avenue were by Americans, the show was stolen by Picasso, Matisse, Cézanne, Gauguin and van Gogh. The conservatism of American art at this date may be judged by the fact that art students, traditionally among the more revo-

Guy Wiggins (1883–1962): 'Wall Street and the Sub-treasury', £10,000.

lutionary groups in any society, actually chose the occasion to burn an effigy of Matisse. The public were disturbed by the Expressionist distortion of the visible world and outraged by the Cubist rejection of natural form; and, of course, the innovative work was savaged by critics.

Yet no artist who had seen the show was left untouched. For some it led to a major shift in direction; for others it produced a determined refusal to be influenced by the dark forces of modernism. American artists were already burdened by Emerson's demand that American art should go it alone and began to see an opportunity. The urban population of America had increased by a factor of 139 during the 19th century. The rabble described by de Tocqueville as dangerous even in the 1830s had been swollen by immigration, natural growth and exodus from rural areas. This provided a wealth of new material for the artists. In the teeming life of the slums, sweat shops, saloons and pool-halls, some artists saw ugliness and degradation; others saw beauty and poetry. Some felt that in this seething cauldron of humanity they could see the true face of America. Others looked for it in the farms and hills; a third group went on painting Greek myths and scantily dressed maidens in deplorably sentimental style, while a fourth group struck out in the direction of European abstraction.

Measured against other periods of American painting, 1910–40 will never be rated as a golden age. Yet when painters of one generation are eclipsed by those of the next, fine work often gets neglected and, in art market terms, undervalued. For not only is this generation surpassed by the later New York School, to the objective critic it lacks the vitality of the international School of Paris that included Léger, Kandinsky and Klee. Even its most gifted members cannot measure up to Picasso, Matisse and other superstars of the period; some may still prove a good buy. But the performance within the group is mixed and the outlook for at least two is unexciting. Reginald Marsh and Raphael Soyer have managed rises of 50% and 150% over the period. Both carried on the social realist tradition of the Ash Can School, Marsh extending the subject range to sensual scenes on Coney Island beach and the dingy flop-houses of the Bowery, while Soyer, along with his brothers Moses and Isaac, chronicled the lives of the poor on New York's East Side. All of them seemed to paint more in resignation than protest. To represent poverty without sentimentality calls for a rare talent. Partly because neither Marsh nor Soyer quite had such talent, and partly because so much of their work is in circulation, no big rise in value can be expected.

John Marin (+210%) and Marsden Hartley (+340%) had both been to Paris before the Armory Show hit New York and on their return began to exhibit in Stieglitz's circle. Marin went on to produce the most forceful abstract Expressionist work of the interwar period, his evocations of landscape and city being infused with a strangely American quality. Hartley abandoned abstraction before 1920 for a straightforward Expressionist style. At the same time a romantic streak ran through his work which might explain its large following today.

The increase of 1000% in Thomas Hart Benton's work is no surprise. He became the artist-champion of conservative middle-brow America.

He scoffed at those who, in the wake of the Armory Show, followed the modernist trail, and contended in his autobiography that modern American art became 'a simple smearing of material, good for nothing but to release neurotic tension. Here finally,' he wrote, 'it became a bowel movement or a vomiting spell.' It was true that in the 1920s a host of artists jumped aboard the international modernist bandwagon, often with the indiscriminate backing of critics. All the same, Benton's condemnation was crude and sweeping.

His own superficially 'truthful' depictions of smalltown America are often no more than folksy idealizations containing as much reality as a Hollywood Western. Along with John Steuart Curry and Grant Wood, who characteristically remarked that all the good ideas he ever had came to him while milking a cow, Benton became a bulwark against a subversive modernism and a leading painter of 'the American Scene'.

Charles Burchfield also took the scenic route though he was not a committed regionalist of Benton's type. His uniquely personal and lyrical interpretation of landscape has won him a big following. Being a prolific and consistent artist, plenty of his work comes on the market and shows a rise of 330% since 1975. The story is the same with the even more prolific Guy Wiggins (+360%). He repeated perhaps too often the snow scenes of New York for which he has become famous, and this probably prevented a faster rise.

Too little of Edward Hopper's work gets sold at auction for the rise to be quantified though the market has certainly been strong. His austere, even scary, vision of the world recurs in most of his paintings. Much of it may be taken as a pictograph of man's

TOP *Edward Hopper (1882–1967): 'House at Essex, Mass.', £60,000.*

ABOVE *John Sloan (1871–1951): 'Burros Threshing', £41,000.*

RIGHT *Joseph Stella (1877–1946): 'Profile of a Woman', £1800.*

isolation, the directness and power of this message raising it far above the efforts of most 'American Scene' artists.

Several other major artists of this period – George Bellows, Charles Demuth, Georgia O'Keefe, Charles Sheeler and Stuart Davis among them – are too rarely sold at auction to be reliably monitored. The available evidence suggests annual growth of at least 10% and the growing rarity of their work makes some acceleration likely.

If the Armory Show presented the public, as Schapiro put it, as an incoherent chorus of individual voices, the proliferation of styles in the ensuing period seems hardly less daunting. The major artists of these years are well established and rising fast; many of those in the middle range have been left behind and may soon catch up.

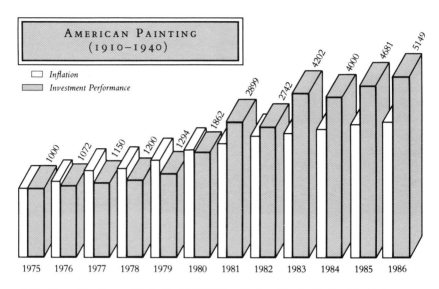

AMERICAN PAINTING
(1910–1940)

☐ Inflation
▨ Investment Performance

1000 1072 1150 1200 1294 1862 2899 2742 4202 4000 4681 5149

1975 1976 1977 1978 1979 1980 1981 1982 1983 1984 1985 1986

Artists: Thomas Hart Benton, Charles Burchfield, William Glackens, Marsden Hartley, John Marin, Reginald Marsh, John Sloan, Raphael Soyer, Joseph Stella, Guy Wiggins

Artist	Mid-market price £	Change since 1975 %
American Painting (1910–40)		
Thomas Hart Benton (*1888–1975*)	21,400	+1000
Charles Burchfield (*1893–1967*)	11,200	+330
William Glackens (*1870–1938*)	24,600	+880
Marsden Hartley (*1877–1943*)	5000	+340
John Marin (*1870–1953*)	7600	+210
Reginald Marsh (*1889–1954*)	1900	+50
Raphael Soyer (*b. 1899*)	2700	+150
John Sloan (*1871–1951*)	7400	+340
Joseph Stella (*1877–1946*)	1800	+70
Guy Wiggins (*1883–1962*)	5300	+360

The New York School and After

During the 1940s and 1950s the New York School produced a body of work that made a lasting impact in the art world. The overall rise in the value of the work done by its leading figures – including Albers, de Kooning, Pollock and Rothko – has been 260% since 1975. The period of recognition is past and the market is now sifting the major figures from the minor.

Each artist was affected by different influences and backgrounds. Not surprisingly the styles they developed also varied; indeed little binds them together except the common experience of living in New York during a period of extreme stress when each was searching for a way of expressing the intense feelings they all shared.

Most styles of painting that have broken new ground in the history of art have at first been greeted with abuse or ridicule. The pace of change accelerated during the last hundred years and it may be that the climax was reached in terms of public outrage in 1913 when Malevich exhibited his *Basic Suprematist Element*, a pencil drawing of a black square on a white ground. Delaunay, Kandinsky and Kupka may in a sense have preceded him with their abstract works but these retained traces of representation; none of them had reduced painting to pure geometrical abstraction before.

Artists may have Malevich to thank for proving that anything was possible in the name of art, yet his work also set a limit to art and left artists to agonize over where to turn next. How far abstract art has developed since then remains a contentious issue, but there is no doubt that an important flowering took place in New York during the 1940s.

TOP *Jackson Pollock (1912–56): 'Four Opposites' (1953), £250,00.*

ABOVE *Arshile Gorky (1905–48): Untitled, £35,000.*

The American people were not prepared to take abstract art lying down. The perennial clash between artist and public reached a new crescendo during the early days of the New York School. From the start there had been a handful of enlightened admirers but these so-called Abstract Expressionists were slow to be accepted. The reasons for this are not hard to understand. Representational art made the critic's job quite easy. The images the artist put on canvas were clearly recognizable and his success in imitating the visible world easily discussed. The artist, the critic and the spectator shared a common vocabulary.

The trouble began when the concept of expression and the artist's intentions began to change. In Goya's *Disasters of the War* the terror and pain of those caught up in the Peninsular War is represented, but their emotions are conveyed with such force because they were also experienced by Goya himself. For most of the 19th century spectators had become accustomed to Academy paintings planned and executed by craftsmen rather than artists in a state of emotional disengagement. That is why sentimentality or false emotion is felt to leave its cold touch on such work.

By the beginning of this century the word 'Expressionism' was used to refer to the artist's intention and ability to render his own subjective feelings although still by means of representational art. There was a limit, it was felt, to how deeply it was possible to infuse a tree, a bowl of fruit or a face with the artist's own feelings. Subject matter could even be seen as an obstacle to self-expression. As a means of conveying the infinitely complicated mental states of the artist, representational art began to seem inadequate.

Furthermore, the spectator must already have his associations with objects in the visible world. Some artists therefore began to recognize that the common ground between artist and spectator was not so common after all. They began to realize that it was difficult to write a message on a piece of paper that was already covered with messages. One solution might be to use forms with which the spectator would be unlikely to have any existing association.

To appreciate abstract art is thought to depend upon a higher level of receptivity than does representational art. To be sure it calls for an act of faith in the sincerity of the artist. One of the main problems with abstract art is that its detractors refuse to believe it calls for any skill or training. Thus, the 'argument' goes, abstract art can never be rare nor can it have any real value.

For many people, abstraction presented a threat to the established order. For them, Abstract Expressionism stood for anarchy in the field of art. In 1949 Congressman George A. Dondero warned the US House of Representatives of the subversive power of new styles in art. With the McCarthy communist witch-hunt still to come, Dondero set the tone by warning that all the 'isms' of the art world were of foreign origin, that that they were the instruments and weapons of destruction and should have no place in American art.

Listing the major movements of recent years, Dondero asserted that Dadaism aimed to destroy by ridicule, Expressionism by aping the primitive and the insane, and Abstractionism by the creation of brainstorms. 'Who', Dondero wondered, 'has let into our homeland this horde of germ-carrying vermin?' It called to mind Hitler's speech delivered twelve years earlier at the opening of the exhibition of Degenerate (i.e., Bolshevik and Jewish) Art.

But the abstract-art bandwagon in America was already moving too fast and its alleged links with communism too weak for the public to accept Dondero's scary picture. If a national character had been hard to identify in American art of the past, here was something distinctively American, even if, as so often before, the pump had been primed by Europeans.

Every good work of art should be a product of its time and no other. The personal influences and external events that bore on each artist of the New York School differed, but two forces bore heavily on one and all – namely the Depression and the Unconscious.

The acceptance of Freud's account of the unconscious had been quicker in parts of America than Europe. Its implications were often discussed by those artists who were once described as the loft-rats of 8th Street, and several members of the New York School underwent more or less successful analyses during the 1940s.

Few artists are able to function without any form of recognition. The battles fought in the studio may be lonely indeed but to have the results of those battles widely if not universally reviled was more than some of these artists could stand. Although art historians find it convenient to attach a label to this group, the absence of a common purpose or method is striking. Most members of the group felt isolated and alienated not just from the mass of American people but frequently from each other. Yet out of these experiences were born works of art that even now are not fully appreciated.

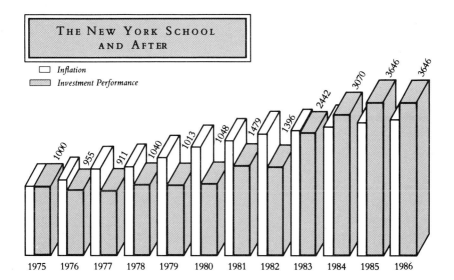

THE NEW YORK SCHOOL AND AFTER

☐ Inflation
▨ Investment Performance

Year	Value
1975	1000
1976	955
1977	911
1978	1040
1979	1013
1980	1048
1981	1479
1982	1396
1983	2442
1984	3070
1985	3646
1986	3646

Artists: Josef Albers, Alexander Calder, Sam Francis, Helen Frankenthaler, Adolf Gottlieb, Hans Hofmann, Paul Jenkins, Franz Kline, William de Kooning, Robert Motherwell, Kenneth Noland, Jules Olitski, Ad Reinhardt, Larry Rivers, Frank Stella, Mark Tobey, Cy Twombly, Victor Vasarely, Andy Warhol, Tom Wesselman

Artist	Mid-market price £	Change since 1975 %
The New York School and After		
Josef Albers (*1888–1976*)	12,200	+30
Alexander Calder (*1898–1976*)	2500	+140
Sam Francis (*b. 1923*)	16,200	+460
Helen Frankenthaler (*b. 1928*)	29,000	+860
Adolf Gottlieb (*1903–1974*)	8900	+470
Hans Hofman (*1880–1966*)	19,200	+400
Paul Jenkins (*b. 1923*)	2500	+220
Franz Kline (*1910–62*)	24,900	+290
Willem de Kooning (*b. 1904*)	21,300	+160
Robert Motherwell (*b. 1915*)	31,800	+640
Kenneth Noland (*b. 1924*)	15,700	+120
Jules Olitski (*b. 1922*)	9500	+150
Ad Reinhardt (*1913–1967*)	20,500	+120
Larry Rivers (*b. 1923*)	14.900	+300
Frank Stella (*b. 1935*)	31,800	+500
Mark Tobey (*1890–1976*)	1700	−10
Cy Twombly (*b. 1929*)	18,800	+260
Victor Vasarely (*b. 1908*)	2900	−20
Andy Warhol (*b. 1930*)	11,700	+260
Tom Wesselman (*b. 1931*)	2000	−50

Further Reading

Lloyd Goodrich and John I. Baur, *American Art of the Twentieth Century* (London, 1962)

Barbara Rose, *American Art since 1900: a Critical History* (New York, 1967)

H. Geldzahler, *American Painting in the Twentieth Century* (Conn., 1965)

M. W. Brown, *American Painting from the Armory Show to the Depression* (Princeton, 1955)

S. Hunter, *Modern American Painting and Sculpture* (New York, 1959)

David Sylvester, *Modern Art, from Fauvism to Abstract Expressionism* (New York, 1965)

H. Geldzahler, *New York Painting and Sculpture 1940–1970* (New York, 1969)

J. T. Flexner, *That Wilder Image: the Painting of America's Native School from Thomas Cole to Winslow Homer* (Boston, 1962)

Jules David Prown, *American Painting from its Beginnings to the Armory Show* (Geneva, 1969)

The German Expressionists

The most turbulent decade in art history ran from 1904 to 1914. During that time one cultural explosion after another shook the art establishment of the West. One of the more revolutionary exhibitions was mounted in 1906 in Dresden by the German Expressionists – Kirchner, Heckel, Schmidt-Rottluff and Bleyl. Other artists, not all of them German, were drawn into their circle – Munch, Nolde, Jawlensky and Kandinsky among others – and together they produced one of the most arresting bodies of work the art world had yet seen.

Since the 1960s their standing has grown internationally, even though the market is still based on German-speaking Europe. The common denominator of their painting styles was a ruthless confrontation with reality and this aspect of their art is particularly admired by collectors today.

The German Expressionist index now stands 270% above its 1975 level. If that performance is rather below the market average, it must be because most art buyers prefer lyrical rather than disturbing images and the intensity of the Expressionist vision and style has tended to restrict demand for their work to a sophisticated and quite small circle of admirers. The big discount to the Impressionists at which they trade in the market is likely to be permanent.

As often happens, the two main groups of artists, *Die Brücke* in Dresden and later *Der Blaue Reiter* in Munich, soon broke up and their members went their separate ways. But the collective impact of their work in Germany had been immense, perhaps as great as that made a generation earlier by Renoir, Monet and their circle. In the 1870s, the French Impressionists were being fiercely denounced by Parisian critics, but, by the turn of the century, they had become, as Emil Nolde put it, the elected darlings of the world.

Nolde found much of the Impressionists' work too sugary for his taste. Along with other Expressionists he was in revolt not only against the hedonistic French but also against the romantic and pseudopatriotic art still favoured by the German academies. The official line on German art had been laid down by the Kaiser Wilhelm II in 1902. 'Art,' he ordained, 'which presumes to overstep the limits and rules I have indicated is no longer art. . . . If art, as now happens all too often, does nothing more than present misery in an even more hideous form than it already possesses, then it sins against the German people.' This was a depressing omen for the new century and indeed a sinister foretaste of the persecution artists were to suffer at the hands of the Nazis thirty years later.

The Expressionists were unwilling to see Berlin become the new capital of Philistia and a laughing stock to the world. A sense of excitement and common purpose was shared not just by artists, but by musicians, architects, poets and dramatists. It was in the cafés – those traditional forums for wild and rebellious debate – this time in Dresden, Berlin and Munich, that plans for a new cultural order were laid. As one of them later recalled, 'We felt like creatures on the first day of creation.'

To find their way towards a new interpretation of reality the Expressionists sought to convey their feelings by rejecting the visible world as their sole point of departure,

renouncing conventional perspective and by the use of urgent brush strokes and often strident colours. It had often been objected that Impressionism made no demands on the intellect.

Goethe once remarked that painting was not based on what man usually sees, but on what he would like to see and should see. This could well have served as a motto for the entire group. For the idea was firmly rooted among them that there was another more important side to reality which could and should be reflected in their work.

As Peter Selz, a leading Expressionist scholar, has noted, they were disgusted by the lack of passion and commitment in the art they saw about them. In the early days the Expressionists had some contact with the Fauve group whose revolutionary work was to outrage all Paris. Yet it would not have been altogether surprising if two art movements with overlapping characteristics had surfaced spontaneously at this time. The same cultural influences were washing over both groups – Art Nouveau (known as *Jugendstil* in Germany and Austria), primitive art, Symbolism, but, above all, Van Gogh, Munch and Gauguin.

Matisse might have been speaking for the Expressionists too when he explained, 'I want to reach that state of condensation of sensations which constitute a picture.' He revealed too that he tried to discover the enduring character of a scene even if in so doing it meant sacrificing its pleasing qualities.

With hindsight it is easy to credit the Expressionists as well as the Fauves with a premonition of impending tragedy. Though the storm was not to break until 1914 the clouds of war were gathering in 1904, and both groups may be seen as sensors and reflectors of the growing crisis.

The sense of oncoming disaster made the drive for self-expression in these artists all the more urgent. Moreover, in giving full rein to this drive the Expressionists were asserting a right which artists had not always been accorded. Since the Renaissance artists were expected to study physiognomy in order to render a subject's emotions by means of gesture and facial expression. It was assumed that the artist's own feelings would be subdued or suppressed altogether. Support for that view waned during the 19th century, but it was the Expressionists who seized on self-expression as a primordial right early in the 20th century. That is one reason why the Expressionists stand as so important a landmark in art history. For them there was more to painting than the representation of the visible world. Driven by an inner necessity, they were determined to represent the invisible but equally important reality they saw in everything that passed before their eyes. The extent to which that inner reality can be represented and the success of the Expressionists in doing so is still debated today.

Ernst-Ludwig Kirchner did his best work during the 1908–16 period. Strong competition between museums has pushed the price of his top paintings to well over £100,000. The general run of his works, however, has risen only 50% since 1975.

Paintings in semi-abstract style dating from after 1928 are less admired. He returned to a natural style in 1936 but this later work is not important. Kirchner's dating of his early work was unreliable; he was apt to knock a couple of years off the true date so as to appear to predate the Fauves.

Erich Heckel's work shows an increase of 180% since 1975. All his important paintings were done before 1914. A lyrical strain is evident even in his severest compositions and particularly in the colourful landscapes to which he returned after 1918. He changed style in 1935 to conform to Nazi requirements and his work up to 1945 is of little interest. Even the work done thereafter, when he was free to paint as he wished, lacks fire.

Karl Schmidt-Rottluff's work is up by 340% since 1975. His best water-colours were done during the 1908–14 period, though the bold use of colour continued into the 1920s. His compromise with the Nazis did not affect his art to the same extent as Heckel's and much of his work done in the 1940s is in strong demand.

Of all the Expressionists Emil Nolde was the most consistent in style and quality. A solitary, religious man, he enthusiastically accepted Schmidt-Rottluff's invitation to join *Die Brücke* in 1906. Schmidt-Rottluff referred to Nolde's 'tempests of colour', and his palette was without doubt the most extravagant of the group. Landscapes are ranked more important than religious works though demand for all subjects and periods is strong. Prices are up 370% since 1975.

Max Pechstein is a minor figure in the group though his work has climbed by 510% since 1975. One of the group's most prolific artists, Pechstein was capable of painting in several different styles. Though he was also an impulsive and uneven artist, his prices doubled between 1983 and 1985 and some reaction may be expected.

The market for top-quality Munchs has never been stronger, but prices for his middle-range work have risen by only 60% since 1975. The 1895–1910 period contains his greatest work. Thereafter, as a rough guide, the later the work the less it will fetch. Although he only participated in some Expressionist exhibitions, Munch was really the forerunner and principle inspiration of the group.

As Kandinsky's girlfriend for many years, Gabriele Münter has usually been labelled a disciple of the great man. Important as his influence was,

Karl Schmidt-Rottluff (1884–1976): 'Frau im Feld' (1919), £33,000.

she is increasingly regarded as a significant artist in her own right and prices are up 480% since 1975. The early landscapes painted while with Kandinsky at Murnau are her most desirable works, though the later work is also rising fast.

Until the turn of the century Christian Rohlfs painted in a more or less traditional style. He then experimented with Impressionism and this cost him his job at the Weimar Art School. Early works are seldom seen in the market and it is the later paintings dating from 1905, after his meeting with Nolde and the other Expressionists, that are most in demand. Prices for the mainstream of his work are up only 60% since 1975 – possibly because he is so little known outside German-speaking Europe.

Alexej von Jawlensky's work is up 250% since 1975. The strongest performance has been for his early work up to 1914 when he was with Kandinsky at Murnau and Munich. As an ex-Russian cavalry officer, he had to leave Germany and stay in Switzerland for the duration of the Second World War. But, wherever he painted, it is his figure paintings, above all heads of women, that command the highest prices today.

Prices for the mainstream of Kandinsky's work have risen only 10% since 1975. His most valuable paintings are those done in Expressionist style between 1910 and 1914. Those of the later Bauhaus and Paris periods in Constructivist style are widely admired but worth less. As a major figure in European art Kandinsky is already well represented in museums and this may help to explain the slow rate of growth.

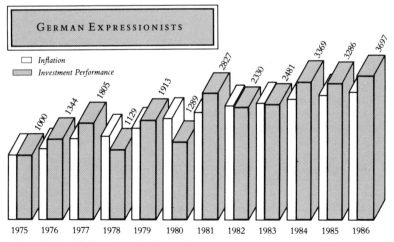

GERMAN EXPRESSIONISTS

☐ *Inflation*
▨ *Investment Performance*

1000 1344 1805 1129 1913 1289 2827 2330 2481 3369 3286 3697

1975 1976 1977 1978 1979 1980 1981 1982 1983 1984 1985 1986

Artists: Erich Heckel, Alexej von Jawlensky, Wassily Kandinsky, Ernst-Ludwig Kirchner, Edvard Munch, Gabriele Münter, Emil Nolde, Max Pechstein, Karl Schmidt-Rottluff

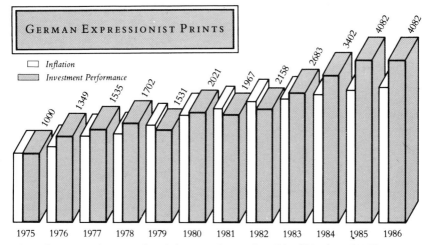

GERMAN EXPRESSIONIST PRINTS

☐ *Inflation*
▨ *Investment Performance*

1000 · 1349 · 1535 · 1702 · 1531 · 2021 · 1967 · 2158 · 2683 · 3402 · 4082 · 4082

| 1975 | 1976 | 1977 | 1978 | 1979 | 1980 | 1981 | 1982 | 1983 | 1984 | 1985 | 1986 |

Printmakers: Max Beckmann, Erich Heckel, Ernst-Ludwig Kirchner, Edvard Munch, Emil Nolde, Karl Schmidt-Rottluff

Artist	Mid-market price £	Change since 1975 %
German Expressionists		
Erich Heckel (*1883–1970*)	3700	+160
Alexej von Jawlensky (*1864–1941*)	16,400	+250
Wassily Kandinsky (*1866–1944*)	21,900	+10
Ernst-Ludwig Kirchner (*1880–1938*)	2200	+50
Edvard Munch (*1863–1944*)	19,900	+60
Gabriele Münter (*1877–1962*)	6900	+480
Emil Nolde (*1867–1956*)	28,500	+370
Max Pechstein (*1881–1955*)	7900	+510
Christian Rohlfs (*1849–1938*)	4600	+60
Karl Schmidt-Rottluff (*1884–1976*)	5500	+340
German Expressionist Prints		
Max Beckmann (*1884–1950*)	800	+170
Erich Heckel (*1883–1970*)	1000	+210
Ernst-Ludwig Kirchner (*1880–1938*)	4900	+300
Edvard Munch (*1865–1944*)	6900	+250
Emil Nolde (*1867–1956*)	2500	+240
Karl Schmidt-Rottluff (*1884–1976*)	2500	+280

Further Reading

C. M. Joachimedes, N. Rosenthal and W. Schmied, *German Art in the 20th Century* (London, 1985)

Barry Herbert, *German Expressionism* (London, 1980)

Carl Zigrosser, *The Expressionists: a Survey of the Graphic Art* (New York, 1957)

Peter Selz, *German Expressionist Painting* (Berkeley, California, 1957)

B. S. Myers, *Expressionism* (London, 1963)

C. L. Kuhn, *German Expressionism and Abstract Art. The Harvard Collections* (Cambridge, Mass., 1967)

The Surrealists

The Surrealists are showing up as the laggards of the art market, having put on just 240% in value since 1975. Considering that this movement in the 1920s was a key development in the history of art the performance is surprising. The explanation lies in the style and subject matter which, with hindsight, always stood to lose favour with collectors in the long term.

A few spectacular prices have recently been paid for works by Dali, de Chirico and Miró but these should not be allowed to mask the sluggish performance of the main body of Surrealist work over a period when the art market has been livelier than ever.

The art world feeds on novelty. Naturally, the contemporary sector must concern itself with living artists, new styles and new theories. But so, paradoxically, do the sectors dealing with earlier generations of artists. The discovery of previously unknown or 'unpublished' paintings, the search for new biographical information and the reassessment of established artists – all this is the staple diet of art galleries and publishers. The test of time is applied on a continuous basis. Since the turn of the century the eye has been stunned by a succession of increasingly 'difficult' styles. And, indeed, the primary and openly acknowledged purpose of many painters has been to shock. During the last thirty years the human eye has grown so accustomed to abstract art it is hard to imagine how much greater the impact of Surrealist painting must have been made when first seen seventy years ago.

Today the pictorial metaphors available for this purpose are almost exhausted. Artists wishing to blaze new trails are searching, without noticeable success, for a truly fresh means of expression. When Malevich exhibited his *Basic Suprematist Element*, in 1913, he made a powerful artistic statement. To the art world it also carried the message, 'From now on anything goes'. Already the revolutionary styles of painting of the 1904–14 period had peeled away at reality to see what lay beneath. The Fauves had dealt iconoclastically with colour and the Cubists had disintegrated form. The last component of a painting to be based in reality was the subject matter itself. In retrospect it seems obvious that reality itself would soon come under attack.

If Surrealist art is defined simply as painting whose subject matter transcends reality, then Surrealism goes back at least to the nightmarish visions of hell painted by Hieronymous Bosch and Matthias Grünewald around 1500. But the term itself was first used by the poet Guillaume Apollinaire in 1916 with a specific and more subtle meaning. He used it to describe the costumes and sets designed by Picasso for the ballet *Parade* performed by Diaghilev's Ballet Russe. These were said to introduce Cubism to the stage, but in trying to convey their impact he described them as *'surréaliste'*.

By this he is believed to have meant that their appearance heightened reality. It was only later in 1924 that André Breton, the coordinating spirit of Surrealism, published a definition. Surrealism, he said, was pure psychic automatism by which it is intended to express, either verbally or in writing, the true function of thought; thought dictated in the absence of all control exerted by reason and outside all aesthetic or moral preoccupation. This rather wayward account served

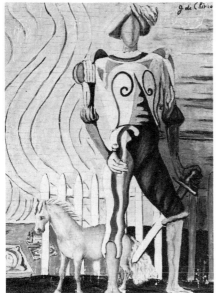

ABOVE *Salvador Dali (b. 1904): 'L'Enigme du Désir – Ma Mère' (1929), £42,000.*

LEFT *Giorgio de Chirico (1888–1978): 'Gentiluomo di Villeggiatura' (1934), £13,420.*

But how can they or should they respond? The idea that they should bend their work to propagandist purposes is generally repugnant, yet to carry on as though nothing had happened would seem worse.

The Surrealist story really begins with Dada, the strangest cultural product of the First World War. In Zürich a small group of French, German and Romanian refugees from military service, driven to desperation (or out of their minds, as many would have it) by the war, responded by founding the Dada movement. A million men had been killed that year in the battles of the Somme. The holocaust provoked this small band to compose and read nonsense poems and sing and argue at the Cabaret Voltaire.

as a lifeline for art critics struggling to unravel the strands of theory and style which the Surrealists seemed to pursue.

Artists are usually more influenced by stresses and crises of a personal rather than national character. Of course they feel the tragedy of war as keenly as anyone – perhaps more so.

The word *dada*, picked at random from a dictionary, was French for a hobby horse or gee-gee. The movement's driving force was an intense disgust with the 'system' in all its manifestations. Disgust with philosophers who attempt to explain, disgust with domination and restriction, disgust with the war and the bourgeois interests that caused it.

Dada was a state of mind – a return to an almost Buddhist religion of indifference. Tristan Tzara, the articulate high priest of Dada, described it as 'a virgin microbe that penetrates with the insistence of air into all the spaces that reason has not been able to fill with words and conventions'.

Dada quickly became an international phenomenon; there was much talk of energy and will, and Dadaists assured the world that they had elaborate plans. No details of these were ever forthcoming and the movement's denial of reality made it unlikely to take off.

The anarchic spirit of Dada was soon assimilated by the Surrealists. Nearly all their most forceful and inspired works were painted during the 1920s and 1930s. Even though the Surrealist *oeuvre* taken as a whole has recently been a disappointing investment, the finest examples have shot up in value.

Market prices from now on will be determined by two opposing considerations. On the one hand, Surrealist art is likely to remain in demand because it is rightly seen as a landmark in the evolution of Western painting. From it developed many of the abstract styles of painting practised since.

On the other hand, seen as a pictorial language, does it remain valid today? Having enjoyed most of the limelight for the last fifty years, Salvador Dali has become for many people the archetypal Surrealist painter. Celebrated though he is, his pictorial statements, in common with those of other members of the 'figura-

TOP *Max Ernst (1891–1976): 'Monument aux Oiseaux', £190,000.*

ABOVE *Max Ernst (1891–1976): 'La Religieuse Portugaise', £250,000.*

tive' school of Surrealism, are essentially incoherent and ultimately unsatisfying.

Automatism or accidentality was

central to Surrealist theory. The idea was that by suppressing conscious selection of subject matter, the artist would somehow draw on a deeper level of experience. But Breton's mistake was to suppose that the raw material presented by the unconscious mind was of greater value than that of the conscious and that it could be used to advantage by artists.

While it was certainly the case that Freud, whom Breton greatly admired, was able to interpret his patients' dreams and unconscious behaviour and so arrive at an understanding of a patient's psychopathology, it did not follow that the paraphernalia of the unconscious which Freud used as a stepping stone to the truth could be successfully transferred on to canvas. For if Surrealist statements are encoded in the artist's private language, how likely are they to mean much, even to an imaginative observer?

The insights offered by psychoanalysis could naturally be of value to an artist, but this did not mean that the uninterpreted contents of a dream, presented statically on canvas and bereft of the dreamer's associations, would constitute a significant aritistic statement.

Although of compelling historical interest, the attempt to put the unconscious *directly* at the service of art was misconceived. The Surrealists chose to paint the messenger and ignored the message.

It was another misconception among artists during the 1900–10 period that artefacts of primitive cultures – Oceanic, African and South American – were created in a state of innocence, an uncorrupted condition akin to childhood in which the noble savages lucky enough to enjoy it were able to produce great works of art. The natural counterpart of this fantasy was expressed by de Chirico as early as 1913. 'To become truly immortal', he said, 'a work of art must escape all human limits: logic and common sense will only interfere. But once these barriers are broken it will enter the regions of childhood and vision.'

This, of course, was another blind alley, and it fell, paradoxically, to psychoanalysis, which had proved so potent an inspiration to the Surrealists, to dispose of the notion of childhood innocence and to demonstrate how intensely children feel greed, aggression, envy and other less attractive traits hitherto reserved for adults.

The artists

Victor Brauner's work is up by a mere 30% on 1975. His important work of the 1930s sells easily, but the wax paintings executed in the 1940s are a difficult market.

Prices of paintings by Giorgio de Chirico have risen 230% over the same period. His 'metaphysical paintings' of the 1912–25 period were of great importance to the Surrealist movement and can fetch up to £150,000. De Chirico left the movement and settled in Rome in 1928. Admirers call him prolific; detractors say he flogged the same ideas to death. Not only was his output considerable, he confused the market in the later stages of his life by issuing certificates of authenticity for paintings he had not painted.

The important works by Salvador Dali of the 1930s have performed well and can fetch up to a million pounds. Minor works of the same period displaying his brilliant draughtsmanship also sell briskly. Nevertheless, the main body of his work has only risen 130% in value since 1975. Dali went rapidly downhill in the 1960s and

1970s and serious collectors shun this highly commercial work. Forgeries of the later period have been rife, and the charge of forging some four hundred Dalis brought against a Spaniard in 1983 further undermined confidence in Dali's later work.

Paul Delvaux prices are substantially unchanged since 1975. The rather repetitive dream-sequences of naked ladies wandering in architectural settings sell readily enough at up to £150,000. The work of the later 1930s and 1940s, when the influence of Magritte and de Chirico was at its height, are likely to do better than the later works.

Prices for Max Ernst's work have fallen to 20% below their 1975 level. The market soared in 1972–3 but dealers found themselves stuck with many unsold canvases. Much of Ernst's work is too cerebral, too difficult to have a wide appeal. Anything important from the 1920s will still fetch a huge price and the California and Arizona landscapes are in steady demand. Otherwise the outlook remains grim.

Joan Miró's work is up 180% since 1975 and demand remains strong. His pure Surrealist phase in the 1920s was short, but his later abstract works are, if anything, more popular. Prices are rising fast for Miró's series of gouaches, *Constellations*, completed in Majorca in 1941. These were based on hallucinations experienced during a period of extreme hunger.

André Masson prices are up 210% since 1975. His Cubist and Surrealist works of the 1920s are in greatest demand. But today there are fewer admirers of his wild and tempestuous style and the market remains subdued.

Paul Klee's work rose sharply in the early 1970s and has climbed by only 190% since. Though he exhibited with the Surrealists, and was much admired by them, he is not regarded as one of them. Yet his involvement with the abstract representation of an inner world makes him an honorary member. The range of quality in Klee is unusually wide, but demand is stronger than the growth rate suggests and some acceleration in prices is likely.

René Magritte was a prolific and uneven painter whose prices are up an overall 190% since 1975. Paintings of his 'Renoir' period in the 1920s and those of the 1930s and 1940s are highly regarded, but the later, more colourful work is in even greater demand. It may be that in the long term the 'impossible' configurations he made his speciality will seem repetitive and a little trite.

Francis Picabia prices fell after 1975 but have since recovered to show an overall gain of 260%. Picabia's early and popular mechanical drawings have been extensively faked, so buyers must be on their guard. Picabia's Dada period contains his best work but he is generally considered to have peaked too early.

Whatever the limitations of Surrealism as a pictorial language, many works have a real fascination, throwing out a challenge to the viewer consisting of both riddle and mystery. But the first shockwaves of Surrealism are getting weaker and this sector should continue to underperform the art market as a whole. Interest has now shifted to the movements to which Surrealism gave birth.

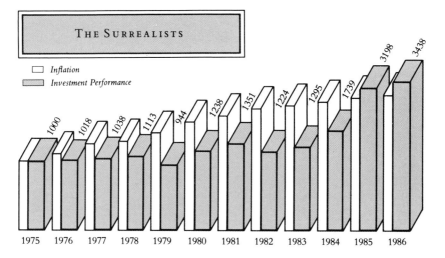

THE SURREALISTS

☐ *Inflation*
▨ *Investment Performance*

1000 · 1018 · 1038 · 1113 · 944 · 1238 · 1351 · 1224 · 1295 · 1739 · 3198 · 3438

1975 1976 1977 1978 1979 1980 1981 1982 1983 1984 1985 1986

Artists: Victor Brauner, Giorgio de Chirico, Salvador Dali, Max Ernst, Paul Klee, René Magritte, André Masson, Joan Miró, Francis Picabia, Kurt Schwitters, Yves Tanguy

Artist	Mid-market price £	Change since 1975 %
The Surrealists		
Victor Brauner (*1903–65*)	10,800	+30
Giorgio de Chirico (*1888–1978*)	22,700	+230
Salvador Dali (*b. 1904*)	14,700	+130
Max Ernst (*1891–1976*)	14,500	−20
Paul Klee (*1879–1940*)	35,300	+190
René Magritte (*1898–1967*)	40,300	+190
André Masson (*b. 1896*)	7500	+210
Joan Miró (*1893–1983*)	30,100	+180
Francis Picabia (*1879–1953*)	7400	+260
Kurt Schwitters (*1887–1948*)	7200	+120
Yves Tanguy (*1900–55*)	30,500	+260

Further Reading

William Gaunt, *The Surrealists* (London, 1972)

Marcel Jean, *The History of Surrealist Painting* (New York, 1960)

Patrick Waldberg, *Surrealism* (London, 1966)

Alfred H. Barr (ed.), *Fantastic Art, Dada, Surrealism* (New York, 1936)

Peggy Guggenheim (ed.), *Art of This Century* (New York, 1942)

H. Richter, *Dada, Art and Anti-Art* (London, 1965)

M. Nadeau, *The History of Surrealism* (New York, 1965)

James Thrall Soby, *Surrealism* (New York, 1968)

Old Master Prints

Most great Western artists of the last five hundred years have created original prints and the tradition is very much alive today. Interest in Old Master prints has fluctuated over the long term though a significant revival since 1975 has left the index up by 320%. To invest successfully in this market calls for real expertise and the finest impressions have risen perhaps twice as fast as the mainstream of the market.

Old Master prints are defined as those made in Europe between 1430 and 1830. The art-form was practised by print-makers all over the continent but until recently collectors concentrated on the big names: Albrecht Dürer, Rembrandt, Adriaen van Ostade, G. B. Piranesi, Canaletto, Jacques Callot and Goya.

The word 'print' used to have a more distinguished meaning than it has today. After the introduction of high-speed printing in the last century, it became important to differentiate between a print made by an artist and the purely commercial product. Collectors, dealers and print-artists still differ at certain points but the nearest they have to an accepted definition runs something like this. An original print is created when the artist works directly on to a copperplate, woodblock or some other matrix. Then, working by himself or with a printer, he uses a printing press to transfer the image he has created on to paper.

Albrecht Dürer is regarded as the father of print-making in the West. He engraved wood and metal with incomparable finesse, producing immensely rich and detailed images. In so doing he transformed print-making from a rude handicraft into an art-form. But even in Dürer's day connoisseurs differentiated between the prints he made and those by Marcantonio Raimondi, for example, who reproduced on copperplates many of Dürer's woodcuts and who, for all his remarkable skills, was basically a copyist. From the earliest days there have been print-makers who *reproduced*, in the form of a print, paintings and drawings originally executed by others. Yet these were often so finely executed that they were ranked works of art in their own right.

But there is a more important distinction. It was discovered during the 19th century that by steel-facing a

OPPOSITE *Lucas van Leyden (1494–1533): 'The Dance of Saint Mary Magdalene'. Engraving (1519), £16,000.*

OPPOSITE BELOW *Albrecht Dürer (1471–1528): 'The Promenade', £600.*

RIGHT *Rembrandt Harmensz. van Rijn (1606–69): 'Christ presented to the People' (1665), £520,000.*

BELOW *Canaletto (1697–1768): 'Ale Parte del Dolo', £1200.*

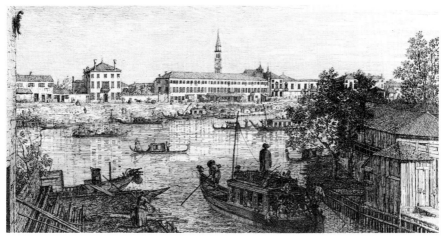

metal printing plate hundreds and even thousands of equally good impressions could be taken without the plate wearing down. Publishers and dealers concluded that if the value of prints was to be maintained, editions would have to be deliberately limited.

The twin concepts of 'original print' and 'limited edition' therefore belong to the age of modern prints. Old Master prints have always been judged by the quality of the impression and other variables that hardly arise in the contemporary field. The status of a print has gradually been downgraded in the public estimation during this century by the avalanche of printed images and words. Yet for today's serious collectors a print is first and foremost a work of art.

Prints were keenly collected in Europe even in Rembrandt's day, though public collections were slow to start. The Boston Museum was offered a collection of 16,000 Old Master prints in the 1880s at $4 a print – well below the going market price – but refused it. New York's Metropolitan Museum only got a Print Room in 1916. Its first curator, W. M. Ivins (Jr), put his finger on the print's mysterious, almost charismatic power. 'A print is not merely an impression,' he wrote, 'it is a picture, an expression of a man and all that is in him.'

During the 1920s appreciation of Old Master prints grew in the United

ABOVE *Jacques Callot (1592–1635): 'Les Grands Misères de la Guerre', £2200 (the set).*

LEFT *Hendrik Goltzius (1558–1617): 'The Holy Family under a Cherry Tree, after F. Barocci'. Engraving, £500.*

BELOW *Albrecht Dürer (1471–1528): 'The Virgin and Child with the Pear (1511), £7500.*

States and Europe, and even sparked off the boom in contemporary prints. The immortal line 'Come up and see my etchings' dates from this period. In London the rush to buy the latest etchings almost became a stampede. Colnaghi's could publish an edition of two hundred prints at £200 and sell out in a week. Some buyers would hurry round the corner to Christie's with their newly acquired etchings and enter them for the next print sale, certain of a quick profit.

But for the print world the 1930–50 period seemed like a new Ice Age. The thriving market of the 1920s had been killed stone dead by the Depression. By 1935 the average price of a Dürer print sold at auction in London sank to £8. Collecting seemed once more to have become the province of academics and art historians. It was not until the 1960s that the major salerooms resumed regular auctions and only in the last ten years that the market began to take off. Print prices had lagged behind the rest of the art market and as prices for paintings of comparable quality moved beyond the reach of the average collector prints seemed a natural alternative.

ABOVE *Martin Schongauer (1445–91): 'Saint John the Baptist', £2400.*

ABOVE RIGHT *Hendrik Goltzius (1558–1617): 'Hercules and Cacus' (1588), £55,000.*

BELOW *Francisco de Goya y Lucientes (1746–1828): 'Esopo el Fabulador, after Velázquez', £3800.*

In the academic world fine arts graduates choosing a subject for a doctoral thesis were finding that every painter worth the name had been covered. They turned to the under-researched world of prints and there they found tracts of uncharted territory including fine printmakers' whose names were not even known.

This growing interest is good news for the market. It means that prints whose origins are in doubt may soon get a firm date and attribution. It also means that museum curators will consider it worthwhile proposing to their trustees the purchase of prints by lesser or newly researched print-makers. In addition, collectors and investors will be more inclined to buy works by fully documented artists.

In the past curators, especially in the United States, have not found it easy to get approval to buy prints by artists whom the trustees do not know by name. This is one reason for the unusually large gap that separates prices for a major Dürer or Rembrandt and a major Aldegrever or Castiglione. Every trustee will have heard of Rembrandt and should raise no objection to spending $50,000 on one of his etchings; on the other hand, a woodcut at $5000 by an important but obscure printmaker has been known to present problems.

The mid-market price for a Dürer now stands at £1000, not a great deal of money for an original etching by one of the world's great masters. But of course £1000 does not buy a great work of art; the finest impressions are believed to have sold for up to £200,000.

Many things go to fix the value of a print, among them the image itself, the quality of the impression, its rarity, its 'state' and overall condition. The quality of the impression is what counts most and only a tiny fraction of those printed are worth so much. The explanation lies in the printing process. When Rembrandt had etched a copperplate, he would often take a trial print and work on it again with a sharp metal point. This latter process, known as drypoint, threw up a tiny ridge alongside the furrows made in the copper. When an impression was taken these ridges held a quantity of ink which appeared on the paper as a smudgy black area. Known as 'burr', this effect is highly prized by collectors though it can strike the uninitiated as an unsightly blemish. Collectors prefer an impression with rich velvety burr because they know it is one of the earliest taken from the plate and closest to the effect the artist was trying to achieve.

But the printing process quickly wore down the ridges that produced the burr; only ten perfect impressions and then another ten of good but declining quality could be taken before the effect disappeared. Thereafter, depending on the thickness of the plate and the depth of the incised line, a thousand more could be taken but none of them would show any burr.

Unfortunately, the valuation process is not that simple. Whenever a print-artist worked on a plate, took a trial impression and worked on it some more, the print was said to exist in two different 'states'. But it wasn't only artists who reworked the plates. When the lines began to print indistinctly the plates would be retouched and sometimes rebitten. This was often done after the artist had died, with several hundred impressions being taken at every stage.

Rembrandt's plates have a chequered history, some being printed from as late as 1910. The French collector Claude Watelet (1718–86) retouched many of them, perhaps with drypoint, to make the impressions he

Ces courages brutaux dans les hosteleries,
Du beau nom de butin couurent leurs voleries;

Ils querelent expres ennemis du repos,
Pour ne payer leur hoste, et prennent usquaux pots.

Ainsi du bien dautruy leur humeur saccommode
Quand on les a souler, et seruis a leur mode.

sold look convincingly early. Several later owners of the plates also re-worked them, but every time a new state was created the link with Rembrandt's original image grew weaker. That is why one Rembrandt print can be worth £25,000 and a late impression from the same plate only £50.

Investors should also beware of skulduggery at the top end of this market. One idiosyncracy of the print world is that collectors are willing to pay at least twice as much for a print that has full margins as for one that has been trimmed to the plate mark, even though the two images may be identical. Forgers are now able to graft full margins on to a trimmed print. Where a print has been damaged they can draw half the print by hand anew. They can also raise the fibres on the verso of a print, introduce whatever watermark is needed to establish it as an early impression, then close up the fibres and leave the operation undetectable with a 20× magnifying glass. Such surgery can raise the value of the print from £2000 to £10,000. The skills needed for such an operation are hard to come by and the going rate is believed to be several thousand dollars. The forger's skills would of course be wasted on a poor impression of a late-state Rembrandt, which is why the lower- and even the middle-quality ranges escape their attention.

Even if these nefarious dealings were more widely known few buyers would be deterred. For the current wave of enthusiasm is anyway happening against the odds. After all, Old Master prints are not only small compared to contemporary prints, they are nearly always black and white. They so conspicuously lack 'wall power' as to be lost in most modern interiors. They are low-

OPPOSITE *Jacques Callot (1592–1635)*: *'Les Grandes Misères de la Guerre'. Etching from the set of seventeen, £2200 (the set).*

ABOVE *Salvator Rosa (1615–73)*: *'The Rescue of the Infant Oedipus'. Etching with drypoint (1663), £540.*

BELOW *Giovanni Benedetto Castiglione (1616–70)*: *'The Creation of Adam'. Monotype (c. 1642), £320,000.*

profile works of art that make their impact through understatement. Consequently, this field could so easily have remained one of the art market's scholarly backwaters.

As it is, American museum-buying is affecting the market and this will keep prices running ahead for top-quality prints. But that does not mean that all top-quality prints cost a fortune. The best impressions of Dürer and Rembrandt prints may cost £25,000 and more, but there is a strong second league of printmakers whose top prices are around £2500. Those are the ones the shrewd investor should go for.

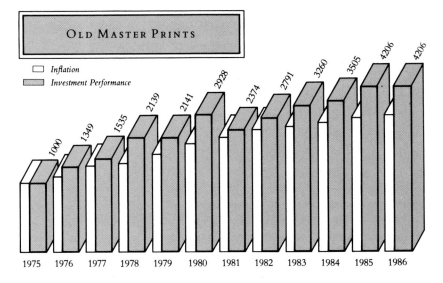

OLD MASTER PRINTS

☐ Inflation
▨ Investment Performance

1000 1349 1535 2139 2141 2928 2374 2791 3260 3505 4206 4206

1975 1976 1977 1978 1979 1980 1981 1982 1983 1984 1985 1986

Printmakers: Jacques Callot, Canaletto, Albrecht Dürer, Goya, Rembrandt

Artist	Mid-market price £	Change since 1975 %
Old Master Prints		
Jacques Callot (*1592–1635*)	600	+390
Canaletto (*1697–1768*)	1700	+340
Albrecht Dürer (*1471–1528*)	1000	+260
Francisco Goya (*1746–1828*)	1300	+240
Rembrandt (*1606–1669*)	1900	+380

Modern Master Prints

The index of 20th century prints is up 340% since 1975. It includes a cross section of major printmakers some of whom, as the individual performance figures suggest, have come into their own only during the last decade while other, greater artists have not performed well since 1975. Though the rises recorded by Braque and Matisse are much smaller than those of Jasper Johns and Roy Lichtenstein, it may be that the two contemporary printmakers have gone through a once-and-for-all upgrading

ABOVE *Joan Miró (1893–1983): Daphnis and Chloe. Etching (1933), £1800.*

RIGHT *Henri Matisse (1869–1954): 'Seated Nude' (1925). Lithograph, £5500.*

such as Braque and Matisse went through during the 1950s and 1960s.

Jasper Johns and Roy Lichtenstein are among the only survivors of a period when print-making was taken up on a large scale. The print boom of the 1960s also drew many a wide-eyed buyer into the market for the first time. The success of serious print workshops in the United States, such as Universal Limited Art Editions and Pratt Graphics Center, gave other galleries the idea of moonlighting in the print market.

A hothouse atmosphere developed as students from art college were signed up to run off editions of several hundred prints for sale to a hungry public at $200 to $300 a time. In prosperous New York of the 1960s culture was a much-desired commodity. Office blocks were going up fast and a new kind of adviser – the art consultant – appeared on the scene. His brief was to cover the acres of bare walls with something of cultural worth. Contemporary prints were a natural solution. Lively, striking, often controversial images were ac-

quired wholesale by large corporations. It was as if the spirit of some 19th century allegorical sculpture, 'Commerce Extends her Hand to Graphic Art', had come to life. Scathing judgements were passed on this new 'Bank Art'; Bonwit Teller opened a print boutique and before long Elizabeth Arden salons together with shops and offices right across the United States had hung their walls with prints.

Of all the print artists then at work, a few were already represented in public collections, some established reputations by the end of the decade but the majority have been heard of no more. The 1960s print boom also made possible dealings that would now be illegal. Some dealers deliberately blurred the dividing line between an original print and a reproduction. Broadly speaking, original prints are those taken from plates worked upon directly by the artist; those made from plates that have been subjected to a photomechanical process are reproductions. This is still the principal distinction, though

TOP *Pablo Picasso (1881–1974): 'Head of a woman in profile'. Etching (1933), £18,000.*

ABOVE *David Hockney (b. 1937): 'Panama Hat'. Etching and aquatint (1972), £1700.*

some artists use photographic processes to create special effects and a precise definition has become impossible.

For the protection of buyers the state of New York enacted that 'art merchants' must provide a written statement for every buyer of a print describing in detail the printing process, the degree of participation by the artist, the paper, the signature, the size of edition and other information which should enable him to decide whether the print deserves to be called original.

In Britain the print boom came a little later and was accompanied by an egalitarian experiment. Editions Alecto, a respected print-publisher, announced, 'We are going to do for prints what Henry Ford did for Detroit'. The idea was that the printing press would supply the world with great art at minimal cost just as it had done with literature. Prints began to be published in unlimited editions and sold at a few pounds a time so that anyone could afford to buy.

The dream was short-lived. Collectors clearly felt that inexpensive prints, let alone those in unlimited editions, lacked cachet. Most buyers, it turned out, were willing to pay a higher price for the knowledge that only so many other people, or preferably only so few other people, would ever own this or that print.

To buy modern prints and paintings calls for a certain courage in the first place, for to do so offers other people an insight into your personality. The artist's struggle to find new means of expression has for some time been driving them to experiment with forms, materials and processes that make their work appear strange and even shocking. An element of self-parody is often present and sometimes a buyer will not know for sure if he is buying a work of art or a joke. To buy any contemporary work of art therefore requires confidence in one's own judgement as well as an act of faith in the serious intent of the artist.

Investors in contemporary prints should take account of the high risks. The more innovative and experimental the artist, the more failures he is likely to have produced in his time. Definitive listings of many leading printmakers have been published and these provide buyers with a view of the artist's output to date. There is usually a broad consensus among collectors on the outstanding images each artist has created and prices for the best of these are high. As time passes the price gap between the most-admired and the least-admired prints widens. Picasso's *Le Repas Frugal* (1904) for instance can now fetch over £20,000 while the less favoured images in the Vollard Suite can be bought for under £1000.

Many of the leading printmakers that were considered outrageous in the 1960s were rated a 'safe buy' by 1975. How has time treated them? And if the market prices reflect degrees of admiration for their work, what is it that accounts for the rise of some and the decline of others? Above all, could these changes have been foreseen? Quite different fates have overtaken some of the leading printmakers.

The market for Jasper Johns has been consistently strong. His standing in academic circles could scarcely be higher and, unusually even among leading artists, every one of his images has been critically acclaimed. His intense pictorial exploration of numerals, letters and other familiar symbols has enabled the viewer to experience them in a new light – perhaps the only aim to which an artist can realistically aspire. His earliest works have risen strongly in value and are now rarely seen on the market. The more recent work has also been selling well at auction and it is clear that Johns's pre-eminence as both artist and printmaker make him the ideal choice for investors.

Rauschenberg, another key graduate of the New York Abstract Expressionist movement, has remained a problematic artist for the market. His work does not translate well into the print medium and collectors sense little involvement by the artist in the printing process. As many as half of the Rauschenberg prints at auction in the course of a year can remain unsold, and this illiquidity makes him an unsuitable artist for investors. Even the major touring exhibition of his work in 1981 did little to stir up interest in his printed work and his prospects in the market are not bright.

The potential of the comic strip as the inspiration of serious art was realised at the hands of Roy Lichtenstein. His early images have become classics of 'pop' history. His dot-and-line method amounts to a visual dialect understood by all. Lichtenstein offers up his images straight and without commentary. He does not mock or idealise and the best of his work derives power from its neutrality. Prices for *Shipboard Girl, Brushstroke* and *Crying Girl*, all published during the 1960s, are up a full 460% since 1975. The later series of Haystacks, Cathedrals and others have become hard to sell and wise buyers will stick to the classics.

Jim Dine's output may be of mixed quality but his mastery of the print process is admired by collectors. Several of his better-known works, including *The Dressing Gowns* and *Realistic Poet Authorised*, are up over

LEFT *Pablo Picasso (1881–1974): 'Woman with flowered corsage'. Lithograph (1958), £13,000.*

BELOW LEFT *Henri de Toulouse-Lautrec (1864–1901): 'Femme au Tub'. Lithograph (1896), £11,000.*

work has been no better. As is the case with other artists Warhol publication prices moved up during the 1960s as his reputation grew. Investors who bought early may have come out on top; those who have acquired their Warhols more recently will be showing a loss.

David Hockney is a print publisher's dream. His style is distinct enough to be recognized from across the street. Collectors can relate easily to his subject matter and his brilliant sunlit colours are a feast for the eye. To complete the package he is, as artists go, a fairly public man with a mildly controversial life style.

Born of working-class parents in England he has made his home in California where his work is widely admired. Nevertheless, the highest prices are paid in London by British and Scandinavian collectors. Every one of Hockney's prints has fared differently in the market, but the overall rise since 1975 is around 430%.

600% since 1975 while others have remained static. Again, it is the earlier prints made before he left Britain which are becoming the serious collector's items.

As the *enfant terrible* of the New York art scene in the 1960s Andy Warhol created some memorable images. The Marilyn and Flower series still sell reasonably well but much of the rest rouses little interest today. The Campbell's soup cans, the Electric Chair series and even his prints of the androgynous Jagger have become an auctioneer's nightmare. Whatever their impact when first published, collectors are unimpressed today. Prices for Warhol's paintings have dropped by 30% since 1975 and the overall performance of his graphic

Some well-known artists such as Josef Albers and Victor Vasarely now have only the most limited following, while barely any of the new generation of artists being published by well-known galleries have created any real interest in the secondary market. Broadly speaking, prints in 'difficult' styles are only saleable at auction if attached to a big name.

The case of Picasso's graphic work is special. Picasso produced just over 2000 prints in the course of his life. They were published in editions of rarely less than fifty, so there are about 100,000 original Picasso prints in circulation. Overall, these have risen in value by 120% since 1975. Nearly a thousand change hands every year and they almost have the status of an international currency. Now that the mid-market price for a Picasso painting is over £40,000 compared to £1500 for a Picasso print, the graphic work is an attractive alternative.

All collectors of modern art would be pleased to own a Picasso, but for some the possession of a Picasso is a 'must'. This element of compulsive buying has driven prices to levels that can only be justified in terms of the magic signature. Some collectors now consider that there is better value to be had among his prints. They recognize that the quality of Picasso's work is very uneven. In fact Picasso is no longer a kind of totem-pole round which art lovers are expected to dance in mindless adulation. The 347 prints Picasso made within the space of six months while at Mougins in 1968 are among the least-admired of his work. The great early works, the set of twelve prints including *Le Repas Frugal*, the Vollard Suite of the 1930s and the linocuts of his wife, Françoise Gilot, done in the late 1950s, are the prints investors should do best with. The Cubist period prints are considered too difficult; the book illustrations hard to display and the 347 series a desperate and not altogether successful last fling.

Several print publishers are now promoting limited editions of 'Picasso prints'. These are created from plates worked on by craftsmen who copy Picasso's paintings or drawings. Needless to say, these have no claim to being original prints and the outlook for them as investments is bleak.

Whenever a print combines artistic quality with rarity it is sure to command a high price. The number of prints making up any edition is therefore important. On the one hand, the very fact that prints are multiples is unconsciously reassuring. Most buyers actually like to feel that some two hundred other collectors will have made the same choice. On the other hand, no collector likes to feel there are ten thousand prints like his own in homes right round the globe.

Publishers find collectors are more influenced in their buying decisions by the image than the size of the edition. All the same, not many publishers attempt editions over three hundred, mainly because the market for more could not easily be created. Investors should be wary of larger editions since the prospects of such prints becoming rare are remote.

Investor-collectors in New York have tumbled to the fact that they can often buy prints for less at auction than they have to pay to print-publishers. Prints made by quite successful artists often fetch a lot less than their publication price when resold at auction. The publishers usually lack the funds as well as the inclination to support their artists in the secondary market. Bidding often stops at around half the current retail price and at this level they are often snapped up by other dealers.

Despite the shifts in taste the print market is growing apace. Turnover in the United States alone runs at over $100 million a year, half of it accounted for by corporate buying. Though print-making is many centuries old, and though the idea of artist and machine combining to create multiple works of art was promoted by the Futurists some seventy years ago, the whole concept of a print as an art-form is perhaps even more dynamic today.

To forecast which printmakers

will be at the top of the tree in the year 2000 is no easy matter. People allege that the art world is fickle. The simple truth behind this allegation is that only some art will stand the test of time. While most art is datable in the sense that Jasper Johns's *Grey Alphabet* may be recognized by those familiar with contemporary art as belonging to a particular period, there is another kind of art which is not only datable but *dated*. This includes, for example, the Warhol soup cans, whose impact and relevance, powerful in their time, have now diminished. Any new work of art can be made to astound; it is only when that work of art is old but retains the power to impress for the thousandth time that it can be reckoned to be great.

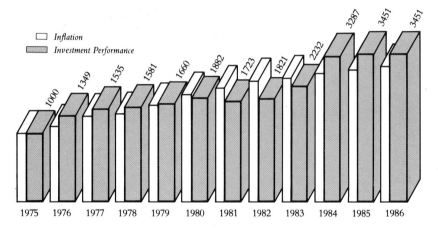

MODERN MASTER PRINTS

Inflation

Investment Performance

1000 · 1349 · 1535 · 1581 · 1660 · 1882 · 1723 · 1821 · 2232 · 3287 · 3451 · 3451

1975 1976 1977 1978 1979 1980 1981 1982 1983 1984 1985 1986

Printmakers: Georges Braque, Marc Chagall, Henri Matisse, Joan Miró, Henri de Toulouse-Lautrec

Artist	Mid-market price £	Change since 1975 %
Modern Master Prints		
Georges Braque (*1882–1963*)	2500	+250
Alexander Calder (*1898–1976*)	240	+70
Marc Chagall (*1887–1985*)	2500	+180
Salvador Dali (*b. 1904*)	300	+130
Jim Dine (*b. 1935*)	1000	+690

Artist	Mid-market price £	Change since 1975 %
David Hockney (b. 1937)	1070	+430
Jasper Johns (b. 1930)	1900	+520
Roy Lichtenstein (b. 1923)	890	+460
Henri Matisse (1869–1954)	4000	+430
Joan Miró (1893–1983)	1200	+140
Henry Moore (b. 1898)	570	+220
Pablo Picasso (1881–1974)	1470	+120
Henri de Toulouse-Lautrec (1864–1901)	2700	+140
Andy Warhol (b. 1930)	860	+270

Leading Dealers

Abbot & Holder
73 Castelnau
Barnes
London SW13
01-748 2416
British and European watercolours and drawings.

John Baskett Ltd
173 New Bond Street
London W1Y 9PB
01- 629 2991
English paintings, drawings and
prints.

Craddock & Barnard
32 Museum Street
London WC1
01-636 3937
Old Master and modern prints.

Thomas Agnew & Sons Ltd
43 Old Bond Street
London W1X 3TD
01-493 3288
Pictures, drawings, prints and
sculpture.

Bury Street Gallery
11 Bury Street
London SW1
01-930 2902
19th and 20th century French
and Scandinavian paintings.

Crane Kalman Gallery
178 Brompton Road
London SW3 1HQ
01-584 7566
Modern British and European
paintings and sculpture.

Artemis Fine Arts (UK) Ltd
15 Duke Street
London SW1
01-930 8733
Old Master and modern
paintings and prints, sculpture
and antiquities.

P & D Colnaghi & Co. Ltd
14 Old Bond Street
London W1X 4JL
01-491 7408
Old Master paintings, drawings
and prints, English paintings,
drawings and watercolours,
European sculpture, furniture
and works of art.

Anthony D'Offay Ltd
9 & 23 Dering Street
London W1
01-629 1578
20th century British and
International Contemporary art.

William Drummond Ltd
11 Bury Street
St James's
London SW1 69A
01-930 9696
*English oil paintings, water-
colours and drawings of the 18th
and 19th centuries.*

Thomas Gibson Fine Art Ltd
9A New Bond Street
London W1Y 9PE
01-499 8572
*19th and 20th century paintings,
drawings and sculptures and
selected Old Masters.*

Alan Jacobs Gallery
8 Duke Street
London SW1Y 6BN
01-930 3709
*17th century Dutch and Flemish
Old Master paintings.*

Hobhouse Ltd
38 Old Bond Street
London W1X 3AE
01-491 1445
*Botanical drawings, 17th–20th
century Indian Company School
painting, European artists
working in India, the Middle
and Far East.*

Richard Green
44 Dover Street
London W1X 4JQ
01-493 3939
*Old Masters, 18th and 19th
century English landscape and
sporting paintings, 19th century
Dutch and French paintings,
and fine prints.*

Oscar & Peter Johnson Ltd
Lowndes Lodge Gallery
27 Lowndes Street
London SW1Y 9HY
01-235 6464
*18th and 19th century British
oil paintings and watercolours.*

Jocelyn Fielding Fine Art Ltd
8 Duke Street
London SW1Y 6BN
01-839 5040
*Old Master paintings and
English paintings and drawings.*

Nigel Greenwood Inc. Ltd
4 New Burlington Street
London W1X 1FE
01-434 3797
Contemporary British art.

Annely Juda Fine Art
11 Tottenham Mews
London W1P 9PJ
01-637 5517
*Contemporary painting and
sculpture, Russian Constructi-
vists, Bauhaus and early 20th
century art.*

The Fine Art Society Plc
148 New Bond Street
London W1Y 0JT
01-629 5116
*Oil paintings, watercolours,
drawings, prints, sculpture,
19th and 20th century designer
furniture, ceramics, glass and
textiles.*

Hazlitt, Gooden & Fox Ltd
38 Bury Street
London SW1Y 6BB
01-930 6422
*18th and 19th century English
paintings and drawings, Italian
baroque and rococo paintings,
19th century French paintings
and drawings.*

Lisson Gallery
66–68 Bell Street
London NW1 6SP
01-262 1539
*British sculpture, European and
American contemporary art
1960 to present.*

Fischer Fine Art Ltd
30 King Street
St James's
London SW1Y 4FQ
01-839 3942
*19th and 20th century paintings
and sculpture.*

Malcolm Innes & Partners
Ltd
172 Walton Street
London SW3
01-584 0575
*Scottish landscape, sporting and
natural pictures and prints.*

Lumley Cazalet Ltd
24 Davies Street
London W1Y 1HB
01-499 5058
*Late 19th and 20th century
original prints.*

The Mayor Gallery Ltd
22a Cork Street
London W1X 1HB
01-734 3558
*Modern American, European
and British paintings, drawings
and sculpture.*

Brod Ltd
24 St James's Street
London SW1 1HA
01-839 2606
*Old Masters, 18th and 19th
century British schools,
Barbizon and Impressionist
paintings, drawings and
watercolours.*

Alex Reid & Lefevre Ltd
30 Bruton Street
London W1X 8JD
01-493 1573
*19th and 20th century paintings,
drawings and sculpture.*

Mercury Gallery Ltd
26 Cork Street
London W1X 1HB
01-734 7800
*20th century paintings, drawings
and sculpture by French,
German and British artists.*

The Parker Gallery
12a–12b Berkeley Street
Piccadilly
London W1X 5AD
01-499 5906
*Old prints, oil and watercolour
paintings of the English School.*

Somerville & Simpson Ltd
11 Savile Row
London W1X 1AE
01-437 5414
*Old Master paintings, drawings
and prints, English watercolours
and paintings.*

John Mitchell & Sons
8 New Bond Street
London W1Y 9PE
01-493 7567
*17th century Dutch and Flemish,
English and 19th century French
paintings and watercolours.*

Partridge (Fine Arts) Ltd
144–146 New Bond Street
London W1L 0LY
01-629 0834
*Sporting pictures, Old Master
paintings.*

Edward Speelman Ltd
Empire House
175 Piccadilly
London W1V 0NP
01-493 0657
*Old Master and Impressionist
paintings.*

Achim Moeller Ltd
8 Grosvenor Street
Bond Street
London W1X 9FB
01-493 7611
*19th and 20th century European
and American masters.*

The Piccadilly Gallery
16 Cork Street
London W1X 1PF
01-629 2875
*20th century watercolours and
drawings, Symbolist works and
art nouveau drawings, modern
British paintings and drawings.*

Spink & Son Ltd
5–7 King Street
London SW1 6QS
01-930 7888
*English oil paintings, water-
colours and drawings of all
periods.*

New Art Centre Ltd
41 Sloane Street
London SW1X 9LU
01-235 5844
*20th century British paintings
and sculpture.*

The Redfern Gallery Ltd
20 Cork Street
London W1X 2HL
01-734 1732
*20th century paintings, sculpture
and graphics*

Michael Tollemache Ltd
15 Duke Street
London SW1Y 6DB
01-930 8733
*Old Masters and 18th and 19th
century British paintings,
drawings, watercolours, prints
and sculptures.*

Tryon Gallery Ltd
22–24 Cork Street
London W1X 1HB
01-734 6961
*Sporting and natural history
pictures, prints, books and
bronzes.*

William Weston Gallery
7 Royal Arcade
Albermarle Street
London W1X 3HD
01-493 0722
*19th and early 20th century
French and European prints.*

Christopher Wood Gallery
15 Motcomb Street
London SW1X 8LB
01-235 9141
*Fine Victorian paintings,
drawings and watercolours,
sculpture and works of art.*

Whitford & Hughes
6 Duke Street
London SW1
01-930 5577
*Fine paintings (1880–1930),
post-Impressionist, Symbolist,
Vienna Secession, Salon and
Academy, Orientalist and Belle
Epoque.*

Waddington Galleries
11 Cork Street
London W1X 1HB
01-437 8611
*20th century paintings,
sculptures and prints by British,
European and American artists.*

Wildenstein & Co.
147 New Bond Street
London W1Y 0NX
01-629 0602
Fine art, painting and sculpture.

FURNITURE

Georgian Furniture

Americans may soon find they own more British antiques than the British. Two hundred million dollars' worth were shipped to the United States in 1985 – a fivefold increase over 1975 – and the figure could reach three hundred million this year.

In 1985, when the pound was at an all-time low against the dollar, Britain seemed like one big bargain basement. Americans swarmed through the antiques markets snapping up any fine 18th century furniture they could find. They have been major buyers of English furniture for two main reasons. First, they do not have enough 18th century American furniture to satisfy demand, and secondly, the English product is often more elegant, usually better made and always carries greater cachet.

Thanks to the strength of American demand, market prices for Georgian furniture have for many years been set in New York. During the 1970s they rose fast enough, but with the dollar now so much stronger against the pound the rate of increase in London has accelerated. This has reinforced the British view that Georgian furniture is a good investment. American collectors go along with this idea and use their strong dollars to buy in the London market and prices get ratcheted up once more. Although there is a circularity about this pattern of buying it is hard to imagine that prices will ever fall far or for long.

The Georgian furniture index is currently showing a gain of 460% since 1975. Unlike many sectors of the art market, medium-quality pieces have been rising as fast as the best. A rise of 270% has been registered by secretaire-bookcases and bureau-cabinets, the comparatively modest rise perhaps being associated with their large size. A rise of 480% was recorded by card tables, side tables and dining-room tables; 520%

One of a pair of George I walnut armchairs, £12,500.

Early Georgian walnut bureau, £4800.

for chairs of all kinds and 640% for mirrors and girandoles.

There has been no significant variation between the performance of walnut, mahogany and satinwood, the three most popular woods of the 18th century. Satinwood rose faster than other woods in the five years to 1980 but now seems to be moving with the pack. Oak is perhaps the only undervalued sector of the market. Country pieces were made in oak well into the 18th century but its heyday ended with the Restoration of Charles II so it forms no part of the Georgian index.

Whatever may happen to market prices, fine furniture is specially enjoyable to live with. Every piece has a personality of its own. Several elements contribute to this – design, size, purpose and, not least, the wood itself. Oak has a workaday earthiness, walnut has a warm, rich texture, mahogany a formal elegance, while satinwood is delicate and bordering on effete.

But where does furniture really stand in the hierarchy of art-forms?

Did the person who recently paid £40,000 for a Chippendale four-post bed at Sotheby's acquire a work of art or a piece of fancy carpentry? Largely because furniture has a clear-cut function it has come to be considered an applied art. Within the art world, in other words, it has been treated as a second-class citizen. But of course this should not be the case. Any object that has a function can also be a work of art. What matters is the amount of creative effort and talent that goes into it. The roof of the Sistine Chapel may have been intended to keep the rain off the people below, but Michelangelo's paintings transform it into a work of art. On a different level, the tribesmen of the Sepik River made hooks on which they hung bags of food so that the rats could not reach them. Very functional hooks they were, yet, because finely carved in the form of cult figures, they rank as works of art.

The enormous value recently placed on fine furniture suggests that it has now been promoted into the first rank of the art world. Most

George I walnut stool, £11,000.

people would still wish to see a gap left between a great Rembrandt painting and a great Louis XV commode, though with the world furniture record standing at $1,600,000 the gap seems to be closing.

Eighteenth-century English cabinet-makers would be astonished to know how much their work is admired today. For they thought of themselves as no better than decent craftsmen. Doubtless they were more inventive than their predecessors and they certainly had a keener sense of style than those who followed them in Victorian times. That is why the 18th century has so much to offer.

There is something unmistakeably English about most Georgian furniture, yet no truly vernacular style ever existed. Nearly all of it incorporates French, Gothic or Chinese motifs. Later, following the excavations at Herculaneum and Pompeii, neoclassical Greek and Roman designs appeared everywhere. Yet somehow all these ideas were filtered through English minds and recreated in peculiarly English form.

Designs were produced by architects as well as cabinet-makers. At the beginning of the century William Kent designed not only Palladian mansions but also richly carved and gilded furniture to put in them. Other architects, including Henry Holland, Sir William Chambers and Sir John Soane, turned their hands to designing furniture, but the greatest of them was Robert Adam, whose neoclassical houses and their contents, conceived as part of a single grand design, are among Britain's most notable cultural achievements.

Furniture designs had been published since the 16th century, but most cabinet-makers were content to work out their own ideas. They responded slowly to changes in fashion,

Pair of George II mahogany armchairs, £121,000.

yet were quick to supply whatever new items of furniture might be needed. In the 17th century a gaming table was basically a chess and backgammon board on legs. By the beginning of the 18th century, gambling fever was sweeping through England and gaming tables with recesses for candlesticks and wells for counters were made in great numbers. George II and his queen gave card parties at which large sums changed hands, and their example was followed by society at large.

The popular games – cribbage, quadrille, Pope Joan and whist – were played by people of all ages and to such an extent that the Countess of Hartford wrote, 'It is actually ridicu-

ABOVE *George III satinwood and rosewood tripod table, £8000.*

BELOW RIGHT *George III mahogany secretaire-cabinet, £75,000.*

cupboards were made throughout the century to hold precious china or books. Chippendale's prettiest pieces incorporate Chinese fretwork and pagodas, making them the ideal display case for oriental ceramics. It was the lightness and strength of mahogany, first imported in quantity in the 1720s, that made possible a decorative door with elaborate and fine glazing bars.

As the leading 18th century cabinet-maker, Chippendale supplied many grand houses and from the surviving accounts we know precisely what his furniture cost. By the standards of the time he does not seem expensive. In the 1770s, the price of a four-post bed with fluted posts and carved cornices was not expensive at £10, though a bedcover and bolster 'fitted with Seasond White Dantzig Downe and feathers' cost about the same, and after all the lace damask and tassels had been added the total came to about £100.

Dining-room tables offered designers so little room for invention that Chippendale didn't bother to

lous, though I think a mortifying sight, that play should become the business of the nation from the age of fifteen to fourscore.' The craze persisted throughout the century and the young bloods of Oxford were reported in 1779 to have staked five hundred pounds on the outcome of a race between maggots.

Other pieces of furniture came into use to cater for changes in habit and life style. Chinese porcelain had been imported on a massive scale since the 17th century. Women were such passionate collectors that, it is said, they traded their clothes for china ornaments.

However the china was acquired, it needed to be protected against breakage and theft. Glass-fronted

include any in the first edition of his famous catalogue 'The Director'. One of his clients was charged £10 for a table of five leaves joined together; similar tables now fetch £5000–£10,000. Even the ten cabriole 'Arm'd Chairs Gilt in Burnished Gold' supplied to the actor David Garrick do not seem too costly at £58.

On the other hand, Chippendale was known to be expensive on special orders. A superb carved frame with large antique ornaments 'exceeding richly carved and highly finished in burnished gold' cost one customer £70 while the glass to go in it, still fabulously expensive in those days, came to £290.

Throughout the 18th century good English furniture cost about quarter as much as comparable French pieces. After the French Revolution in 1789, London became the marketplace for the furniture and paintings of aristocratic French refugees. But the market was swamped and by the early 19th century the price of French furniture was dropping. English furniture prices were hit even harder.

Towards the end of the 19th century French furniture became all the rage in the United States. The fashion for drawing-room suites with Gobelins tapestry panels was at its height and in 1900 French furniture was selling for roughly ten times the price of English.

But this lowly status for English furniture did not last long. Percy Macquoid's *History of English Furniture* (1904–8) opened the eyes of the British to their fine achievement in this field. Macquoid made a withering attack on Victorian design and proclaimed that the long romance with beauty that had lasted in England for eight centuries ceased suddenly in 1820.

Before Macquoid, hardly a piece of English furniture would have sold for more than £500. Ever since, the gap between French and English has been closing. Compared to French furniture, English is still seen by some collectors as the plain country cousin, yet just as many now seem to prefer its more restrained styles.

ABOVE LEFT *George III ormolu-mouted rosewood library table, £6000.*

BELOW *George I giltwood mirror, £8500.*

Of all English arts and crafts, furniture is the least researched. Whereas silver is stamped with a maker's mark, porcelain usually bears a factory mark, and most paintings are signed, furniture is very seldom marked and can only be attributed to a maker when the account sent to the client has survived. Documented furniture is rare outside the houses supplied by Chippendale and other leading makers. In all other cases attributions have to be made on stylistic grounds, though this is fraught with problems. For in practice, the three great seminal design publications of the century – Chippendale's *The Gentleman and Cabinet-maker's Director*, Robert Adam's *Works in Architecture* and Thomas Sheraton's *The Cabinet-maker's and Upholsterer's Drawing Book* – were bought by competing craftsmen throughout England who freely adapted or pirated the designs.

At one time almost any piece of mahogany with curly rococo decoration was attributed without qualms to Chippendale. Now, salerooms catalogue furniture by reign or period –

late George II, for example. They describe its form and decoration but, unless they have documentary evidence, do not ascribe it to a particular maker.

All that could change before long. A dictionary of English furniture-makers listing several thousand names is due to be published in 1987. A

BELOW *George I giltwood side table,* £6000.

OPPOSITE *George III mahogany dressing chest,*
£3000.

ABOVE *George III satinwood and fruitwood*
Pembroke table, £10,000.

RIGHT *George III mahogany card table, £2000.*

second phase to this project could be
an illustrated publication linking furniture of particular designs to specific
makers. This could make the field
more interesting to collectors and
investors. But what no book can fully
explain is how to spot the almost
invisible restorations that are carried
out these days.

A great deal of old English furniture has taken a beating and parts
have needed to be replaced. Few feet
can stand on damp stone floors for
two hundred years without rotting
away. And, apart from being kicked
and scraped, many pieces will have
been attacked by worm. The condition of furniture makes a crucial
difference to its value, so, unless you

know what to look for and are willing
to spend time on the floor inspecting
every inch for authenticity, it pays to
have any piece you plan to buy
checked over by a professional.

The auction rooms handle many
of the fine Georgian pieces appearing
in the market, though 80% of them
are bought by dealers. That is a
higher rate than in other sectors and
raises the question, 'Do private buyers
have reason to be nervous?'

No one should forget that auctioneers act first and foremost for the
seller. A surprisingly high percentage
of the lots on offer are described as if
they had left the cabinet-maker's
premises that morning. The salerooms decline responsibility for errors

of description and urge buyers to satisfy themselves that lots are accurately described. Dealers often claim to find the descriptions absurdly flattering, while auctioneers put such talk down to the not-so-friendly rivalry that smoulders away between them. Both sides probably have a point, but at all events investors need not be put off. Provided the price you pay for a piece reflects its condition, 15% annual growth over the next ten years looks probable.

GEORGIAN FURNITURE

☐ *Inflation*
▨ *Investment Performance*

1000 1300 1815 2062 1856 2062 2095 2332 3032 4093 5582 5582

1975 1976 1977 1978 1979 1980 1981 1982 1983 1984 1985 1986

Components: a selection of George I, George II and George III chairs, bookcases, card tables, commodes, side tables, bureau-cabinets and mirrors

French Furniture

Eighteenth-century French furniture is widely agreed to be the finest furniture ever made. It was very expensive at the time and has remained so ever since. Between 1950 and 1970 it rose in value by 400% – well under 10% every year – so some acceleration since then was to be expected. The evolution of price in this field is hard to monitor, though the rise since 1975 is estimated at 340%.

The supremacy of French furniture has meant that it never seemed cheap and was more often overpriced by

RIGHT *Pair of Louis XV beechwood fauteuils,*
£5000.

BELOW LEFT *Louis XVI secretaire à abattant, once*
owned by Marie-Antoinette, £900,000.

BELOW RIGHT *Louis XVI porcelain-topped centre*
table, £55,000.

comparison with other works of art.
Ten pieces of French furniture were
sold in 1882 at an average price of over
£6000. Some had fetched more than
the £9000 the National Gallery in
London had paid a few years earlier
for Leonardo's *Virgin of the Rocks*, and
the going rate for a Rembrandt at the
time was £3000 to £6000. By 1965
the position had been reversed, or, as
some see it, corrected. The record for
a piece of French furniture then stood
at £63,000 while a Rembrandt had
been sold for over £800,000.

The virtuosity of the French cabinet-makers commands admiration.
Working within the limits set by the
function of each piece, they produced
effects of elegance, prettiness, har-

monies of line, colour and proportion
that highlight this furniture in the
field of art. Prices are now determined
largely by the American market
where French furniture has been the
preferred taste of New York and other
decorators for the past thirty years.

Prices have risen faster for so-called
'case furniture' than for 'seat furniture'. Commodes, tables and chests
are not only less likely to be damaged
than the various pieces of furniture
made to be sat upon. In addition,
many people choose to sit on modern
sofas and chairs because they are more
comfortable, but are very much in
the market for elegant pieces that
enhance a drawing room.

Eighteenth-century French styles

ABOVE *Pair of Louis XV beechwood fauteuils,*
£5000.

ABOVE RIGHT *Louis XVI giltwood fauteuil,*
£3000.

RIGHT *18th century French banquette. One of a*
pair, £5000.

range from the Versailles look to the quite crude, but more human, country or provincial pieces that have a strong earthy appeal. Good-quality country furniture has risen faster than its polished Parisian counterparts. This may be because it is more versatile, looking good in the drawing room or the kitchen, and partly be-cause for many people the Versailles look in the 1980s is simply unacceptable.

Boulle furniture has risen in line with the rest though prices depend very much on condition. All French furniture calls for highly skilled restoration, but Boulle pieces in particular can deteriorate badly, with bits

Louis XVI ormolu-mounted bois satiné bureau à
cylindre, £3500.

Louis XVI mahogany table à écrire, £4000.

of tortoiseshell and brass wire protruding, and may take thousands of pounds and some years to put right.

Straight-talking dealers will admit that the French furniture market is a jungle. French dealers love what they call the *condition anglaise* or English country-house condition: a somewhat derelict-looking commode, for example, rather dirty, missing a few pieces, but basically untouched for a long time. This would be taken to Paris for 'Americanization' – the age-old surface would be scraped away and it would be French polished anew. This constitutes legitimate, if regrettable, restoration. But there are restorations which go too far.

A *bureau plat*, for example, can cost anything from £1000 to £200,000. The valuation depends on the date, the quality of the mounts and veneers, the colour, the style and the name of the *ébéniste*. French restorers in particular are clever at working up a dull 19th century *bureau plat*, perhaps even of German or Austrian origin, into something more desirable and into a higher price bracket. The upgrading might include rechasing the mounts, adding a band of inlay for a classier look, bleaching the bare wood on the underside to make it look lighter and older, and even applying the stamp of a famous maker. Spending £5000 on a £5000 *bureau plat* could lift it into the £50,000 range.

This is one reason why buyers are so keen on provenance. It isn't only snobbery; it is a protection against buying a fake. Any piece that has spent a hundred and fifty years in the same person's house is unlikely to have been interfered with.

However, French furniture should still prove to be a fine investment. Objective and expert advice is not that easy to find, but it is essential for anyone planning a trip into the jungle.

ABOVE *Louis XV ormolu-mounted kingwood bureau de dame, £5000.*

ABOVE *Early Louis XV kingwood and floral marquetry commode, £5000.*

ABOVE *Louis XV giltwood mirror, £11,000.*

Victorian Furniture

The market for Victorian furniture has been climbing nearly as fast as that for Georgian. Furniture which would have been dumped without hesitation by dealers thirty years ago is returning to favour and is thought of as amusing and good value for money, or even fashionable. Many people, however, still regard Victorian furniture as a cultural aberration – a blemish they would prefer to see erased from the national record.

Yet prices for even the most ordinary pieces are up 310% since 1975. The Victorian furniture index includes some of the horrors of mass production, showing all the flamboyance, or, as admirers would have it, charming exuberance, of Victorian taste. But throughout the Victorian era there was a succession of architects from Pugin to Mackintosh who were producing designs for furniture which is now in demand by museums in the United Kingdom and abroad.

The all-time low in terms of public esteem for Victorian furniture was reached in the 1930s. Not even the best pieces were taken seriously. It was then that John Betjeman gave his friend Evelyn Waugh the Philosopher's Cabinet designed and painted by William Burgess. The two men were not in the habit of giving each other expensive presents and there is little doubt that Betjeman picked up the cabinet for only a few pounds. A similar cabinet was sold in 1973 for the then staggering £8400, but the sale in 1983 of the Philosopher's Cabinet itself for £45,000 – a rise of 430% over the decade – shows how opinion has swung back in favour of Victorian furniture.

Most Victorian furniture was derivative in the worst possible way. Designers corrupted the styles they borrowed and pandered to their newly rich customers by loading every piece with vulgar ornament. It was not surprising that William Morris, the apostle of the Arts and Crafts movement, is reputed to have been sick at the Great Exhibition of

1851. He was not alone in recognizing that furniture design had reached a new low.

A reviewer of the exhibition noted:

The hunger after novelty is now insatiable: heaven and earth are racked for novel inventions and happy is the man who lights upon something, however *outré*, that shall strike the vulgar mind and obtain the run of the season. . . . We imitate every extant school. We can execute Chinese and Athenian with the same facility. We can forge – perhaps that is the most appropriate term – an Egyptian obelisk, or a Corinthian capital, a so-called Gothic moulding or a Sèvres cup. . . . We are the most skilful mimics but what do we create?

Victorian yew-wood marquetry and parcel-gilt draw-leaf dining table, £700.

OPPOSITE *Victorian mahogany centre table, £1500.*

Middle-class Victorians seemed to confuse ornament with beauty. The more an object was adorned the more beautiful it became. Plain surfaces were anathema to them and even Elizabethan panelling was torn out or covered over with garish new wallpapers. In the 18th century carved and inlaid furniture had been handcrafted at considerable expense and could only be afforded by the rich and aristocratic. These were the people the parvenus of the Industrial Revolution most wanted to ape. So, during the 19th century when moulds and carving machines made it cheap and simple to adorn furniture, manufacturers went to town.

A sideboard at the National Trust's Charlecote Park gives an idea of the extravaganza to which furniture could be subjected. In addition to cupids tending vines and reaping corn, goats' heads and a menagerie of dead game, the backboard is surmounted by a selection of gods associated with the idea of Plenty. This orgy of decoration, on what might be seen as an altar to the gods of food and drink, may mark another new low in Victorian taste; but the climb back to a higher artistic plane was retarded by such arbiters of taste as John Ruskin who declared the sideboard 'worthy of Michelangelo'.

Sometimes two or more styles were combined on one piece of furniture with the unhappiest results. A mid-century guide to furniture-making listed original designs in the Grecian, Italian, Renaissance, Louis XV, Gothic, Tudor and Elizabethan styles. But it was the Gothic that fired the Victorian imagination most. The novels of Sir Walter Scott had re-kindled interest in medieval chivalry; romantic tales of dashing heroes made a pleasant contrast to life in an increasingly materialist society. Neo-Gothic buildings, both public and domestic, proliferated and were naturally furnished in matching style. But the most benevolent critics have found hardly a stick of furniture to admire from the first thirty years of Victoria's reign, and even the craftsmanship fell far short of continental standards. This had become painfully obvious at the 1851 exhibition and foreign craftsmen were welcomed into the trade during the 1850s and 1860s.

During the 1860s a distinction began to be made between standard lines turned out in the factories and so-called 'art furniture' produced by firms employing artists and architects such as Webb, Burgess, Dresser, Eastlake and Talbert. It was not unusual for architects to involve themselves with the furniture of the houses they designed but it was unfortunate that many who did so in the late 19th century were strongly influenced by ecclesiastical designs.

The Gothic style had of course been used in the Middle Ages for secular as well as religious buildings but for most Englishmen it smacked of the established Church. It was inevitable that when Victorian architects, who were already caught up in the Gothic revival, began to design furniture for the home it would have an air of sanctity about it.

Given the opportunity they introduced stained glass into ordinary windows; their benches looked like monks' settles; their tables and cupboards as though they had strayed from the vestry; their chairs seemed to have been made for prelates rather than people; even a humble firedog was made to look like a monstrance. To modern eyes most of this furniture is associated with a pious and moralistic era. It may command high prices today but it is bought for its solidity and good value in relation to modern furniture rather than for its beauty or elegance.

Throughout the period almost any resurrection of an earlier style emerged the worse for its Victorian modification. But there were exceptions. The renewal of trade with Japan in the 1860s after its 250-year seclusion brought Japanese prints,

ABOVE *Mid-Victorian kneehole desk in Louis XVI style, £2500.*

OPPOSITE *Mid-Victorian oak library table (13th century domestic style), £1500.*

ceramics and lacquer on to the market. The hacks of the furniture industry quickly tacked Japanese ornament on to standard items so as to offer the latest 'Japanese' designs. This 'instant' Japanese furniture was a gross travesty of Japanese design which only a very few designers, such as E. W. Godwin and Christopher Dresser, ever took the trouble to understand.

The company formed by William Morris in 1861 turned out well-constructed workaday furniture for the ordinary household. Many of his designs were based on old English chairs of village manufacture. In the 1870s his ebonized wooden armchairs retailed at £1 and the three-seater settees at £2. Morris was more occupied with textiles, ceramics, printing and his somewhat simplistic political philosophy than he was with furniture, but he felt passionately about craftsmanship and this is reflected in the pieces manufactured by his company. Many of the company's finest designs, whether based on an old Sussex armchair or a Japanese altar, came from the architect Philip Webb.

These were extensively reproduced by the trade but any proven Morris Company originals can be worth several hundred pounds.

A key designer of the late 19th century whose work is now being bought by museums is Charles Rennie Mackintosh. His style was way ahead of its time and so had little success in his native Glasgow and even less in London. Among his few Scottish patrons he counted the Misses Cranston who, in the 1890s, launched a somewhat optimistic campaign to stamp out Glasgow's appalling drunkenness by providing a chain of tea-rooms to which its thirstier citizens could repair in time of need. Mackintosh designed the chairs for these, but his strange art nouveau style was little appreciated and for the last fifteen years of his life he went back to painting. A Mackintosh desk of revolutionary design has fetched £130,000 and a rare suite of white bedroom furniture has changed hands for over £210,000. As with so much of the more interesting Victorian and Edwardian pieces, the craftsmanship of Mackintosh's furniture is not exceptional but the conception is unusually daring.

The importance of Mackintosh and the other architect-designers in the history of design will just about underwrite a steady rise in value for their work. It seems that even mass-produced Victorian furniture must continue to appreciate, though its lowly status in the antiques world makes a strong investment performance unlikely.

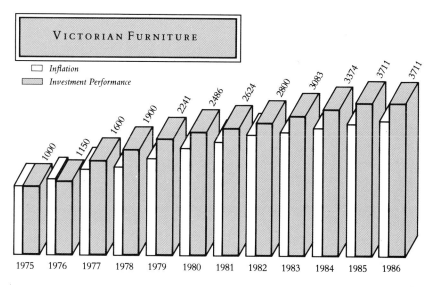

VICTORIAN FURNITURE

☐ Inflation
▨ Investment Performance

1000 1150 1600 1900 2241 2486 2624 2800 3083 3374 3711 3711

1975 1976 1977 1978 1979 1980 1981 1982 1983 1984 1985 1986

Components: a selection of cabinets, centre tables, library tables and writing tables

Further Reading

Ralph Edwards, *The Shorter Dictionary of English Furniture* (London, 1964)

Joseph Aronson, *The Encyclopaedia of Furniture* (London, 1965)

Christopher Gilbert, *The Life and Works of Thomas Chippendale* (London, 1978)

Frances Collard, *Regency Furniture* (Woodbridge, 1985)

Christopher Payne, *Nineteenth-century European Furniture* (Woodbridge, 1981)

John Andrews, *Victorian, Edwardian and 1920s Furniture* (Woodbridge, 1980)

Ralph Fastnedge, *Sheraton Furniture* (Woodbridge, 1983)

C. Claxton Stevens and S. Whittington, *18th Century English Furniture: The Norman Adams Collection* (Woodbridge, 1983)

Rachael Feild, *Buying Antique Furniture* (London, 1984)

Dealers

Norman Adams Ltd
8–10 Hans Road
London SW3 1RX
01-589 5266

Apter Fredericks Ltd
265–267 Fulham Road
London SW3 6HY
01-352 2188

H. Blairman & Sons Ltd
119 Mount Street
London W1Y 5HB
01-493 0444

Richard Courtney
112–114 Fulham Road
London SW3 6HU
01-370 4020

Jonathan Harris
54 Kensington Church Street
London W8
01-937 3133

W. R. Harvey & Co Ltd
67–70 Chalk Farm Road
London NW1 8AN
01-485 1504

Jeremy Ltd
255 King's Road
London SW3 5EL
01-352 3127

Mallett & Son Ltd
40 New Bond Street
London W1Y 0BS
01-499 7411

Stair & Company Ltd
120 Mount Street
London W1 5HB
01-499 1784

O. F. Wilson Ltd
3–6 Queens Elm Parade
Old Church Street
London SW3 6EJ
01-352 9544

SILVER

English Silver

The overall rise in the value of English silver made between 1660 and 1900 is 250% since 1975. This represents an acceleration over the 1950–75 period when the growth rate was an annual 10%. Within the index the highest rate of growth at 310% has been achieved by Regency silver whose massive elegance is much admired in the United States. Next comes Georgian and Queen Anne silver at 240% and Victorian at 210%.

Investors can still expect a growth rate of 10% to 15% for very good quality silver but the less interesting pieces will not do so well. Silver has always sat a little uneasily on the frontier between art and craft. A pair of rococo candlesticks with strong sculptural qualities can be taken seriously as a work of art. A clumsy 19th century dinner service on the other hand can amount to no more than many artless chunks of metal.

The link between the market value of a piece of silver and its melt value depends on the artistry it is judged to possess. The lower its artistic value the closer its cash value will be to the value of the silver of which it is made. An outstanding piece by Paul de Lamerie, one of the greatest of English silversmiths, may be worth fifty or more times its melt value. A small Lamerie salver weighing 12 ounces, for example, might be worth £3000 or £250 an ounce. The clumsy dinner service weighing 200 ounces may sell for £2000 or just double its melt value if the silver price were standing at £5 an ounce. The metal-intensive pieces are more responsive to movements in the silver bullion price. If the price of silver went up to £10 an ounce, the dinner service could well double in value too. The Lamerie salver and other 'art-intensive' pieces might rise by between 10% and 20% – only to the extent that market sentiment would generally be more buoyant.

Charles II flagon (1678), £5000.

Investors need to remember that there is a vast amount of undistinguished English silver in circulation. One London auction house sells at least fifty thousand lots a year, the workaday or damaged pieces often close to melt value. During the 18th century, when silver cost just 10 pence an ounce, quite modest households were able to afford a few pieces of silverware, and during the 19th century, when for much of the time silver cost 25 pence an ounce, ownership widened even further.

English silver was not consciously collected or preserved until the late 19th century. The long-standing link with silver coinage meant that silver plate was regarded as the next best thing to cash. About 95% of all the silver made up to the time of the Restoration in 1660 was probably melted down. Even towards the end of the 19th century silver of all periods was going into the melting pot so that it could be refashioned in the latest style.

The most serious losses of silver plate were at times of political upheaval, such as the Wars of the Roses, with the result that only about four-hundred pieces of medieval English silver have survived. During the Civil War twelve Oxford colleges handed over all their silver to Charles I so that the troops could be paid. After the Restoration the richer classes began to make good the losses they had sustained in the recent Civil War, equipping the great houses they built with furniture and silver plate. But even 17th century silver is scarce today – probably less than 1% of the lots sold at auction.

The first period investors can realistically collect is Queen Anne. The Huguenots who arrived from France in the late 17th century included many fine silversmiths and

FROM TOP *Pair of Queen Anne candlesticks by John Elston, Exeter (1706), £3500.*

Queen Anne porringer, by John Perryman, Falmouth, £5000.

George II cake basket by Edward Wakelin (1749), £2800.

their influence on the design of English silver was immense. Such men as Pierre Harache, Pierre Platel, David Willaume, Augustin Courtauld and Paul de Lamerie derived their styles from the French provinces where the townspeople had wanted their silver ornamented but not as flashy as it was at the court of Louis XIV. Their contribution to English decoration was to reintroduce order where motifs of flowers and leaves had been allowed to straggle uncontrollably over an entire surface. The return to a formality of decoration was received with admiration and relief by their new patrons and though the competition was resented at first their meticulous standards were soon emulated by their English rivals.

The price of silver from this and every other period is governed by the status of the silversmith, the quality of the piece (not necessarily the same thing), its usefulness today, its condition and its associative value.

The quality of workmanship is at least as important as aesthetic quality. In the world of silver the machine age

Pair of George II butter-shells by Paul Lamerie (1746), £34,000.

began in the 18th century, and many collectors buy nothing dating later than 1770. By then Matthew Bolton had a warehouse in London where silversmiths could come and buy all the ready-cast handles, legs and small pieces they wanted. Many items could be soldered together in a few hours and taken along to Goldsmiths' Hall to be assayed, hallmarked and stamped with the name of the 'maker'. The simple designs of the Classical Revival style were ideally suited to mechanical production. By the 1840s silver and plated wares from Sheffield and Birmingham dominated the production of spoons, forks, salt cellars, casters, candlesticks and teapots.

Elaborate or commissioned pieces were still handmade in the traditional ways, but the first phase of the gradual takeover by machinery makes earlier pieces all the more desirable.

One of the dampers on the silver market has been the tiresome fact that silver has to be cleaned. Nobody

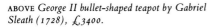

ABOVE *George II bullet-shaped teapot by Gabriel Sleath (1728), £3400.*

ABOVE RIGHT *Set of four George II candlesticks by Edward Wakelin (1757), £52,000.*

RIGHT *Pair of George III silver-gilt wine coolers by Paul Storr (1810), £30,000.*

wants to display silver in tarnish-proof bags, and long-term silver polishes do not work very well. Many people regard time spent cleaning silver as time wasted and the incentive to get rid of unused silver is strong. The dinner table, however, has proved an exception. As a result, pieces of silver that enhance the dinner table are in greater demand than ewers, nutmeg graters and so on. People are still willing to clean (or have cleaned) candlesticks, coasters, cutlery, salvers and coffeepots, but the list does not go far beyond that.

Grand or interesting associations can raise prices a long way. Pieces made for royal or noble households and bearing their coats of arms are in great demand. Straightforward snobbery plays a part here but there is another, better reason. Grand patrons were the best form of advertising available to a silversmith and he would devote the greatest care to the pieces they ordered. Presentation salvers inscribed to historical figures are highly prized and this has provided the rogues of the market with a

profitable line in fake inscriptions. The new engraving will always be rubbed down to simulate decades of polishing but a keen, suspicious eye will usually pick out something amiss.

The artistic appeal of different styles of silver will not change significantly among longstanding collectors, though new groups of buyers will often make an impact on the market. Collectors in the southern American states have been pushing up prices for Regency period silver for at least ten years. Paul Storr has become something of a cult figure among such buyers, yet in speaking of his workmanship it should be remembered that a silversmith of his period normally relied on outworkers for casting, chasing and engraving. Sometimes very little work would actually be done on Paul Storr's premises, and as often as not none by the master himself. The quantity of silver bearing Paul Storr's mark is huge and is unfortunately growing even today as a stream of quite presentable fakes from Italy arrives on the market.

Paul de Lamerie himself is known

LEFT *George III candelabrum by William Tuite (1764). A pair, £10,000.*

ABOVE *William IV silver-gilt vine-leaf fruit dish by John Watson, Sheffield (1834) £2000.*

to have had over forty employees at his workshop at one time and his output was correspondingly large. It is quite likely that he never touched the majority of pieces that bear his mark, yet his quality control was excellent. The high standard never faltered and for that reason his mark on any piece lifts its value at least 100% above its nearest rivals.

Whereas in the field of Old Masters the slightest suspicion of a painting being wholly or partly done by the hand of an assistant is enough to bring its value crashing down, nobody seems to expect a master silversmith to have had much to do with any individual piece. It seems then that the leading English silversmiths were no better at the job than those they employed. If they had been, experts would be able to tell for certain which pieces were their own work.

The big rise in the price of Victorian silver during the early 1970s has not been followed through. Elaborate and flamboyant centrepieces were made by Garrard and other leading makers from the 1830s, sometimes featuring Arabs, blackamoors, camels and so on. These monsters often weighed in at over 1000 ounces, and in the early 1960s when silver was selling at 40 to 50 pence an ounce they would not have fetched more than £1 or £2 an ounce. In the early 1970s Arab money pushed prices for such pieces up to £30 to £50 an ounce but there has been little change since.

Even so, Victorian silver as a whole is now treated more respectfully. Whereas nearly everything of the period used to be catalogued simply as Victorian, details are now given of the date, the maker and the style. Several names, including George Fox, Hunt and Roskill and the Barnard and Hennell families, are emerging as important makers, and before long will be uttered in the same breath as Paul Storr, Eliza Godfrey and Paul de Lamerie.

The silver bullion market has fluctuated widely over the years and however irrational any link might be between its price and that of fine

George III silver-gilt wine labels by Benjamin Smith (1808), £2300.

antique silver, there may still be some psychological connection. From 35 pence an ounce in 1920 the price slid to 5 pence an ounce in 1931, but climbed quite steadily to reach 50 pence an ounce in early 1967 when currency fears began to sweep the precious metal markets. The sterling crisis helped to push the price of silver to 90 pence in November and throughout that year the price of antique silver in the auction rooms kept climbing. The November devaluation of the pound from $2.80 to $2.40 explains in part why, by the end of the year, Georgian coffeepots and candlesticks were going for double their estimates.

It seems that some buyers who heard that silver was rocketing took this to mean that antique silver must be rising, or would soon rise, at a similar rate. Furthermore, the law did not at that time allow UK residents to buy gold, so for many investors silver seemed the natural alternative as a hedge against a weakening pound. A pair of good George II candlesticks that was worth £1000 in 1966 reached £3000 to £3500 in early 1969. The bubble burst in the summer and by the end of the year they were back to £1000. Many dealers went out of business and prices did not move into new high ground for another ten years.

Memories of this episode were painfully fresh in dealers' minds when Bunker Hunt and his associates moved into the silver market in 1979. Their manipulation of the futures markets nearly left them in a position to fix the world price. The colossal buying programme eventually pushed the price to $40 an ounce (£18) in February 1980. During the preceding year the antique silver dealers had been watching the bullion market nervously to see if the wild spiral in prices of the late 1960s was about to be repeated. Prices for bullion-related silver had begun to rise strongly. But canteens of 19th century flatware were selling for below the melt price during the last stages of the boom, and it was as if the market sensed that such levels could not be sustained for long. Dealers were sometimes in a position to buy goods at auction below their melt value and take them straight along to the bullion dealers to be melted.

But Bunker Hunt and his co-speculators were soon tripped up by a change in the commodity exchanges' regulations and the silver price fell back to $8 in a matter of weeks. Over the period of the Hunt boom, art-related items also climbed in price, not more than 20% to 30%, and fell back when the bullion markets subsided.

One of the more irrational aspects of the silver market is the large premiums paid for pieces that happen to have been made in some provincial town. Up to 100% extra will be paid for pieces from Scottish or Irish provincial towns. In the case of Chester, Norwich and the Channel Islands, premiums can be anywhere between 30% and 100%. In most cases the premiums have nothing to do with quality and vary according to the date of the piece. The earlier the piece the greater the premium. The trade is still prejudiced against pieces made in India and even silver made in Birmingham and Sheffield is sometimes rated below London.

Among the small collectable pieces of silver, price trends have been mixed. Vinaigrettes are selling at around the same prices as ten years ago; fine English snuffboxes rarely appear in the saleroom and this market too seems to be running out of steam. Caddy spoons have fallen by the wayside but matchcases have been surprisingly buoyant. All antiques connected with wine have been booming; corkscrews and coasters have performed well, and the market for wine labels has risen very fast, but fine and interesting examples are scarce.

Now that new canteens of silver tableware retail at £30 to £50 an ounce it is possible to buy complete sets of 18th century English silver more cheaply by buying at auction. Odds and ends of 18th century table silver often sell at little more than twice their melt value.

ABOVE *Pair of Regency silver-gilt wine coasters by Paul Storr (1814), £10,000.*

BELOW *George IV wine waggon by Benjamin Smith (1827), £2500.*

BOTTOM *George III pair of entrée dishes and covers by Paul Storr (1800), £4500.*

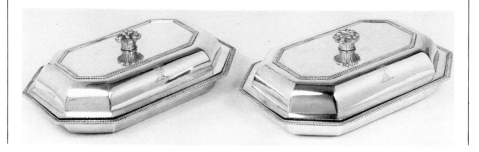

Silver sales in Britain and the United States are now dominated by the trade and illegal auction 'rings' operate widely. Private bidders are often run up by the ring and either end up being outbid or forced to pay an inflated price. Many collectors pay a dealer 5% or 10% commission to bid on their behalf. Even after paying the commission, this often gives the buyer a lower base-price than if he had had to contend with the ring.

Victoria. Oval soup-tureen and cover, by Samuel Hayne and Dudley Cater (1845), £4200.

Silver Marks

In 1238 the official standard for the purity of English silver plate became the same as for English silver coins at 11 ounces and 2 pennyweights per troy pound. The troy scale – with the exception of the pound – is still used for precious metals today.

24 grains = 1 pennyweight (dwt)	
20 pennyweights = 1 ounce	
12 ounces = 1 pound	

English silverplate was therefore 92.5% pure, the rest usually being made up of copper. This was referred to as the sterling standard from the little star known as a starling that appeared on the silver pennies in circulation at the time.

Hallmarking was introduced in 1300 and this has given buyers of English silver some protection ever since. The statute required that each piece of silver be punched with the mark of a leopard's head as a guarantee that it was sterling standard.

In 1363 every goldsmith was re-quired to register a mark by which his work could be distinguished. Until the end of the 17th century some symbol or rebus of the crafts-man's name was often used. The records of craftsmen's marks before 1697 were lost and craftsmen were required to re-register their marks in that year as the first two letters of their surnames.

The date-letter that enables every piece of English silver to be precisely dated came into use in London in 1478. The Goldsmiths' Company has used a cycle of twenty letters, one for each year with i and j treated as one, similarly u and v, and omitting the last four letters of the alphabet. One cycle was distinguished from another by changing the style of the letter – Roman capital, Lombardic, lower case Roman and so on – or the shape of the shield in which it was placed.

In 1544 came the lion passant guardant (a walking lion with its face turned towards you) and this has re-mained the standard mark for English silver up to the present day, except between 1697 and 1720 when the purity of silver was raised to 11 ounces and 10 pennyweights per pound (95.8%).

With the New Sterling Act of 1697 the hallmarking system was changed and four new marks introduced. The first was to be the first two letters of the silversmith's surname, the second was to be the figure of a woman 'commonly called Britannia', and the third a lion's head erased (with a jagged neckline) in place of the leopard's head and lion passant guardant. The fourth was to be the variable mark used by the Warden of the Goldsmiths' Company to identify the year in which the piece was made. A further Act of 1700 laid down separate arrangements for the provincial and Irish assay offices. Silver plate made from 1784 to 1890 was punched with a further mark of the sovereign's head to show that duty had been paid.

Fakers have always been a problem for investors in silver. They have been active in England for the last five years applying fake marks to modern imitations of 17th and 18th century silver. Seventeenth-century beakers and early 18th century coffeepots are among their most recent lines and many collectors, particularly from overseas, have been duped. Buyers are often inclined to look less critically at goods when they are offered at 'bargain' prices and the result is usually disastrous.

There are no easy ways to settle the question of authenticity. Fakes sometimes betray themselves by having slightly wrong-looking proportions; sometimes the marks look fresh or are applied in unusual places; sometimes the surface of the metal looks and feels too hard.

But other less subjective methods can be used. Spectrographic analysis and wet chemical techniques can indicate the quantities of impurities present in a given piece of silver and these are now used to date the object itself. The ingenious but inconclusive theory rests on the idea that refining techniques have become more efficient over the centuries. Modern silver is very unlikely to contain more than thirty parts per million of gold, whereas in the 18th century it was common for silver to contain more than a hundred times as much. An '18th century' coffeepot, for instance, found to contain only thirty parts per million of gold, is very likely to be a fake. The Antique Plate Committee of the Goldsmiths' Company provides any member of the public with a free authenticating service.

Victoria. Pair of five-light candelabra (1885). Maker's mark R.H. and R.H., £4800.

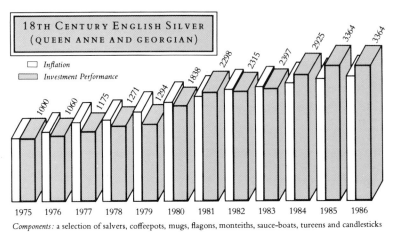

18TH CENTURY ENGLISH SILVER (QUEEN ANNE AND GEORGIAN)

☐ *Inflation*
▨ *Investment Performance*

1000 · 1060 · 1175 · 1271 · 1294 · 1838 · 2298 · 2315 · 2397 · 2925 · 3364 · 3364

1975 1976 1977 1978 1979 1980 1981 1982 1983 1984 1985 1986

Components: a selection of salvers, coffeepots, mugs, flagons, monteiths, sauce-boats, tureens and candlesticks

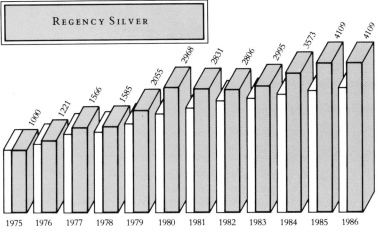

REGENCY SILVER

1000 · 1221 · 1566 · 1585 · 2055 · 2968 · 2831 · 2806 · 2995 · 3573 · 4109 · 4109

1975 1976 1977 1978 1979 1980 1981 1982 1983 1984 1985 1986

Components: a selection of tea urns, wine coolers, entrée dishes, wine coasters, tureens and candlesticks

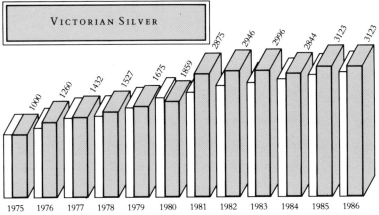

VICTORIAN SILVER

1000 · 1260 · 1432 · 1527 · 1675 · 1859 · 2875 · 2946 · 2096 · 2844 · 3123 · 3123

1975 1976 1977 1978 1979 1980 1981 1982 1983 1984 1985 1986

Components: a selection of wine waggons, soup plates, cake baskets, tea services, salt cellars, soup tureens and claret jugs

American Silver

American silver might be expected to have performed strongly as an investment. So why is it up only 240% since 1975? There has been no real upswing of interest in American silver over the last decade – not at least on the scale seen in other fields of Americana. Collectors are more fearful than ever of burglaries – though it is not clear why they consider silver more vulnerable than paintings or ceramics. Many found insurance premiums too high and cashed in unused or unwanted pieces around 1979/80 when Bunker Hunt drove the price of bullion silver to $40 an ounce.

As in other countries demand remains strongest for silver that enhances a dinner-table. The formal tea party, on the other hand, is becoming rare. Consequently, the market for tea services and tea urns has been flat. The price of an attractive set made in the 1820s stands at only 150% above its melt value while clumsy sets sell for even less. Nobody foresees a comeback for the tea party so prices can move at best in line with the bullion price.

The heyday of silver-collecting in the United States was from 1920 to 1950. During that time the nation's silversmiths were arranged in their appropriate pecking order and this holds good today. No unsung masters are waiting to be discovered so no sudden re-ratings are in prospect.

By far the most desirable period of American silver is the 18th century, yet the three major silver sales Christie's hold every year include no more than twenty pieces of that date. Prices for this silver have always been strong with plenty of museum interest, but there is not enough of it around to keep collectors satisfied. Rare and beautiful things will always

Cream pitcher by Joseph Richardson (Jr), Philadelphia (c. 1785–1810), £700.

be in demand yet, paradoxically, the extreme rarity of 18th century American silver deters collectors and makes them move on to other fields.

A steep drop in price separates the top flight of American silver from the enormous range of 19th century wares. Collectors are not attracted by the later material because of its mechanical sameness. A few important makers were still at work in the 19th century, including William G. Forbes of New York and Samuel Kirk of Baltimore whose style was influential for a generation.

Though Paul Revere is the best-known of American silversmiths and supposed also to be the finest, most experts rate the work of Myer Myers of New York more exciting. And if Myers rather than Revere had made the famous ride from Charleston to Lexington, his work would certainly be worth more than Revere's today.

Revere was a colourful and versatile man. During the Depression of the mid-1760s, when silver was hard to sell, he turned to dentistry. The state of the art may have been primitive but there was no shortage of patients; women had often lost half their teeth by the age of twenty. Revere's first advertisement in 1768 claimed his teeth would look 'as well as the Natural', but offered no guarantees on chewing.

In the same year he made his best-known piece, the 'Sons of Liberty Bowl', commissioned to commemorate an act of defiance to George III. The colonists' demand for 'no taxation without representation' had been pressed for years, but eventually the Massachussetts House of Representatives sent letters to the other American colonies asking for support. This drew from London a royal order to rescind the letter. That order was defied by 92 of the 109 representatives. Toasts were drunk at all patriotic gatherings to the 'illustrious 92' and Revere engraved and published a print lampooning the seventeen who had cravenly voted to rescind.

Revere's big moment came seven years later. Warned that the English were planning an expedition to Lexington to arrest the rebel leaders Adams and Hancock, and to Concord to seize the rebels' stock of arms, Revere set out by night to alert them. Longfellow's poem has Revere arriving in Concord at 2 a.m. to warn the inhabitants, though he was in fact arrested by English officers two miles short of his destination. But the poem's stirring lines not only consolidated Revere's reputation as a national hero, it transformed the value of his silver as well.

As it is, a tankard by Revere will fetch $40,000–$50,000 at auction against $20,000–$25,000 for one by

ABOVE *A Cann by John Symmes, Boston (c. 1767), £3000.*

BELOW *Sugar urn, Philadelphia (1785–1810), £600.*

OPPOSITE *Porringer by Paul Revere (1760–1800), £12,500.*

Eighteenth-century American silver should continue to outperform 19th century silver though the best performance may well be achieved by pieces that predate the Revolution. The ideal investment piece should be by a known maker and marked accordingly. Not only must it be genuine, its authenticity must be undisputed. The value of an item pronounced genuine by two experts will be reduced if it is doubted by a third. It should be well documented – that is, listed in inventories or the maker's daybooks or, better still, published in a respected antiques book or periodical. Lastly, it should be readily useable today, as with the paraphernalia of the dinner table.

From the time silverware was first made in Boston around 1650 until the time of the Revolution, the craft of a silversmith was highly regarded and known to demand special skills. This seemed to justify the high cost of the product, while the close link between money and the metal itself helped to create an image of luxury. After the Revolution silver began to be mechanically rolled out in mills rather than forged by hammer from an ingot. Thinner sheets could be used and instead of being hammered from a single piece, hollow-ware was often made from pieces of silver cut out and seamed together. Such shoddy work does not make for a sound investment. By the early 19th century machines were in full swing stamping out bands of ornament and cut-out decoration that could be soldered on in next to no time. And by 1801 machines were producing spoons and other flatware at the rate of 180 an hour.

Myers and $7500–$10,000 by a run-of-the-mill silversmith of the same period. A porringer by Paul Revere will be sold for $18,000 while another by an accomplished but less-celebrated craftsman makes just $2000. Even a spoon by Paul Revere can be worth $2000 or ten times the price of one by an ordinary maker.

Within the index, metal-intensive pieces such as tea sets have done least well. Condition has a bearing on performance; anything in its pristine state will not only be more valuable, its value should rise faster. For example, few tankards came through the latter part of the 19th century unscathed. The temperance movement was then at its height, and tankards, so flagrantly associated with alcohol, were given a spout as a kind of fig leaf and put into service as water pitchers. Many have been changed back again, but their owners' *démarche* into tee-totalism has cost them dear. A mid-18th century tankard in its original condition can be worth $10,000; changed to a pitcher, its value is $2500.

The high value of silver by Paul Revere and other leading makers makes it a natural subject for the faker, and his task is made easier by the absence of English-style hall-marks.

In the United States the only mark stamped on silver is usually that of the maker. Fakers of English or American silver try to imitate the form and decoration of an antique piece down to the last detail. Though you might expect any self-respecting faker to stick closely to his model, many pieces give themselves away by uncharacteristic ornament. When, as more often happens, form and decoration look about right, the expert looks to see how the parts are soldered together.

A simple kind of fraud enables some rogues to cash in on the premium paid for American over English silver. Among 18th century English silversmiths were several with the initials PR or MM. By erasing three hallmarks and leaving just the maker's monogram, inexpert collectors can be persuaded that the initials stood for Paul Revere or Myer Myers.

Although early American makers sold silver that still bore the marks of their tools, and this is accepted as part of their rough charm, today's fakers give themselves away by exaggerat-

ing the roughness. Some of the early Virginia and Connecticut silversmiths turned out crude pieces but never as crude as the modern efforts to duplicate them.

At present auction rooms are turning away more fake Revere pieces than they can find genuine ones to sell. Since so much of Revere's work is either in, or destined for, museums, prices for what remains on the market are certain to keep rising.

Even if American collectors wanted to collect 18th century American silver it is now too rare. Faced with the choice of collecting American 19th century silver or English 18th century – and prices are not far apart – many opt for English silver. Throughout the 19th century every well-off American family would present their daughter on her marriage with a pair of candelabra, a set of flatware, of which three thousand different patterns were available in 1900, and a tea set. As investments, the outlook for most of these is not bright. Better that they should be kept as treasured possessions or sold rather

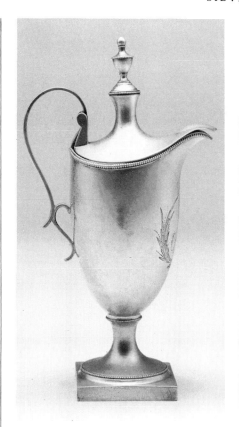

OPPOSITE *Teapot, bearing marks of William Grigg and Gerrit Schank, New York City (c. 1785–95), £2500.*

ABOVE *Cream pitcher by Charles Moore and John Ferguson, Philadelphia (c. 1801–5), £900.*

ABOVE RIGHT *A punch strainer by Benjamin Burt, Boston (c. 1755–80), £2800.*

RIGHT *A caster by Andrew Tyler, Boston (c. 1715–25), £5000.*

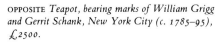

than be held in the hope of becoming very valuable. Although the prospects for early American silver are better, there are too many off-putting factors for this market to climb at all fast.

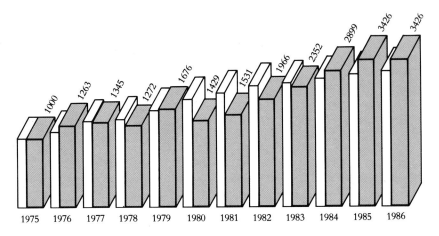

18TH AND 19TH CENTURY AMERICAN SILVER

☐ Inflation
▨ Investment Performance

Components: a selection of bowls, julep cups, teapots, meat-dishes, coffeepots, casters and sugar tongs

Further Reading

Michael Clayton, *The Collector's Dictionary of the Silver and Gold of Great Britain and North America* (Woodbridge, 1985)

Ian Pickford, *Silver Flatware: English, Irish and Scottish 1660–1980* (Woodbridge, 1983)

Peter Waldron, *The Price Guide to Antique Silver* (Woodbridge, 1982)

Charles James Jackson, *An Illustrated History of English Plate* (New York, 1911)

Seymour B. Wyler, *The Book of Old Silver English – American – Foreign* (New York, 1975)

Arthur G. Grimwade, *London Goldsmiths 1697–1837. Their Marks and Lives* (London, 1976)

Michael Clayton, *Christie's Pictorial History of English and American Silver* (Oxford, 1985)

Dealers

Armitage
4 Davies Street
London W1Y 1LJ
01-408 0675

J. H. Bourdon-Smith Ltd
24 Mason's Yard
Duke Street
London SW1Y 6BU
01-839 4714

Collingwood of Conduit
 Street
46 Conduit Street
London W1R 0HE
01-734 2656

M. Ekstein Ltd
90 Jermyn Street
London SW1Y 6JD
01-930 2024

Harris (Antiques) Ltd
Old Bond Street House
6–8 Old Bond Street
London W1X 3TA
01-499 0352

Brand Inglis Ltd
9 Halkin Arcade
Motcomb Street
London SW1
01-235 6604

Richard Ogden Ltd
28–29 Burlington Arcade
London W1V 0NX
01-493 9136

S. J. Phillips Ltd
139 New Bond Street
London W1A 3DL
01-629 6261

S. J. Shrubsole Ltd
43 Museum Street
London WC1A 1LY
01-405 2712

Spink & Son Ltd
5–7 King Street
London SW1Y 6QS
01-930 7888

PORCELAIN

Chinese Porcelain

To outsiders this market is quite puzzling; for it is one where legendary Japanese dealers battle it out with Chinese millionaires to secure strange little bowls that the uninitiated might use to feed the cat. However, the unique status of Chinese ceramics is unassailable in the context of world culture and in no other field has the marriage of art and practicality been more successful. For that reason the market in the long term should be safe, and prices are edging up.

Much of the buying power for top-quality Chinese ceramics is now concentrated on Hong Kong where auctions were first held in 1973. The market has grown over the last decade and changed the investment outlook in the process. Competition for early Ming porcelain and the Imperial wares of the Qing dynasty is strong.

The index of Ming and Qing ceramics is up 340% since 1975 but there are signs that prices have moved on to a plateau. This is a market that has been volatile in the past and further upsets could well lie ahead.

In 1982, when the future of Hong Kong hung in the balance, dealers in Chinese ceramics found the going very tough and auction prices fell sharply. But the market rallied as soon as the Anglo-Chinese agreement was announced and prices for the best material moved up to a new peak. The weakness of the Hong Kong dollar had enabled American collectors to pay what seemed enormous prices in the local currency.

Whereas in the mid-1970s the Hong Kong Chinese showed little interest in the ceramics of the earlier Tang, Song and Yuan dynasties, they are now beginning to appreciate their more cerebral qualities. They also recognize that these are undervalued alongside the Ming and Qing that they have traditionally collected. A top-quality Ming bowl, for instance, may fetch $300,000 against $60,000 for a Song bowl of comparable quality. Some people fear that Ming and Qing wares rose in value so far

OPPOSITE *Pair of famille rose fish bowls*, £20,000.

ABOVE *Iron-red decorated dragon dish, Kangxi period*, £650.

BELOW *Pair of blue and white garden seates, late 18th century*, £3400.

during the 1970s that the rate cannot be sustained in the 1980s.

Nobody has forgotten the market upheaval of 1972–4 and any significant rise in prices now brings with it fears that another collapse lies just around the corner. It was a strange constellation of events that set the market ablaze in 1972. Japanese buying became hectic that year; with accelerating inflation and a soaring Tokyo stock market collectors anxiously began switching out of the yen. Sotheby's Hong Kong sales were just beginning and in London a spate of investment-buying pushed prices sky high. As the first Europeans to trade with China in the 16th century, the Portuguese had a long-standing interest in Chinese ceramics and a handful of rich Portuguese collectors were also active in the market. One million dollars was paid for a 14th century blue-and-white Ming bottle and Sotheby's predicted the ceiling to be a long way off.

A good *famille rose* dish of the Kangxi period that would have fetched £8000 in 1971 was up to

£50,000 by early 1974. The crash was sudden and unforeseen. During 1974 increased oil prices began to bite into the Japanese economy. Several major Japanese collections were being formed by industrial corporations for prestige and tax-saving reasons. Funds available for these rapidly dried up.

In the UK, share prices collapsed by over 50% during 1974 leaving investors with little enthusiasm for Chinese or any other ceramics. In April 1974 a *coup d'état* in Portugal left one collector in prison and drove others out of the market. By the end of 1975 the *famille rose* bowl had plummeted to $10,000. It is now back to $50,000 but the rate at which this market could collapse is etched in every dealer's memory.

Chinese export wares have risen by 260% and, provided they are in perfect condition, should rise steadily. The Chinese modified the form and decoration of their ceramics to suit their various export markets. Their products were instantly successful in the West and by the early 18th century Europeans were importing on a huge scale. The account of a visiting Jesuit mentions that in 1713 the Imperial Factory at Jingdezhen employed over half a million. But the ceramic art of China had depended to a great extent on simplicity of form and purity of colour. The attempt to marry up these to a Western style of painting was not always successful and a gulf separates the Chinese and Western taste.

For over two hundred years Europeans were only familiar with ceramics made and exported for their market. Only in the late 19th century did they begin to see the evidence of China's great ceramic history stretching back several thousand years. As a result of excavation, looting and trade, China's early classical wares

began to be more widely known and appreciated in the West.

Early Ming may still be the most valued of all periods but Yuan and Song are now beginning to catch up. The horses, camels and other funerary wares of the Tang dynasty once held little appeal for Chinese collectors, mainly because they thought of them as stolen from their ancestors' tombs. Now these are sought after throughout the Far East.

Investors need to be cautious in this field, for experts regularly disagree on the age of the items they appraise. High prices have made faking more attractive than ever and the quality of the fakes has improved. In the Hong Kong market the reign mark on the foot of any important piece is considered essential. When there is no such mark, the faker grinds away the glaze, paints a suitable reign mark, applies new glaze and refires the entire piece. Fortunately there are tell-tale signs; the new glaze seldom matches up with the old and the rim of the foot will look speckled after being refired. Another favourite fraud is to take a plain white Qing bowl, enamel it in *famille rose* style and so raise its value by a factor of ten.

A European visitor to China in 1912 was the first to see fake Tang horses and camels coming off a production line, but these would fool no one today. On the other hand high-quality fakes are streaming out of Taiwan. The TL or thermolumi-

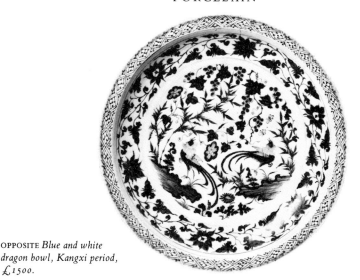

OPPOSITE *Blue and white dragon bowl, Kangxi period, £1500.*

ABOVE *Dish painted in underglaze blue. Ming (14th century), £5000.*

nescence test, which measures the time that has elapsed since a piece of clay was last fired, is widely used on any piece purporting to date from Tang or earlier times. The test has proved reliable and is insisted on by many collectors.

But the test is inconclusive on more recently fired ceramics so investors are thrown back to stylistic judgement. Only after years of studying and handling these ceramics do collectors begin to understand the artistic language of the Chinese potter and in time anything out of keeping with that language calls attention to itself.

Official reproductions of important pieces are now being made at Jingdezehn. When ordered from overseas the pieces are marked with the name of the importer but they can also be bought without factory marks at the factory itself. Though finely made, they sometimes give themselves away by slightly wrong glaze, form or texture. Moreover, since the originals are well known, and would cost £200,000 or £300,000 apiece, collectors are not likely to be taken in.

For the last six years visitors to Beijing have been able to buy genuine Chinese ceramics at the official stores. So far nothing of importance has been offered; most pieces sell for under £500 and can usually be bought more cheaply in the West.

All collectors, but the Chinese in particular, are fastidious about damage. In Hong Kong the value of any piece having a crack – even though invisible to the naked eye – would be reduced by half. Cracks are regarded as more serious than chips since there is always the risk that they may turn into a full break.

The darkest cloud looming over the investment scene now is the growing spate of ceramics arriving in the West. From ancient times until around 1600, the dead were buried with the ceramic or bronze artefacts which were thought to be needed in the afterlife. The population of China has always been vast, so the quantity of fine objects now lying a few feet below ground from the Tang, Song, Ming, and even earlier dynasties, is also vast. The Chinese veneration for

ABOVE *Blue, iron-red and white dragon bowl, Yongzheng period, £1500.*

OPPOSITE *Coffeepot milk jug and a pair of coffee cups and saucers en suite (c. 1745), £5000.*

their ancestors has been weakened in the recent ideological turmoil and grave-robbers feel easier about their work. All they need apart from a spade and a torch are Christie's and Sotheby's catalogues – now the standard reference works – to enable them to select the items worth looting.

The illegal export trade has boomed since 1980, one dealer having reputedly made £10 million over the period. More importantly though, prices in the West are being tested by this new supply. Dealers are inclined to play down the seriousness of the situation, and it may even be true that very fine and rare items will always remain so. The outlook for run-of-the-mill pieces is no longer so bright.

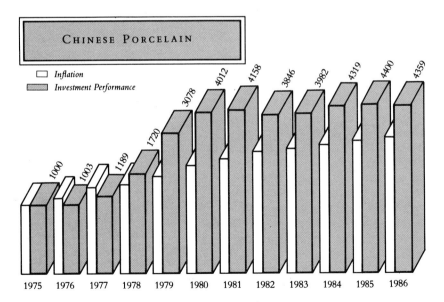

CHINESE PORCELAIN

☐ Inflation
▨ Investment Performance

1000 1003 1189 1720 3078 4012 4158 3846 3982 4319 4400 4359

1975 1976 1977 1978 1979 1980 1981 1982 1983 1984 1985 1986

Components: Ming and Qing vases and covers, fish bowls, jars, pilgrim bottles, bowls, saucer-dishes and stem-cups

Meissen

The Meissen index stands at 370% above its 1975 level, suggesting an annual growth of 15%. All the pieces on which the index is based were made and decorated during the great period of production at Meissen that ended with the Seven Years War of 1756–63.

Porcelain of the second most desirable period from 1774 to around 1800, while Marcolini was director of the Meissen factory, has performed as strongly, though 19th century Meissen as a whole has risen more slowly.

Within the index of early Meissen, teapots, cups, saucers, tureens and other functional pieces have risen by 450%; snuffboxes, cane-handles and other knick-knacks of the period by 470%; figures by 430%; and armorial plates from the grand dinner services by 340%.

Performances vary within each group, the higher rate of growth usually being achieved by any piece that is rare in itself or that is unusual or outstanding in form or decoration. Broadly speaking, pieces painted or enamelled by the independent outworkers known as *Hausmaler* have climbed as fast as those decorated at the factory. *Hausmalerei* played an important part in the development of German porcelain and pieces that can be identified as having been decorated by the more important *Hausmaler* such as Hunger, Seuter and Bottengrüber can command extra high prices.

The pre-eminent position of Meissen among European porcelain factories now seems well established. By 1700 Chinese porcelain was being exported to the West on a massive scale, yet no European had been able to discover the secret of its manufacture. When Johann Böttger happened upon the right ingredients in 1708, there was a flurry of industrial espionage and Meissen became the Silicon Valley of 18th century Europe.

Since then, Meissen porcelain has been highly prized, not because it was

Octagonal sugar box and cover (1723–5), £8500.

the first in Europe but because nothing as fine has been made since. At times, other European factories have been more admired and prices have fluctuated. Since around 1960, however, Meissen's status as market leader has been confirmed. The rise in prices has been steady and the outlook for early pieces as an investment is good.

Not everyone saw Meissen porcelain as a work of art. Not long after the first Meissen figures were made, the German art historian Johann Winckelmann described them as 'idiotic puppets' and his jibe has not been forgotten. On the whole, however, appreciation of Meissen has grown steadily.

In 1805 three fine figures modelled by Kändler sold at auction for 50 pence apiece; today they would be worth between £1000 and £2000 each. Prices were particularly high around 1900. A showy, crinoline group sold for £1100 and might fetch no more than £5000 today. Though the trend has been rising over the long term, it has been affected by German buying.

In 1931, fears of another round of hyper-inflation produced a strong market, but after the war Meissen could be bought in Germany for next to nothing. German collectors had no money and their erstwhile enemies were in no mood to buy. Even Chelsea porcelain at this time was fetching higher prices. In the 1960s the resurgence of the German economy created strong demand from native collectors and it was then too that German museums began to rebuild collections lost or destroyed during the war. Apart from the late 1970s, when the pace of German economic growth slackened, conditions have generally been buoyant.

Meissen admirers are to be found worldwide, though the greatest buying power outside Germany is in the United States. Regular auctions including fine Meissen porcelain are held in New York, Geneva, London and Munich, but because the leading dealers and collectors operate internationally there is little if any advantage in buying in one place rather than another.

ABOVE *Figure of a jay, modelled by J. J. Kändler (c. 1745), £11,000.*

ABOVE RIGHT *Baluster vase and domed cover painted with Chinese figures (c. 1730), £14,000.*

BELOW *Painted snuffbox and cover with two-colour gold mounts (c. 1650), £6500.*

With demand so well spread Meissen seems a prime candidate for investment, and indeed there is still good-quality Meissen porcelain of the early period available for under £2000.

Meissen ranges from beautifully modelled figures of people, animals and birds to the functional plates, tureens, cups, saucers, candlesticks and so on, usually known as wares. Sometimes these were quite simply decorated and at other times ornately, as in the case of the enormous dinner services ordered by Count Sulkowski, Count Brühl and other grandees.

A single dinner plate from the spectacular Sulkowski service now fetches £3500 compared to £1000 in 1975. Each piece in the service is decorated with the arms of Count Sulkowski and scattered Japanese flower sprays. Surprisingly, a forty-five piece dinner service, painted with bouquets of flowers, made in 1750 and with just five pieces damaged, was recently sold at Christie's for £3200. That figure compares with £1600 currently being charged for forty-five similar

pieces of modern blue-onion design Meissen. There can be no doubt that the earlier set will prove the better investment.

There are also the knick-knacks of the period – snuffboxes, cane-handles and scent bottles. All have proved a sound investment over the last decade, though performances vary from a rise of 600% for the best-known figures to just 100% for a simple teapot.

When Johann Böttger, a Saxon chemist, discovered the secret of making porcelain in 1708, the Chinese had already had a thousand years of manufacturing experience behind them. The commercial value of Böttger's discovery was not lost on Augustus the Strong, Elector of Saxony. At many European courts, especially those with financial problems, belief in the arcanum, or secret of making gold, was still firmly rooted. Böttger's early reputation was built on his supposed ability to convert molten metals into gold by the addition of a mysterious elixir, and every ruler wanted him as court alchemist. When he could no longer conceal his inability to make gold, the Elector commissioned him to develop new industries and moved him to the Jungfern fortress in Dresden where large kilns had been installed. Here, this gifted man, treated throughout his life more like a criminal than a scientist, produced Europe's first white and translucent porcelain.

Meissen's first half century was the

OPPOSITE *Sultan seated on an elephant driven by a Moorish mahout modelled by J. J. Kändler and P. Reinicke (c. 1750), £1500.*

ABOVE *Figure of a leopard modelled by J. J. Kändler (c. 1745), £2200.*

period of its greatest artistic vitality, brought to an end by the Seven Years War in 1756. After Saxony's defeat by Frederick the Great of Prussia, Meissen lost many of its ablest decorators, moulders and painters to the new porcelain factories springing up in Germany.

Though conceived as both a business and a creative venture, to satisfy the king's love of luxury, the factory was undercapitalized from the start. Augustus proposed that the debts it had incurred to private finance houses be paid off in porcelain, and for a time this surprising arrangement worked well. But later Böttger had to borrow heavily to maintain production.

As a business Meissen may always have been a shambles, but the artistry

of its products, the modelling and decoration, has not been surpassed. In the 1720s a style of chinoiserie painting was developed by the brilliant Johann Gregor Höroldt. During this period some forty painters and their apprentices were engaged as decorators. Höroldt clearly cannot have painted the countless pieces attributed to him. As many as five different hands may have been involved in decorating each article – one for the rim, one for the flowers and so on – and this explains the remarkably consistent quality achieved.

After 1730 form began to assume greater importance than decoration, and for forty years modelling at Meissen was dominated by Johann Joachim Kändler. The figures he created are the most sought after of any period. Though copied throughout Europe, the ersatz versions never achieve the style and vigour of Kändler's originals. Sometimes he worked with other modellers – notably Peter Reinicke and Johann Friedrich Eberlein – on forms that were to

Shaped armorial dish (1741–2), £2800.

become standard lines at Meissen. The concept of a limited edition did not exist during this period, so nobody knows how rare Meissen figures and wares really are. The moulds for figures would have been used again and again as sales dictated and it is known that some of Kändler's moulds were still in use at the end of the 19th century.

The figures in the Italian Comedy series inspired by prints by Riccoboni are among the most popular today. Prices depend partly on the quality of decoration and range from a few hundred pounds up to several thousand. The figures of Scaramouche, Harlequin, Columbine and Pantaloon are represented in jaunty or humorous mood. So too are the series of craftsmen – the tinker, the mason, the shoemaker and others. These highlight the 18th century aristocrat's vision of the working classes, all jovial, well fed and happy in their work. To complete this fantasy of a well-ordered world, they are portrayed at their daily work but attired in gleaming Sunday best.

As parts of a series these appeal strongly to collectors whose goal is often to complete a set. Perhaps the best known of all the series is the monkey band. In 1805, a set of seventeen players sold for £17; a hundred years later a set sold for £235; in 1963 for £3150 and it would reach £15,000 to £20,000 today.

But, as with all works of art, there are pitfalls for the unwary. Chips, cracks and stains on any piece of porcelain seriously reduce its value, so investors should examine pieces they plan to buy with the greatest care, and, of course, take out comprehensive insurance as soon as they are at risk. On viewing days before porcelain auctions, dealers can be seen prodding with pins at arms and legs to locate cleverly concealed repairs. Similarly, they will hold up a dish or bowl on the fingers of one hand and give the rim a sharp flick with the forefinger of the other. If there is no musical ring, some minute or invisible crack must be present. Since it is to such fastidious porcelain collectors that the investor may even-

Pair of two-handled wine coolers (mid-18th century), £1800.

tually want to sell, he should heed their preferences for pieces in perfect state.

The factory mark that a piece bears can also affect its value. The AR monogram, standing for Augustus Rex, was used at an early date to indicate that the piece was delivered to the king for his own use or for presentation to someone else. The presence of the monogram suggests that the piece is of outstanding quality and this can add 50% to its value. Some twenty other marks were used at Meissen – mainly variations on KPM (Königliche Porzellan Manufaktur) and the better-known crossed swords which appeared in 1722. Most have been forged without let-up from the earliest days – the AR monogram was used extensively by a Madame Wolfsohn in the last century until the factory took action against her. Crossed swords also appear where they do not belong and investors must familiarize themselves with the genuine marks or use a reliable dealer as protection.

Most of the Meissen now appearing at auction outside Germany is being bought by German and Swiss dealers. For UK collectors prices will be determined partly by the strength of the German and Swiss currencies, for while they are in the ascendant London will seem a bargain basement – as it has seemed to American collectors in 1985–6. But whatever the exchange rates may be, Meissen's fundamentals as an investment are sound and profits over the long term are almost assured.

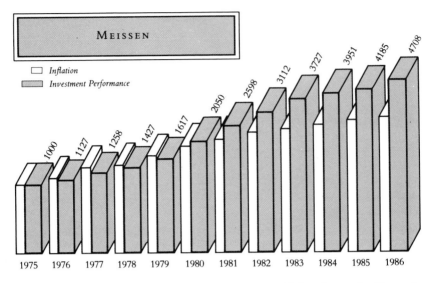

MEISSEN

☐ Inflation
▨ Investment Performance

1000 1127 1258 1427 1617 2050 2598 3112 3727 3951 4185 4708

1975 1976 1977 1978 1979 1980 1981 1982 1983 1984 1985 1986

Components: a selection of tea bowls and saucers, tureens, teapots, armorial plates, figures and snuffboxes of the 1720–50 period

Vincennes and Sèvres

Over the long term Sèvres prices have moved erratically. The field is complicated by the existence of so many fakes and no satisfactory index can be compiled. Nevertheless, the rise in value since 1975 is estimated at 200%, most of it having occurred in the last two years.

The sudden jump may be due to collectors realizing that Sèvres prices had simply been left behind during the 1960s and 1970s, but also to the transformation of demand for top-quality pieces following the decisions taken by several American museums, including the Getty in Malibu and the Nelson Atkins in Kansas City, to form collections of French decorative art.

Investors should aim, above all, for the early pieces made at Vincennes and those made at Sèvres after the factory moved in 1756.

Of all European porcelain, Vincennes and Sèvres are the trickiest. There are only five eagled-eyed scholars in the world whose judgement on the vital question of authenticity is considered sound. Most other ceramics experts, including museum curators, will admit to feeling uneasy in this field. Imitations of Vincennes and Sèvres, whether conceived as forgeries or not, certainly outnumber the genuine and the effect on the market has been serious. Moreover, since dealers have plainly been short of

expertise, collectors have had good reason to lose their nerve. Most Sèvres porcelain is distinguished by a strong background colour and this helps to determine its value to collectors. A simple mug decorated with flowers on its natural white ground might be worth £500; a similar mug having a *bleu céleste* or light blue ground would sell for £1000, whereas another example with the famous *rose pompadour* ground might be worth £5000. Though the remarkable pink colour named after La Pompadour was not so-called in her day, she was an ardent admirer of Vincennes and Sèvres. The daybooks of Lazare Duvaux, the leading porcelain dealer in Paris, for the years 1748–58

show her to have been by far his best customer.

The ornate trappings of aristocratic life in 18th century France are not to everyone's taste. Furniture, silver, porcelain, clothes and even manners reached a peak of overpowering extravagance. An English visitor to Versailles in 1765 remarked that he could see magnificence all right, but no beauty anywhere. Even now tourists come reeling out of France's gilded châteaux and palaces, stunned by the opulence but having learned something too about the causes of the French Revolution. Art historians differ on the status of such ostentatious works. The craftsmanship and design may have been superb, but if

the overall effect is to debauch the eye, the whole plan must surely have miscarried.

Most porcelain factories have passed through periods of decline yet have often emerged with renewed creativity. Collectors become familiar with these cycles and choosy about the periods they will buy. In the case of Sèvres, the 1790–1820 period is generally passed by. Things looked up again around 1840 but by 1870 a commission was appointed to look into the degeneration of aesthetic standards. It found that the feeling for decoration at the factory was weak and that evidence of appropriate training, and indeed the very principles of art, were absent.

Carrier-Belleuse was appointed Director of Art soon afterwards and he persuaded two other sculptors, Rodin and Dalou, to collaborate in restoring standards. But in the 1880s copies of Sèvres porcelain began to flood out of other European factories to meet the rising demand. Genuine but plain early Sèvres wares were ruthlessly 'upgraded' to satisfy the taste for richly ornamented porcelain.

Prices for Sèvres had fallen over the 1803–14 period as French refugees raised money by selling in London – plates were selling at around five

ABOVE *Ecuelle, cover and stand (1781)*, £2200.

LEFT *Biscuit group of Le Valet de Chien (c. 1776)*, £1200.

shillings apiece – but picked up sharply under the impact of the Prince Regent's buying until his death in 1830. In the 1860s French industrialists began to share the English taste for 18th century French works of art and prices soared. The 1870s and 1880s were the height of the boom. In 1875 the Earl of Dudley paid £10,500 for a three-piece garniture for a chimney-piece – a higher price than had yet been paid for any work by Leonardo da Vinci. He also bought a pair of potpourri vases in apple green and *rose pompadour* for £6825 which were resold in 1963 for just £5800.

The market fell in the 1890s, picked up again in the 1900s and fell sharply again during the First World War. Many of the 'copies' were mere parodies of the forms originally made at Sèvres; only the lavish decoration and sentimentalized figures gave a vulgar impression of the originals.

During the 19th and early 20th centuries Sèvres was the most collected of all European porcelain, and its popularity was nearly its undoing. By the 1920s the huge scale of the forgery problem began to be appreciated. In addition to the copies made outside France, there was a vast number of 'half-forgeries'. These were undecorated white pieces, often with firing marks or other defects, which had been sold in England during the dark days of the early 19th century, and were later convincingly enamelled and glazed in the Sèvres style by Minton and other English factories. Many of these still circulate in the market and when identified change hands for about a quarter the price of a genuine example.

That this remains a real problem today is shown by the experience of one wealthy New York collector. Over the years he spent substantial sums on his Sèvres, all of it bought from a reputable dealer. On taking it recently to a New York auctioneer, he was surprised to learn that in their opinion most of the pieces were 'wrong'. Assuming the auctioneer is right, the collector has no remedy against the dealer who sold them in good faith and would no doubt stick to his opinion that every piece was genuine.

It was the recognition of such hazards, coinciding of course with the Depression, that caused a collapse of prices during the 1920s. Only recently has the outlook begun to brighten. The meticulous kiln records as well as sale records kept at Sèvres have been studied. Furthermore, a humble cup and saucer will often bear enough marks to identify the painter, the gilder, the potter and the year of manufacture. Recent research has filled in many of the remaining gaps and investors who buy pieces of known provenance and from reputable dealers and auctioneers can do so with more confidence than before.

Collectors recognize that the finest porcelain of many factories was produced in their early years. This is not an irrational preference of the kind that moves book collectors to buy first editions. It comes from seeing

Plate from the Du Barry Service (1771), £200.

that the freshness, vitality and even experimental character of the early pieces have more to offer than the mechanical, albeit more accomplished, work of later periods.

From the entire range of Vincennes and Sèvres porcelain, the most promising investments are the small- to medium-sized pieces dating from before 1772. In 1745 Vincennes was granted the sole right to gild its porcelain. This privilege, which passed to Sèvres with the move in 1756, was on the whole exercised with moderation and taste. Occasionally the gilding on even the early Vincennes pieces seems heavy, and it is this flamboyantly 'rich' look that is going out of fashion today.

The flowers which accounted in the early days 80% of production are also expected to underperform. Over the years many have been detached from their brass or copper stems and vases in which they were arranged; and in any case the taste for porcelain mounted in ormolu has waned.

The unglazed white 'biscuit' figures by Falconet and other leading sculptors which changed hands at the turn of the century for around £1000 are worth the same or less today. Although the modelling and technical quality are astonishing, the figures have a cold unfinished quality and

demand for them is unlikely to return.

Other types of Sèvres that are likely to prove good investments include the figures of children inspired by the paintings of Boucher and modelled in the factory. The most sought-after modellers include Chanou, Goubert, Deperrieux, Hubert and Blondeau. Similarly, certain painters are known for their exquisite handling of particular subjects – Jean-Louis Morin for shipping scenes, Etienne Evans for birds, Charles-Nicolas Dodin for *putti* and other figures, François Aloncle for birds and animals and Claude-Charles Gerard for pastoral subjects. Although the overall quality of painting was high, some early painters achieved surprisingly kitsch results which investors should take care to avoid.

It goes without saying that any piece having an established connection with the French royal family will not only carry a premium, but should prove a better investment. Demand for material with a royal association is likely to continue even if the rest of the market is flat. Furthermore, any piece made at Sèvres for the royal family will always be of the best quality and such pieces normally outperform the rest.

The royal connection with Sèvres could hardly be stronger. Louis XV became sole proprietor of the enter-

OPPOSITE *Pair of tea bowls and saucers (1773),*
£2000.

ABOVE *Pair of seaux à bouteilles (1770), £14,000.*

prise in 1759 as well as its most important salesman. At the annual exhibitions at Versailles he sold off the porcelain to members of the court at prices he himself set. It was considered unwise to resist the royal offers and business boomed.

The royal connection with Sèvres was maintained when Louis XVI succeeded his grandfather in 1774. But the factory gradually sank into debt and by 1790 was barely able to pay its workmen. In 1793 a gang of revolutionaries spent four hours smashing the moulds of every bust or figure associated with the old regime.

Nowadays Sèvres is regarded as elitist porcelain *par excellence* – an ostentatious child of its time, as decadent as the regime under which it flourished. Yet at its most restrained it may be seen as a peculiarly French fusion of prettiness and elegance.

The current revaluation of Sèvres could continue at an annual rate of 10% to 15% for the next decade. Though the heavily ornate 19th century pieces have shared in the recent rise, investors would be wiser to stick to objects made before 1770.

Chelsea

The Chelsea porcelain index is up 235% over 1975 and prospects for further growth are good. As in other sectors of the ceramics market, prices have moved erratically over the long term. Demand outside the UK is minimal, so prices are affected by the state of the UK economy. As the index shows, the recovery since 1982 has been impressive and there is no reason now to expect any significant reappraisal which might cause prices to collapse.

From its beginnings in 1745 to its sale and merger with Derby in 1769/70, the Chelsea factory moved through four distinct periods. These are named according to the marks applied to the wares and are distinguished by the different pastes used as well as by changes in form and decoration. Sprimont, the founder of

Cabbage-leaf bowl. Red Anchor period, £1200.

the factory, was a silversmith and many of the earliest models derive from objects that existed in silver or bronze.

The early pieces from the Triangle period (1745–9) seldom appear on the market, so investors should concentrate on the years 1750 to 1763 which take in the Raised Anchor (1749–52), Red Anchor (1752–7) and part of the Gold Anchor (1757–69) periods. It was then that the finest wares were made, the later Gold Anchor period yielding the grossly overgilded and decorated pieces that many collectors shun.

Within the index, Raised Anchor and Red Anchor period wares have performed least strongly with rises of 200% and 250%, while Gold Anchor period is up 280%. It also emerges that functional pieces such as plates, saucers and bowls have risen more slowly than figures and groups.

Joseph Willems is thought to have arrived at Chelsea in 1749 and it is to him that most of the models are attributed. It has to be recognized that his modelling, though sometimes lively

and pleasing, lacked the finesse of his German counterparts. The thicker glaze used on Chelsea porcelain also had the effect of blurring the details and this combined with the painting to give many of the figures rather gormless expressions.

Even so, prices for figures and groups in good condition have been rising strongly. A peak was reached in 1919/20 when Gold Anchor vases and urns made in imitation of Sèvres were fetching £2000 and more apiece. For most of the 18th and 19th centuries Chelsea porcelain did not command high prices. Figures were sold in the 1760s for five shillings each and dinner plates for two shillings. But the lowly status of Chelsea ended in the Gold Anchor period when the Sèvres imitations proved so popular. For most of the 19th century Chelsea figures were considered folksy and provincial compared to Meissen, and were worth only a fraction of their German rivals until around 1930 when rich collectors began to take an interest.

Prices held up reasonably well

ABOVE *A billing dove, tureen and cover. Red Anchor period, £14,000.*

BELOW *Chelsea Figure of a dancing man. Gold Anchor period, £2500.*

during the Depression but collapsed at the beginning of the war. Pairs of important figures that might have made £3000 ten years earlier changed hands for £50 to £150. An asparagus tureen that made £36 in 1941 was sold again in 1963 for £1450 and would today be worth £8000.

But prices recovered fast even during the war and a second boom developed around 1950. Any figure in good condition commanded £1000 minimum and by 1957 the famous Tyrolese Dancers group was fetching £3600. The explanation for these prices cannot be found in the state of the British economy which was then barely recovering from the austerity of the war; prices were particularly strong in New York where a handful of collectors were forcing them higher.

Even in the early days, German porcelain enjoyed a higher status than English. In 1748 the British minister in Dresden was presented with a china dinner service for thirty people costing £1500. Such enormous prices gave German porcelain an image of

ABOVE *Pair of saucer dishes. Raised Anchor period,*
£600.

BELOW LEFT *Mercury and Venus. Gold Anchor*
period, £2000.

BELOW RIGHT *Plate of silver shape. Raised Anchor*
period, £1500.

luxury. German factories could therefore aspire to produce works of art while the English needed to sell a high proportion of functional wares to survive. The English factories that went heavily for figures ran into difficulties; Longton Hall was closed in 1760, Bow suffered a serious setback in 1763 and Chelsea's financial problems became acute in the same year.

Its problems had been increased by the Chinese porcelain that flooded into Europe during the 1760s. Many

factories found they could only continue economically by producing
larger and more expensive pieces. In
the 1780s the price of Chelsea porcelain fell as cheaply produced Wedg-
wood creamware swamped the market. Even the larger pieces could be
bought cheaply; at a clearance sale in
1783 a garniture of five urns made just
twelve guineas. It was not until the
early 19th century that Chelsea acquired some rarity value.

The finest of all English porcelain
was made at Chelsea between 1750
and 1756. That alone gives it sound
credentials as an investment. From
its earliest days the factory had borrowed heavily from Chinese and
Japanese styles. And nearly all the
tureens that appeared in the 1755
catalogue in the form of rabbits,
cauliflowers, asparagus and so on
were taken directly from Meissen
originals. However derivative Chelsea porcelain may have been, it has a
powerful appeal to English collectors.
If the groups of rustic lovers, mas-
queraders and Italian comedy figures
seemed cruder than their European

ABOVE *Decagonal saucer dish,* £1500.

BELOW *Teapot. Red Anchor period,* £1000.
Bowl and cover, £1800.

Pair of plates, Kakiemon style. Red Anchor period,
£900.

rivals, that to an English collector is all to the good. It is part of their simple charm. In the long term it is the less garishly decorated porcelain of the Raised and Red Anchor periods that should outperform the ornate work of the late Gold Anchor period.

There is a good deal of genuine but unmarked Chelsea porcelain in circulation, but pieces that bear genuine factory marks are currently worth 20% to 30% more. It is always unwise to attribute and date porcelain by its marks, and especially so in the case of Chelsea. Only about half the pieces

bearing anchor marks are genuine. Large quantities of 'Chelsea', 'Sèvres' and other European porcelains were openly produced by Samson and other Parisian firms in the second half of the 19th century. Some are quite persuasive but worth less than half the real thing. Investors should therefore be careful to buy only from reputable dealers and auctioneers. These severe fluctuations in the Chelsea market make timing especially important. At present levels prices are realistic and the market looks set for further growth.

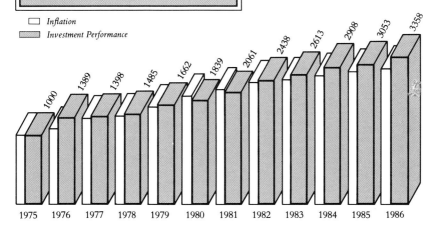

CHELSEA PORCELAIN

☐ *Inflation*
▨ *Investment Performance*

1000 · 1389 · 1398 · 1485 · 1662 · 1839 · 2061 · 2438 · 2613 · 2908 · 3053 · 3358

1975 1976 1977 1978 1979 1980 1981 1982 1983 1984 1985 1986

Components: a selection of figures, teapots, dishes etc. of the Raised, Red and Gold Anchor periods

Further Reading

Peter Wilhelm Meister and Horst Reber, *European Porcelain of the Eighteenth Century* (London, 1983)

Hugo Morley-Fletcher and Roger McIlroy, *Christie's Pictorial History of European Pottery* (Oxford, 1985)

Anthony du Boulay, *Christie's Pictorial History of Chinese Ceramics* (Oxford, 1984)

Michèle and Cécile Beurdeley, *Chinese Ceramics* (London, 1974)

Henry Mason Garner, *Oriental Blue and White* (London, 1970)

Margaret Medley, *The Chinese Potter* (Oxford, 1976)

S. Valenstein, *Handbook of Chinese Ceramics* (New York, 1975)

Paul Atterbury (ed.), *The History of Porcelain* (London, 1982)

Geoffrey Godden, *Eighteenth-century English Porcelain* (London, 1985)

Peter Bradshaw, *18th Century English Porcelain Figures, 1745–1795* (Woodbridge, 1981)

John Ayers, *Far Eastern Ceramics in the Victoria & Albert Museum* (London, 1980)

George Savage and Harold Newman, *An Illustrated Dictionary of Ceramics* (London, 1974)

Dealers (European Porcelain)

Delomosne & Son Ltd
4 Campden Hill Road
London W8 7DU
01-937 1804

Jan van Beers
1–7 Davies Mews
London W1
01-408 0434

Winifred Williams
3 Bury Street
London SW1Y 6AB
01-930 4732

Graham & Oxley
(Antiques) Ltd
101 Kensington Church
Street
London W8 7LN
01-229 1850

Earle D. Vandekar of
Knightsbridge Ltd
138 Brompton Road
London SW3 1HY
01-589 8481

Chinese Porcelain

Grosvenor Antiques
27 Holland Street
London W8
01-937 8649

Bluett & Sons
48 Davies Street
London W1Y 1LD
01-629 4018

Eskenazi Ltd
Foxglove House
166 Piccadilly
London W1V 9DE
01-493 5464

Sydney Moss Ltd
51 Brook Street
London W1Y 1AU
01-629 4670

Spink & Son Ltd
5–7 King Street
London SW1Y 6QS
01-930 7888

GOLD

OVER THE last five thousand years gold has acquired an almost mystical status in the human mind and people are often confused about its credentials as an investment. Since 1970 its performance has been erratic to say the least. Yet, although its reputation is tarnished, gold still weaves a magic spell over half the investment world.

Even Lenin recognized that in a capitalist society gold was a necessity, though he looked forward to a communist future when gold could be used to cover the walls and the floors of public lavatories. Lenin's dream may not come true for some time, so investors can meanwhile take a view on gold.

The gold world is divided into two camps. One comprises the 'gold bugs' who believe that a return to a currency backed at least partly by gold would bring order and growth to the economies of the world. They now argue that this would require some increase in the price of gold and therefore rank it as an attractive investment.

Their arguments are as follows:

1 A gold-backed currency would ensure economic stability and restore confidence.

2 Growth in the world money supply would be determined by increases in the world stock of gold. Since this is currently expanding at around 2% a year, inflation and interest rates would drop sharply.

3 The universal acceptability of gold gives it a supreme advantage as a world currency. Moreover, whatever has happened to other stores of value, gold has remained valuable throughout every crisis in history.

The latest attempt to resurrect an official role for gold was discussed at the United States Gold Commission in 1981. The hearings produced little to please the gold bugs so for the time being any ideas of official revaluation must be ruled out.

The other camp, known as the 'barbarous relic school', was so named after the contemptuous reference to gold made by John Maynard Keynes whose economic theory has been influential since the 1920s. This school argues that:

1 A gold-backed currency introduces a rigidity into the economy, forcing it to accept severe recessions and even depressions if, for example, a sudden oil-price increase led to a high rate of inflation.

2 If a currency is tied to gold, the money stock cannot be expanded when economic conditions call for a stimulus.

3 It would be strategically unwise to depend on a metal when three-quarters of new supplies originate in South Africa and the Soviet Union.

4 It is basically absurd to extract a metal from deep in the earth only to bury it again in holes dug for the

purpose beneath, for example, Fort Knox and the Bank of England.

5 The reintroduction of gold as an integral part of the international monetary system hinders the acceptance of more sophisticated concepts of credit such as special drawing rights.

What is gold's impressive reputation as an investment based upon? A hundred years ago, when the South African gold fields were opening up, the price of gold was still fixed at £4.25 an ounce. In 1931, when Britain went off the gold standard, the price was the same, but in the meantime the cost of living had increased by about 60%. So, although gold had provided no income at all over that period, and its value had declined in real terms by 37%, most people continued to regard it, quite irrationally, as a fine investment.

The new price of $35 an ounce fixed by the United States in 1934 gave gold holders a profit of nearly 70% even though the price in the London market had been creeping up in anticipation of the change. The sterling price rose to £12.40 an ounce following the devaluation of 1949 and again to around £16.40 after the 1967 devaluation.

Admittedly, the increase from 1931 to 1986 (taking a base price of £240) is an impressive 5600%. Seen as a UK-based investment this is highly satisfactory, yet it must be remembered that the growth in dollar terms has been just 840%, which means that any 'growth' over and above that is thanks to the collapse of sterling – rather than to any fundamental investment quality in gold.

From the end of the $35-an-ounce era in 1970 to 1985 the increase in sterling terms amounts to 1500% (£15 to £240). But many analysts regard 1970 as an unrealistic base date from which to measure gold's performance and prefer to take the average price over the 1974–6 period – by which time gold had caught up with other commodities after its fixed-price experience. Looking at it in dollar terms (to avoid flattering the growth rate by building in continued benefits to UK holders from the slide in sterling) we have an average price of $148. Taking the gold price in 1986 at $330, the growth rate over the 11-year period comes to just 123%, while UK inflation over the same period was 175%.

But, as the index on page 178 illustrates, a lot happened in between and analysts are constantly searching for a formula that can be used to predict movements in the price. A few are beginning to feel an affinity with the alchemists of old who faced the equally hopeless task of turning base metal into gold.

But analysts are paid to make reasoned forecasts or intelligent guesses at the least. Whatever their inclination they cannot spin a coin or consult tea leaves. There is a worldwide network of markets enabling investors to trade right round the clock and they look to analysts for daily advice. Analysts maintain that the gold price responds to inflation rates, interest rates, exchange rates, banking crises, the oil price, the size of the Soviet grain harvest and perhaps even East–West tension. But does it? The answer is yes, but nobody knows quite how.

Production of gold in the non-communist world has been rising gently for the last six years and the trend is expected to continue. Annual Soviet production is estimated to have varied between 270 and 450 tons in recent years and is forecast to reach 450 to 500 tons a year in the 1990s.

The Soviet Union sells gold through its Zürich-based Wochzod Handelsbank, shrewdly unloading a large tonnage at the time of the invasion of Afghanistan when the price touched $850. If foreign currency is needed to buy grain from the West, sales may be made from the stockpile as well as from current production. If the Soviet external trade account is in surplus no sales at all may be necessary. Soviet gold managers are regularly in the market as buyers too and analysts are continually trying to read their actual positions and intentions.

On the demand side, by far the largest end use for gold today is carat jewellery. It is actively traded throughout the Middle and Far East where the mark-up over melt value is normally between 5% and 30%. The quality of machine-made chains and bracelets (mostly made in Italy) at around 30% over melt value is acceptable, but the pieces of Middle Eastern workmanship are as crude as one might expect at only 5% over melt value.

Sophisticated econometric models have been designed in the West to forecast the gold price, yet many people believe that the women buying or selling gold in the *souks* of Saudi Arabia are a better guide to its next move. During the winter of 1979/80, while investors elsewhere were piling into the market and driving the price to $850, the Saudi women were selling fast, convinced that the price must soon collapse.

As sold in the Middle East, gold jewellery is an acceptable way of investing in gold, but in Europe and North America, where the mark-up is usually between 200% and 300%, buying for investment makes little sense. Jewellery demand in the West is less sensitive to the price of gold

than to the state of the economy. It is predictable that if a Western economy is booming, carat jewellery sales will rise even if the gold price is high. In India on the other hand, the excellent harvest of 1984 enabled farmers to purchase an unusually large quantity of gold (145 tons) in preparation for their daughters' weddings. But who can forecast demand for next year? Fabrication of jewellery in Turkey rose to 100 tons in 1976 but by 1984 other more attractive investments – mostly high-yielding bonds and property – had reduced the figure to three tons. It is factors such as these that make predicting the gold price so difficult.

Rising demand for gold used in the field of electronics depends partly on demand for consumer durables. In the 1970s efforts to economize in the use of gold by substituting palladium-nickel and other alloys, and by thinner gold plating, caused a drop in demand. But the practical limits to this trend have been reached. In defence and aerospace where performance is vital gold is not threatened by other metals. Overall demand for gold in electronics and in other industrial and decorative uses is forecast to rise slowly.

The outlook for gold demand in dentistry on the other hand is bleak. The Germans put more gold in their teeth than any other nation. The figure was 28 tons in 1979 but has now dropped to 14. The second largest consumer was the United States, but there too consumption fell by over half in five years. Most people now prefer to have their teeth fixed with natural-looking ceramic compounds and gold usage is likely to drop further.

Gold used in medals, medallions and fake coins has been stable over the last few years though down on the late 1970s. Fake coins in this context means the facsimiles of official coins struck outside the country of origin. Saudi Arabia, for example, struck 22 tons worth of fake sovereigns, double eagles and other coins in 1984. Lighter and less pure than the genuine coins, these are often linked up to form a bracelet in the Middle East. Recent legislation requiring manufacturers to stamp each fake with the caratage of the gold could affect sales.

Private mints produce standard items such as St Christophers and medallions to commemorate events ranging from the Olympic Games to the Chinese Year of the Rat. These are usually marketed as having some investment potential, though the heavy mark-up over melt value – often several hundred per cent – makes it very unlikely that a buyer will ever get his money back. A few medallions marketed in the early 1970s did manage to climb above their original retail price though this owed nothing to their artistry; buyers were simply baled out by the massive rise in the gold price.

The US five-year medallion sales programme ended in 1985 having achieved poor results. Opinion is divided on the reason; some say poor marketing was responsible, others that Americans are too canny to buy mass-produced medallions at 10% or so over gold value when bullion coins such as the krugerrand and mapleleaf are readily available.

Gold used in official gold coins has dropped sharply from 290 tons in 179 to 108 in 1985. The South African krugerrand, which came from nowhere in 1970 to dominate the market with 194 tons in 1978, has been losing ground to the Canadian mapleleaf, the other major bullion coin selling at around 3% over melt value. Since the United States ban on

importation of krugerrands as part of the pressure exerted on the South African government to end apartheid, sales have dwindled to around 25 tons. There is no doubt that bullion coins and gold bars will always be the leading vehicles for investment in physical gold. Yet many governments, including the British and American, have grabbed the chance to levy tax on those buying gold in this form. VAT is currently chargeable in the UK at 15% and taxes up to 8% are payable in certain American states. This encourages buyers to hold their gold in tax havens to escape the tax, but it also deters people from buying at all since an important attraction of gold is that the owner has it on hand in preparation for some unspecified emergency.

The greatest obstacle to forecasting the gold price is that none of the factors accepted as affecting it is consistent in its impact. The widely acknowledged relationship between gold and the dollar, whereby a strong dollar is supposed to result in a weak gold price and *vice versa*, is anything but constant. Goldman Sachs found that over thirteen years the expected correlation had occurred only 29% of the time. And when in September 1985 the United States and its five major trading partners agreed that the dollar should fall by 25%, the gold price barely stirred. This reflected too the market's scepticism that central banks were capable of engineering such a move.

Nor do serious incidents that might flare into a confrontation between the superpowers always trigger a movement in the gold price. The all-time peak of $850 in 1980 was thought to have been caused at least in part by the Soviet invasion of Afghanistan. Yet the price began a sharp slide soon after. Similarly, the price reached another peak with the outbreak of the Iran–Iraq war but fell fairly steadily for the next twelve months.

The reason may be that an international crisis will cause the more jittery members of any society to buy gold as a form of insurance against the day when paper securities are valueless and property is in ruins. But when that slice of demand is satisfied, a crisis such as the failure of the attempt to rescue the American hostages in Teheran will not bring buyers back into the market. Rather, they will sit back and enjoy the security afforded by their recently purchased gold and the price will not be disturbed. That is why major international crises do not always trigger buying in the gold market. Furthermore, this kind of panic-buying is mainly done by wealthy people whose home territory is threatened and who have the right to reside elsewhere. At present, there are few individuals who fall into this category.

As for the link between gold and the oil price, there is no doubt that when oil prices soared during the early 1970s many millions of petrodollars went into gold. However, all the evidence now suggests that Arab buying of gold is quite unrelated to the oil price. Some analysts work on the hypothesis that an ounce of gold should be worth 13 barrels of Saudi light crude oil. The charts they draw show that the variance from the 13-barrel line has swung from 10 to 40 barrels over the last twenty years, so the link is by no means strong. It is also argued that a rising oil price will produce a higher rate of inflation in the industrialized world, yet again the correlation is irregular.

A more logical link may be seen in the relationship of gold to interest rates in the United States. The real interest rate in the United States –

that is, prime rate minus the rate of inflation – remained historically high at 7% to 9% from 1981 to 1986 and provides the best explanation for the lacklustre performance of gold. It took double-figure inflation and very low or negative real interest rates to produce the great surges in the gold price of 1974 and 1979. Without a comparable interest rate as backdrop, gold is very unlikely to break through $400.

Another plausible cause for a stampede into gold might be the financial Armageddon some bankers have been predicting for years. A major banking crisis brought about by a Third World default began to look more likely than ever in the mid-1980s. The idea that Brazil, Peru and other multibillion dollar debtors should be doomed to a state of more or less indefinite austerity so that American and other commercial banks could be sure of raising their quarterly dividends began to make even bankers feel uneasy. Yet even if the debtor nations declared a moratorium, and commercial banks had to be propped up by central banks, the actual benefits of holding gold are not immediately obvious. Furthermore, the Mexican banking crisis in the summer of 1982 produced a short-lived jump in the price, created mainly in the futures markets. But the demand for physical gold simply was not there and the price soon fell back.

The factors that go to establish the gold price have recently shown themselves to be more complex and inconsistent than ever. A sound case can be made for a price of $600 in the near future, but the case for $200 can be made equally convincing. Many investors would actually prefer to see the price moving erratically between the two, for stability offers less scope for profitable trading. But ultimately, gold is more likely to gratify an investor's psychological needs than increase his wealth. Certainly the growing insecurity that has created a religious revival in many parts of the world from the United States to Iran suggests a retreat into fantasy with which faith in gold is entirely consistent.

The Background

Between 1500 and 1850 about 150 million ounces of gold was mined. From 1850 to 1933 when gold lost its monetary role, 950 million ounces was mined, most of it minted as British sovereigns and American dollars. In a move to restore a stable currency after the inflationary period of the Napoleonic Wars, Great Britain issued new gold sovereigns in 1817 weighing 0.2354 of an ounce. The American five-dollar piece or half eagle issued twenty years later contained 0.2419 of an ounce of gold, making the exchange rate $4.86 to the pound.

The sterling price of £4 4s 11½d had been set when Isaac Newton was Master of the Mint in 1717 but gold coins were not widely used in the 18th century. It was only after gold was discovered in California in 1849 and later in the century in Australia, Alaska and South Africa that enough of the metal was available for a monetary function to be established.

During the Depression, when other commodity prices were falling, gold, thanks to its official status, held its price. Precisely this kind of behaviour fostered the illusion that gold possessed some special characteristic – some intrinsic stability that insulated it from ordinary market forces.

Britain went off the Gold Standard in September 1931. The United States followed in April 1933 but went back on to a gold exchange standard in January 1934 with the dollar devalued to 59.06% of its old parity. The new gold price of $35 an ounce was to remain fixed until 1968.

In 1944 the Bretton Woods Conference restored gold to its former status as the ultimate reserve asset, the pivot and numeraire of the new system of fixed exchange rates. Under this system, an ounce of gold was again to be worth $35 and the US government assumed a legal commitment in 1945 to maintain the convertibility of the dollar into gold on the demand of any foreign central bank. Such was the commercial and industrial strength of the United States at this time that a balance of payments deficit seemed inconceivable. Moreover, the United States then held $20 billion worth of gold or 60% of the world's official reserves and no one scented danger in this commitment.

Yet by the late 1950s the US balance of payments shifted into deficit. The US Treasury 'gold window' was doing a brisk one-way business as Britain, France and other countries cashed in their surplus dollars for gold. The flaw in the Bretton Woods system was that it was based upon uncertainty. For if it were certain that the price of gold in dollar terms would never rise above $35, what would be the point of holding gold? Why not hold dollars which could at least earn interest? Each time a bar of gold passed out of the US Treasury gold window, it could be taken as an expression of disbelief that the dollar value of gold really was fixed for all time.

In the autumn of 1960, the weekly Treasury reports of American losses through the gold window were making the front page of the *New York Times*. In 1961 negotiations between the leading central banks led to the creation of the Gold Pool. This was an agreement whereby the Bank of England would sell enough gold on behalf of the eight leading central banks in the London market to keep the price at $35. The arrangement worked well enough in the early years but in late 1967 losses from the Gold Pool were running at up to $100 million a day.

Attempts were made to dam the flood, but with gold market speculation now focusing squarely on the dollar, the crisis came in March 1968. On Monday 11th Gold Pool losses were $118 million, on Tuesday $103 million, Wednesday $179 million and by lunchtime Thursday $220 million. At 3.00 p.m. President Johnson stopped Pool operations. The governors of the Gold Pool banks met in Washington on March 16th and settled for the long-canvassed proposal for a two-tier system. The central banks agreed to buy and sell gold among themselves at $35 but not to deal in the London market which would be left free to find its own level. The recent waves of speculation had been based on the expectation of a new official price for gold, so that when the market reopened there was no one on whom the speculators could unload their holdings and prices rose to only $38. Later in the year it reached $43 but with increased offerings from South Africa in 1969 the price drifted back to $35.

By 1971 the United States was heading for a trade deficit of $23 billion and financial markets began to sense an impending dollar crisis. For the week 7–14 August, the US Treasury reported an outflow from dollars into gold and reserve assets of $3.7 billion. On 15 August Nixon closed the gold window.

The Smithsonian Agreement of December 1971 devalued the dollar against other currencies by between 6% and 17% and raised the official price of gold to $38 an ounce. The free market price finally lifted off that year and broke through $100 for the first time in 1973.

Further Reading

Timothy Green, *The New World of Gold* (London, 1985)

R. Jastram, *The Golden Constant* (New York, 1977)

Consolidated Gold Fields: Annual Reviews 1969–1986

J. K. Galbraith, *Money* (London, 1975)

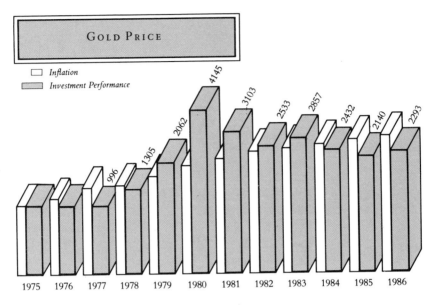

Average gold price in US dollars, 1974–76= 1000

Gold

US$ per ounce – Annual Averages

1974	158.80
1975	160.87
1976	124.79
1977	147.71
1978	193.51
1979	305.85
1980	614.63
1981	460.13
1982	375.64
1983	423.68
1984	360.72
1985	317.33
1986	*

DIAMONDS

MEN HAVE adorned their wives and girlfriends with diamonds for over three thousand years. Today diamonds are still admired in jewellery but increasingly thought of as investments. So much so that a market specifically for investment diamonds was developed during the 1970s. Prices climbed steadily for a few years, then rocketed during 1978–80 and have been falling ever since.

As investments, diamonds have got themselves a bad name. Investment counsellors and bankers have made soothing noises about prices becoming stable but since the headlong dive began in the spring of 1980 nobody in the trade has found a way to re-establish confidence. For the diamond market has a similar problem of confidence as gold. Once its reputation for stability takes a beating it can take many years to win back.

The investment saga of the 1970s included a host of cautionary tales for investors, many of which are little known today. Of all the diamonds mined today, 90% are used for cutting, drilling and other industrial purposes. The remaining 10% are pure enough in colour and clarity to be used in jewellery. These are graded into many hundreds of categories. Those with the fewest internal flaws – known as inclusions – and which come closest to being colourless are rarest of all. Naturally these have always been in demand for jewellery and because prices for these were seen to rise steadily investors took to buying such top-quality stones unmounted.

But when dealers began to offer loose stones at prices ranging from £1000 to £20,000 a carat, buyers were puzzled. To their untrained eyes the stones looked pretty much the same, and even under the loupe – a ten-times magnifying glass used throughout the trade – it was not easy to see the tiny inclusions that explained the great differences in value, nor to distinguish the equally important variations in colour. It was all very well taking a dealer's word for it, but what if another dealer, to whom you might later wish to sell, claimed your stone was of poorer quality than you had been led to believe? The answer seemed to lie in an accepted grading system backed up by certificates issued by independent laboratories which would record the precise characteristics of each stone.

This reassured investors up to a point; but what if they were sold an inferior stone whose quality was 'guaranteed' by a certificate that had originally been issued for a better stone? The solution offered by dealers was to sell the stone sealed in a transparent plastic case along with a microfilm of the certificate. No switching would therefore be possible.

But a further problem arose. Although most laboratories used the same grading terminology, some applied more rigorous standards than others. The result was – and still is – that a 1 carat stone graded D Flawless – signifying it to be of the purest colour and without inclusions – by a laboratory of the highest standing may be worth $12,000, while another given the same grades by a less respected laboratory will have a market value of only $8000. Only one laboratory – the Gemological Institute of America – enjoys the confidence of the whole diamond investment community and even they have been known to slip up.

In the light of these problems investment in diamonds calls for extreme caution. Between 1975 and 1979 prices rose by 380%, so with perfect timing an investor could have done well. By 1981, however, prices had fallen by almost half and are now back to the level of 1977. But none of these calculations takes account of tax or dealing margins. The Belgian newspaper *L'Echo de la Bourse* devotes a monthly feature to the diamond market quoting 'interprofessional' buying and selling prices. To these, it warns, must be added a 10% to 25% or an even higher margin that the ordinary buyer should expect to pay. The payment of V A T at 15% in the United Kingdom, 25% in Belgium and even higher rates in some countries – all of it unrecoverable by a private investor when selling – makes diamond investment even less attractive.

During 1978 diamond investment companies sprang up in Europe, the United States and Japan. Dealers found it easy to hype the market and prices began to rise by around 10% a month. Dealers not only worked on outrageous margins, they frequently induced investors to buy by offering buy-back guarantees. The price of the 1 carat D Flawless rose from $15,000 in 1978 to $64,000 in

March 1980. Silver, gold and platinum were also climbing fast at the time. De Beers saw how prices were moving in the diamond exchanges and raised prices by 30% in August 1978, on top of recent rises of 46%. But the bubble burst in May 1980 and by June 1986 the index of 1 carat investment grade stones, that is, D to H in colour, Flawless to V S2 in clarity (see page 186), was standing 75% below the average for 1980. Furthermore, investors wishing to sell have found themselves swimming against the tide. For the diamond trade is designed to flow in one direction only – from mine to cutter to polisher to wholesaler to retailer to investor. Inevitably the high mark-ups along the line were bound to result in pitifully low offers being made to investors who wanted to cash in.

The collapse in 1980/1 seriously damaged confidence and pushed many investment companies to the wall. International Diamond Corporation, the largest of the American diamond investment companies, went bankrupt in 1982. The Federal Trade Commission and several states filed legal actions on the grounds that the company had misrepresented the prices of its diamonds and failed to warn customers of the risks involved in investing in diamonds.

Even though the claims of so many companies to be able to resell stones on behalf of investors may not have amounted to much in practice, while they were still trading investors could at least hope one day to turn their stones back into cash.

A UK diamond investment trust was nearly launched in 1981 inviting members of the public to subscribe five million pounds for investment in diamonds. The draft prospectus claimed a rise in top-quality diamond prices of 2000% over the previous ten

years and though the directors claimed that no material fact had been
omitted from the prospectus, there
was no mention of the diamond
industry being, as the authoritative
Belgian magazine *Diamant* had just
put it, 'wholly in recession', nor that
in the last quarter of 1980 'a true crisis
[had] developed'. A *Sunday Times*
article exposing the risks evidently
prevented the trust from going ahead.

For all the adverse comment in the
trade and general press on the investment diamond market, you might
think only a handful of hermits were
now unaware of the dangers. Yet
quite a few investors are still coming
forward eager to get into the market.
Diamonds, like gold, have a psychological hold over the man in the
street and, although diamonds are the
commonest of all precious stones –
100 million carats have been mined
in the last ten years – they still enjoy
an image of great rarity and value.

So far none of the major auction
houses sells investment diamonds of
the kind sealed in a pack and therefore
impossible to wear, though Christie's
and Sotheby's have recognized the
new sophistication of jewellery
buyers by including the laboratory
grading of important stones in their
catalogues. This top slice of the market, catering for oil sheikhs, film stars
and the private jet set, is less sensitive
to revelations about the diamond
market, but it does respond to movements in world stock markets. A man
with a ten-million dollar portfolio
hardly thinks about the investment
performance of a necklace costing
$50,000. He is probably buying it for
a woman-friend because, as De Beers
puts it, 'Love is forever', or for the
simple pleasure of giving, and not
because he thinks the market is about
to pick up. Similarly, buyers like the
Arab sheikh who ordered ten identical

diamond bracelets from Harry Winston are not going to be affected by a
hiccup in the market.

But if newcomers to the market
find it absurd that a diamond costing $50,000 looks the same to the
naked eye as one priced at $10,000,
he now has a further hazard to contend with. Jewellers can have the tiny
inclusions in a diamond lasered out
and the holes filled with a substance
of the same refractive index, so that
even under magnification the difference becomes still harder to spot.

The ethics of this practice are still
being debated by jewellers in the
trade press. After all, treating a
$1000 diamond by laser at a cost of
$35 and then selling it for $2000 without telling the customer strikes most
people as questionable. As matters
stand now, some jewellers disclose
and some do not. Since jewellery
buyers do not normally take a loupe
with them when they go shopping,
and since the disclosure of lasering is
optional in most countries, there can
be no doubt that large numbers of
diamonds are bought without the
buyer being aware that they have
been lasered.

Another hazard, though far less
common, is the irradiation of stones
to improve their colour. Very occasionally a fancy-coloured diamond
can be valuable in its own right, but
it has to be just the right shade of pink
or canary yellow, for example.
Thanks to their extreme rarity this
has been one of the only bright spots
of the market. Usually, however, the
lower their colour ranks on the scale
from pure white to muddy brown,
the less valuable are the diamonds.
There is of course an instant profit to
be made if the colour of a stone can
be improved by bombarding the surface of the stone with neutrons. A
gemologist can spot about half the

cases of an irradiated stone using a hand spectroscope; in other cases special laboratory equipment is needed.

Valuing Diamonds

A 1 carat diamond can be worth anything from $1000 to $50,000 depending on four main factors known as the 'four Cs': Clarity, Colour, Carat and Cut.

Clarity

No diamond is absolutely flawless. Anything that interferes with the passage of light through a diamond reduces its value. There are several diamond grading systems that set out to quantify and qualify the imperfections in a stone. With the jeweller's loupe, tiny inclusions invisible to the naked eye are noticeable and these can significantly reduce the value of a stone.

The most widely accepted system makes use of the following terms:

F = Flawless
VVS 1 = Very very small inclusions
VS 1 = Very small inclusions
SI = Small inclusions
P = Piqué

The three middle categories are further divided into VVS 1 and VVS 2 and so on.

Colour

There are at least a dozen colour-grading systems in practice throughout the world making use of letters, numbers, adjectives and even the names of mines to describe colours ranging from pure white to yellow. Diamonds are so nearly pure carbon that the purest give the impression of being quite white. Yet in nearly all gem diamonds traces of nitrogen and other impurities absorb some of the colour in white light giving each stone a more or less yellowish tinge. Dealers often grade the colour of a stone by comparing it with a set of master stones.

The alphabetical scale beginning with D for pure white and running down to H is the accepted scale for all investment diamonds. The scale runs down to M but it would be unwise to buy a stone for investment that was graded below H.

Carat

The accepted unit of weight in the diamond trade is the carat, equivalent to 0.2g. The word is taken from the Greek name for the locust tree, *keration*, whose fruit was a black pod full of beans. Centuries ago, Middle-Eastern pearl traders noticed that the dried beans were remarkably uniform in weight and so adopted them as the unit of weight for pearls. At the beginning of this century the carat was given an internationally agreed value of 0.2g, each carat being divided into one hundred points.

The price structure of the diamond market now reflects the investor's preference for stones weighing exactly or slightly over one carat, exactly or slightly over two carats and so on. Thus a stone weighing 98 or 99 points will be worth perhaps 10% less than the 1 carat stone because the psychological threshold has not been reached.

Cut

The cut of a diamond must take advantage of its three optical properties – refractivity, reflectivity and dispersion. When light enters a transparent substance at any angle other than the perpendicular, the path taken by the light deviates. The refractive index of diamond is high at 2.42, which means that by perfect faceting the light that enters a diamond can be made to bounce around inside.

The reflectivity of a diamond is also high. Whereas light falling perpendicularly on glass would reflect only 4%, diamond reflects 18%.

A diamond's third and most important optical property is dispersion. As light moves through the diamond it is broken up, or dispersed, into all the colours of the spectrum and these return separately to the eye producing the diamond's famous sparkle and fire.

In the valuation process a diamond which has been cut in an old-fashioned style that does not make full use of the diamond's optical properties will be valued according to the estimated weight of the stone after it has been recut as a brilliant and the cost of the recutting operation.

As for size, diamonds do not have a constant value per carat. A 2 carat stone will not be worth twice as much as a 1 carat stone of the same quality, but more likely three times as much. Similarly, a 3 carat stone may be worth five times as much as the 1 carat stone. This semi-exponential increase in value for every increase in weight is a recognition that the rarity of diamonds exactly corresponds with their size.

The value of a diamond can also be reduced if its edges are abraded, if the facets are wrongly angled, if it is badly polished and even if it fluoresces under ultraviolet light.

Synthetics and Simulants

General Electric in the United States was the first to announce in 1955 that it had successfully created a synthetic diamond. The process used was basically a repetition of the heating and squeezing of carbon that is believed to have produced natural diamonds 120 miles below ground 120 million years ago. Gem-quality diamonds of 1 carat have been made but the high pressure and temperature needed makes the process viable only for the industrial-quality diamonds that can be made more quickly. For the time being it is cheaper to dig gem diamonds from the earth than to produce them synthetically.

Simulants are diamond look-alikes but made in other materials. Marcasite, rock crystal and paste were being made in the 18th century but several cleverer and more deceptive simulants have reached the market since. The properties of simulants can be tested in several ways, one of which will invariably expose them for what they are. Paste tends to have abraded edges to its facets and its refractive index is lower than that of diamond. Diamonair too has a lower refractive index; it also has a higher specific gravity, though its 'fire' is strong enough to imitate a diamond. Strontium titanate is too soft to be polished as highly as a diamond, yet its dispersion is five times that of diamond and gives a quite spectacular sparkle. Cubic zirconium, which also has an impressive sparkle, is widely used today but the colours look a little weak and soapy.

The Background

Diamonds in their natural state look rather like soda crystals and were probably ignored by primitive man in favour of prettier stones such as rubies and emeralds. By about 800 BC some polishing skills had been learnt in India and diamonds began to be worn.

The Romans are known to have bought them for their magical powers. Several emperors collected precious stones and, according to Pliny, Caligula's wife was smothered in precious stones whose great value she was ready to prove by showing the receipts. In the Middle Ages they were believed to have the power to cure lunatics and win lawsuits. According to Hindu tradition they had medicinal value, though when diamond powder was prescribed to the ailing Pope Clement VII in 1532 he failed to survive the fourteenth spoonful.

Elizabeth I of England possessed some diamonds, although portraits usually show her clothes profusely decorated with pearls. In the 17th century the diamond came into its own when trade with India brought more diamonds into circulation in Europe and when, in around 1650, Vincenzio Perruzzi invented the early form of brilliant cut which showed the diamond's great brilliance and fire for the first time.

India was the world's only source of diamonds until the 18th century. A French jeweller, Jean-Baptiste Tavernier, visited the Golconda Valley near Hyderabad in 1683 and reported seeing 60,000 men, women and children shovelling soil from the River Kristna into pans and washing away the sand in the hope of finding diamonds. Some of the largest diamonds ever found came from India and many are still among the family jewels of Indian princes.

Diamonds were discovered in Brazil in 1725. The alluvial deposits were worked by 40,000 black slaves who dug the gravel by spade and carried it to special washing compartments. White overseers seated on high chairs and holding long whips supervised this part of the operation. Any slave finding a diamond weighing over $17\frac{1}{2}$ carats was rewarded with his freedom.

Brazil took over from India as the world's largest supplier of diamonds until the diamond fields of South Africa began to be worked in the 1860s. Africa continues to be the largest source of diamonds though vast new deposits were discovered in Western Australia in the 1970s, notably at Ashton. Production from this source is expected to run at a peak of 25 million carats a year from 1985. Less than a fifth of this amount will be of gem quality but even so confidence in the diamond-producers' ability to maintain, let alone raise, prices has not been bolstered by this news.

The discovery of major diamond deposits in the Soviet Union was announced in 1954. About 25% of the world's annual production is accounted for by Soviet diamonds. A fifth of this output is of gem quality and is sent to London for sale by De Beers and, increasingly, in already polished form to Antwerp.

The Outlook

Gem diamonds compete with other luxury goods such as fur coats and other precious stones. But their intrinsic appeal could not be more solidly based and there can be no serious threat to demand. After all, the attention-seeking aspect of jewellery is well understood. From the moment diamonds were perceived to be beautiful and attractive they also became valuable. And as soon as they became valuable they became desirable.

The recent development of the market for investment diamonds sealed in a pack shows that the attraction of diamonds as a store of wealth and as an investment has been conflated with, if not superseded by, their physical attraction.

The outlook for demand for large diamonds as a symbol of wealth is mixed. On the one hand, rich people, for reasons of social conscience or from fear of violent crime, like to keep a lower profile these days. Auction houses note that the strongest reason for selling jewellery today is that the owners do not have or do not take the opportunity of wearing it.

The quantity of large stones from old-established mines is declining, but rising production from the Soviet Union and Botswana is already proving hard to absorb. In the past a key selling point for large diamonds was that as mines were worked out fewer were discovered. That may still be true but the overall production figure is rising.

The Central Selling Organization is the marketing arm of De Beers through which the main diamond producers, including the Soviet Union, sell their production. The CSO handles 80% of all gem dia-

monds sold. Nearly all of these pass through London where they are sorted into 2000 grades of colour, clarity, weight and shape. These rough stones are offered at fixed prices to some three hundred dealers, known as the direct buyers, ten times a year. At these sales, known as 'sights', a dealer is offered a parcel of diamonds on a take it or leave it basis.

Leaving aside their role as investments, gem diamonds are luxury goods for which demand can fall sharply during a recession. In the past the CSO has sought to stabilize prices at such times by offering fewer diamonds at their sights and adding the rest to their stockpile. It was argued that this artificially induced stability in diamond prices benefited everyone in the diamond industry from miner to retailer. Yet this was not enough to prevent serious hardship and numerous bankruptcies throughout the industry during the 1979–82 recession.

De Beers reported that the encouraging trend of polished diamond sales was maintained into 1986. That may be good news for mining companies and retail jewellers. Meanwhile, the slide in the price of investment grade stones is levelling out. Given strong world stock markets, prices should stabilize at 1986 levels but no better performance is currently in prospect.

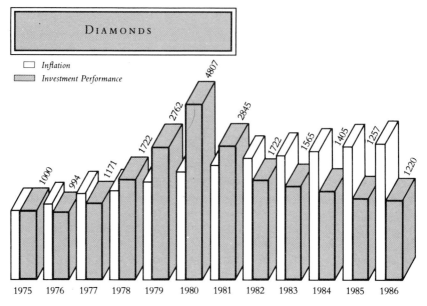

DIAMONDS

☐ Inflation
▨ Investment Performance

1000 994 1171 1722 2762 4807 2845 1722 1565 1405 1257 1220

| 1975 | 1976 | 1977 | 1978 | 1979 | 1980 | 1981 | 1982 | 1983 | 1984 | 1985 | 1986 |

Components: twenty-five 1 carat diamonds ranging in colour from D to H, and in clarity from Flawless to VS2. Adapted from the index published by the Diamond High Council in Antwerp. Figures are based on dollar prices.

Further Reading

Eric Bruton, *Diamonds* (London, 1970)

Godehard Lenzen, *The History of Diamond Production and the Diamond Trade* (London, 1970)

S. Tolansky, *The History and Use of Diamond* (London, 1962)

Timothy Green, *The World of Diamonds* (London, 1981)

Michael Weinstein, *The World of Jewel Stones* (London, 1958)

COINS

THE COIN market as a whole has risen by 110% since 1975. That overall figure takes in three indexes – Ancient Greek and Roman, United States and United Kingdom coins. Without the index of US coins, which has risen in sterling terms by 260% but only 130% in dollar terms, the overall figure would come down to 55% – one of the worst performances of any sector of the alternative investment market.

The market has reached three peaks over the last twenty years – in 1967/8, 1973/4 and 1979/80 – and it is tempting to interpret this as the coin market's regular six-year cycle. The real significance of these dates, however, is that they coincide with periods of high activity in the precious metals markets.

The price of silver bullion doubled in the year to May 1968; the price of gold doubled in the year to January 1974 and trebled in the year to January 1980. There seemed to be two basic reasons why the coin market should have responded so directly to precious metals. First, many numismatic coin dealers also deal in bullion coins – that is, coins whose value is based almost entirely on the intrinsic value of the metal they contain. Turnover was heavy while the gold price was rising and these dealers made large sums both from dealing and from their personal positions in the market. One natural home for their profits was numismatic coins.

The second reason is sometimes hard to believe but it seems that a surprising number of investors, on hearing that silver and gold were rising fast, have assumed that by buying any attractive old coin in silver or gold they will be getting a place on the bandwagon. They ignore the important point that the value of the gold in a coin valued by collectors for historical, aesthetic or any other reasons may be a small fraction of its market value. These buyers imagined that they were taking a position in a market which would respond to movements in bullion prices but as soon as this wave of buying was over coin prices fell back.

However irrational it may seem, a recovery in the gold price is still likely to inject life into the coin market. Dealers and auctioneers have seen many false dawns since prices fell in 1980 but some still expect to see coin prices recover gradually even if the gold and silver markets do not.

Generalizations about the coin market are nearly always misleading. There are dozens of national markets, each one dependent on the state of the domestic economy, the level of its currency and the trend in the collecting/investing population. Each market is also stratified in terms of price and quality. Demand for coins in the finest condition may be strong, and yet for the same coins in the lower grades it may be non-existent.

Over the last decade the growing

importance of grading has transformed the market. The gap in prices between coins in EF (Extremely Fine) condition and VF (Very Fine) condition and between other grades has been widening. In the United States collectors are getting more and more obsessed with condition. The accepted grading system is more elaborate, running from a top mark of MS (Mint State) 70 down to Fa (Fair) 2. The differences between MS 67 and MF 65 may not be visible to the naked eye, but the better coin may be worth as much as five times more than the other. Such distinctions make it easy for dealers to run circles round the amateur.

The case against coins as an investment today appears to be strong. Collectors have been put off by several developments, not least the rising number of counterfeits in circulation. These range from superb coins struck from dies engraved by Wilhelm Becker in 19th century Germany to a whole range of gold coins struck in Beirut in the 1970s. An international bureau was set up to circulate blown-up photographs of the coins to dealers showing the details by which they might be recognized. Damage has also been done by Franklin Mint and others promoting limited editions of coins and medals at prices up to ten times the value of the metal in which they were struck.

This would not matter if the artistry of these pieces justified such a price. But it so happens that when resold these are very seldom worth more than the scrap value of the metal.

The gold price itself has twice fallen by 50% over the last fifteen years and this instability has shaken confidence in coins. Furthermore, the supply of gold is expected to rise through to 1990 at least and prospects for a recovery are not encouraging.

Another deterrent to collecting coins is that although at their best they rank indisputably as works of art, they are more difficult to display than paintings, ceramics and silver and are therefore inclined to be passed by in favour of art-forms that are more easily shown and appreciated.

The poor investment performance of coins has itself put off existing and would-be collectors. Over the last twenty years UK coins rose in value by over 1000% but the greater part of that rise occurred in the early 1970s and the momentum of the market then has never been recovered. Although dealers can hardly hope for a drop in the market, many feel coins are just too expensive to attract new collectors. They also complain that the coinage of today compares unfavourably in design with the great artistry of earlier periods and is therefore unlikely to stimulate the younger generation to collect.

Buying Coins

1 Avoid coins in grades lower than EF 30.

2 Beware of coins that have been 'tooled up' – that is, where the details have been sharpened up in an attempt to improve the grade.

3 Be cautious about coins that appear to be bargains. They could be counterfeit.

4 Buy coins that are easy to sell. When the market is weak demand dries up for all but the best material.

Ancient Greek and Roman Coins

Ancient Greek and Roman coins have been a disappointing investment for some time. The index has risen just 35% since 1975 and in some cases prices have not yet climbed back to the heady levels reached in 1972–3.

New collectors in this field sometimes assume that ancient coins are rare, likely to be worn and are certain to climb in value. These assumptions are wrong. Millions of ancient coins have survived and more are coming to light all the time. Though most would be graded somewhere in the bottom half of the scale (see table on page 196), a good many are still in near-mint condition and it is only these that are of interest to serious collectors. These are also the coins that investors should go for. The case for getting into the market now is by no means strong, though if this field is ever going to catch up the ground it has lost the capital gain made by buyers today would be large.

Between 1971 and 1973 ancient coin prices rose by 100% to 200%. It was then that the gold price which had been shackled at $35 an ounce by the central banks for thirty-six years was finally freed to find its own level and duly soared to $200. Ancient coin prices dropped by 50% or more in 1974 reflecting the movement in gold. They resumed a steady climb through to 1980, by which time they had doubled again.

High interest rates and the deepening recession then deterred collectors and investors from buying. A spate of newly discovered hoards had also rocked the market, and ancient coins still have a nasty habit of turning up several hundred at a time. Whenever this happens it is not only the price of the coin in question that is affected; confidence in the whole market takes

Lucania, Heraklia (c. 433–400 BC), didrachm, £800.

Sicily, Syracuse (c. 414–407 BC), dekadrachm, £5500.

Sicily, Syracuse, Hieron (275–215 BC), 16-litrai, £700.

a knock. In 1980 a London dealer was offered forty Athenian silver *tetra-drachms*. Assured that this constituted the entire hoard, he took a chance and bought the lot. Soon he discovered other dealers who had swallowed the same story and bought similar numbers. The market was awash with Athenian *tetradrachms* – another thousand or so were in circulation – and prices fell.

Throughout Europe and around the Mediterranean metal detectors are turning up more than enough Roman and Greek coins to worry investors. This weekend treasure-hunting is popular because there is much to be found and prospectors seldom come back empty-handed. The fact that it is illegal in some parts of the Middle East seems to bother nobody.

Although at its lowest coin-collecting may be no more than a socially acceptable form of hoarding, in the case of ancient coins there are good reasons why demand should always be strong. In the first place, both the Greek and Roman series constitute uniquely important sequences of historical data. The Greek series in particular throws light on the individual character and development of the city states. The coins depict heroes, gods, animals, local products and stories from local mythology. All of them help the historian to build a more complete picture of Greek civilization.

But to most collectors the historical value is subordinate to the artistry that runs through the series. A French numismatist rhapsodized over Greek coins as 'so many fragments taken from the frieze of the Parthenon' and they are rightly ranked as works of art. No coinage has ever quite managed to rival the creative vitality of the ancient Greek. In their culture it

Sicily, Syracuse (c. 380 BC), gold 100-litrai, £14,500.

Constantius I (AD 305–6), 4 Aurei, £28,000.

Septimius Severus, Caracalla and Geta, Aureus, £6000.

Septimius Severus, Julia Domna, Caracalla and Gerta, Aureus, £9000.

was not only the coins that were admired but also the men who engraved the dies. Many cut their signature into the dies and are therefore known by name today. The coins engraved by Kimon and Euanetos in Syracuse during the 5th century BC are among the most beautiful of all coins. Not often seen in the market today these Syracuse *dekadrachms* can be worth over £10,000 and if nicely struck could yet be a sound investment.

One of the idiosyncracies of the coin market is that some dealers are choosy about their customers. Some look over their prospective buyers as though they were being asked for their daughter's hand in marriage. Some suitors are not even shown the trays containing the best coins and may end up buying grade two material.

Dealers have been known to regard investors as brazen and vulgar – in short, unworthy custodians of any great coin and the less scrupulous have been known to make the straightforward investor pay for his motives in another way. For it follows that the less a buyer cares about a coin the less he will notice its finer points and the more easily he can be swindled. The grading of all coins is subjective, but in the case of ancient coins it is not only the wear that can be in dispute, it is the overall impression made by a coin and known in the trade as its 'style'.

As might be expected with hand-struck coins, some images are more accurately centred than others. Furthermore, the quality of the strike will depend on how early in the life of the die it was taken, and also on how hard and clean a blow it was struck. None of these factors lends itself to precise grading. Also of great interest to collectors are the subtle shades of metallic colour, known as

Caracalla and Geta, Aureus, £16,000.

Hadrian, Aureus, £2600.

Marcus Aurelius, Aureus, £300.

Postumus (AD 259–68), Aureus, £3000.

'toning', that old coins have acquired over the years.

These are the nuances of an ancient coin that go to establish its real value and no new collector or investor can expect to understand them fully. So investors who cannot be discerning about coins should try to be doubly discerning about coin dealers.

Septimus Severus, Aureus, £4700.

Caracalla, Aureus, £10,000.

Faustina, Aureus, £4000.

Price movements for coins in the Roman series have been steadier than for the Greek, perhaps because there are even more collectors to iron out the shifts in supply and demand.

The most remarkable feature of the Roman coinage – and an obvious theme for investors – is the series of portraits of the emperors running from 31 BC to AD 476. They are a tough-looking bunch and it is tempting to read into their features the characters so well known to history. Caligula looks cruel and capricious, Claudius amenable and wise, and Nero fat and psychotic.

Not only does the political history of Rome come to life through its coinage, her economic fortunes can also be followed through the weight and fineness of her coins. The costs of administering the Roman Empire were partly borne by the revenue from issuing coins. By the time of Caracalla the silver denarius which had been the cornerstone of the system was debased to just 40% silver. Later, things got so bad that the state refused to accept its own coin in payment of taxes and insisted instead on silver bullion. Demand for all this historically evocative material is strong and has been since the surge of interest in ancient coins that came with the Renaissance. Investors need have no fears of a sudden collapse in the market. But nor should they on present evidence expect anything but sluggish growth over the next decade.

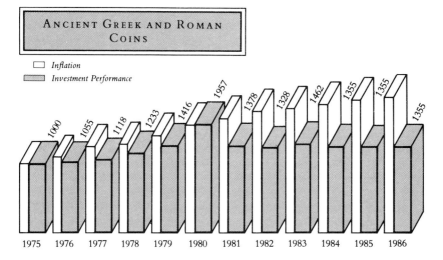

ANCIENT GREEK AND ROMAN COINS

☐ *Inflation*
▨ *Investment Performance*

1000 · 1055 · 1118 · 1233 · 1416 · 1957 · 1378 · 1328 · 1462 · 1355 · 1355 · 1355

1975　1976　1977　1978　1979　1980　1981　1982　1983　1984　1985　1986

Components: a selection of Greek and Roman silver and gold coins, including Sicilian and Athenian *tetradrachms*, Lucania Metapontum Stater, Alexander III Stater, Ptolemy II Octodrachm, Julius Caesar Denarius, Caligula Sestertius, Otho Denarius, Hadrian Aureus and Constantine I Solidus

English Coins

The English coin index is up 60% since 1975. Within this figure gold coins have climbed 30% and silver 90%. If such growth rates are to be repeated in future the field would hold little interest for investors. Perhaps the most disappointing aspect of the index is that the gold coins managed a rise of just 60% between 1975 and 1980 when the gold price was rising strongly. Gold coins in Extremely Fine condition are up 60%, while those in Very Fine condition are up only 25%.

Reasons for the weakness of the English market are broadly similar to those in other markets. An extra factor affecting gold was the run-off during the mid-1970s of the premium at which British sovereigns then traded. As the krugerrand came to dominate the bullion coin market in the United Kingdom investors began to recognize that a 50% premium over melt price for a coin that had been minted in millions made no sense. There was even a time when half sovereigns, because they were in such demand for use in jewellery, fetched more than sovereigns.

The discovery of hoards has upset the market from time to time. The William I silver penny was once among the rarest Norman coins until a hoard of 8640 was unearthed in Hampshire in 1833 and it became one of the commonest overnight. Less spectacular finds are being made all the time. Most coins are found in poor condition but even these do the coin market no good. The Lebanese counterfeiters created havoc with the market for George III spade guineas, Victoria Gothic crowns and Victoria jubilee five pounds. All had been central to English coin-collecting, but now had to be treated with the greatest caution. The George III spade guinea worth £125 in 1975 is worth no more today; the Queen Victoria Gothic crown has managed to double to £275; and the Queen Victoria five pounds is up just 20% at £450.

English coin collectors have also been put off by the promoters of commemorative coins and medals. The proliferation of *proof* or *specimen* coins issued in the mid-1970s would not have mattered so much if they were not also promoted as investments. Often the 'limited issue' argument was used – even by the Royal Mint – to persuade buyers of the coins' investment potential. Whereas previously a limited issue might have numbered 500 to 10,000 sets and so justified some claim to rarity, the Royal Mint's 'Last Sterling' souvenir set was believed to have run to three-quarters of a million.

Several private mints in Britain and the United States profited by the surge of interest in coins during the 1960s by marketing limited editions of medallions. The Shakespeare Medals for instance, marketed in 1971

Scotland, Charles I, £1500.

Elizabeth I, sovereign of 30 shillings, £1800.

Victoria, proof halfcrown (not used) (1864), £2800.

Elizabeth I, halfcrown (1602), £2100.

Charles II, 5 guineas (1679), £6800.

William and Mary, guinea (1694), £1750.

George I, 5 guineas (1716), £6000.

Charles I, triple unite (1644), £8000.

Charles II, 5 guineas (1669), £8800.

George IV, pattern five pounds (1826), £5600.

at £220, contained £28 worth of silver. The Kings and Queens of England set had about the same retail and melt values; gold medallions and coins were usually better value at three to five times their melt value. The editions were said to be limited, though the final figure is thought to have been fixed only after all the applicants' cheques had been counted.

Since then, salerooms have often turned away would-be sellers explaining that they stand little chance of recovering more than the melt value of the metal they contain. More often than not such sets have been bought by investors who are least able to stand the loss.

During the early 1970s the Swiss and Japanese were known to have bought into English coins; a few outstanding collections came on the market, including rare Scottish gold coins, and were sold for record prices.

Lecturers were even in demand for numismatic study groups and the future looked bright. But as the gold price began to slide during 1975/6 interest slackened into apathy. Collectors who had been horrified by the investor invasion were not willing to pay the new inflated prices and shrewdly waited for prices to fall. Nobody quite expected prices to stagnate for so long and dealers are mystified that coins in what used to be thought collectable condition are finding no takers.

The English coin market has simply been transformed. Buyers are only interested, whether they think of themselves as collectors or investors, in coins that are right up in the top 5% or 10% of the grading scale, for only they are acceptable to the fastidious eye and only they on past evidence stand a chance of performing well.

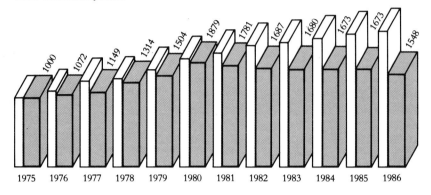

ENGLISH COINS

☐ Inflation
▨ Investment Performance

1000 1072 1149 1314 1504 1879 1781 1687 1680 1673 1673 1548

1975 1976 1977 1978 1979 1980 1981 1982 1983 1984 1985 1986

Components: 100 gold and silver coins from William I to Elizabeth II

UK Coin Grading Scale

FDC *Fleur-de-coin.*
Mint state, unused, flawless, without any wear, scratches or marks.

Unc. *Uncirculated.*
A coin in new condition as issued by the Royal Mint, but, owing to modern mass-production methods of manufacture, not necessarily perfect.

EF *Extremely Fine.*
A coin that shows little sign of having been in circulation, but which may exhibit slight surface marks on very close inspection.

VF *Very Fine.*
Only slight traces of wear on the raised surfaces; a coin that has had only slight circulation.

F *Fine.*
Considerable signs of wear on the raised surfaces, or design weak through faulty striking.

Fair.
A coin that is worn, but which has the inscriptions and main features of the design still distinguishable, or a piece that is very weakly struck.

Poor.
A very worn coin, of no value as a collector's piece unless extremely rare.

Note:
'Proof' signifies a coin struck with extra care from special dies with mirror-like or matt finish. It does not describe the state of preservation.

American Coins

The index of American coins is up 260% in sterling terms since 1975. Most of this rise is accounted for by the fall in the value of the pound against the dollar. The rise in dollar terms has been just 110%.

From 1975 to 1980 prices rose strongly. In the final year the rise was fuelled by profits taken in the silver and gold bullion markets. Prices dropped back in 1981 and drifted lower still in 1982 and 1983. Dealers were talking of recovery during 1984 and 1985 and saleroom prices now confirm that the market is nearly back to its 1980 level.

There are two million coin collectors in the United States and the number is rising. Of these only 5% would spend over $500 on a coin and it is they who determine the course of the market. For them the $20 double eagle, containing just under one ounce of pure gold, has been a favourite though sometimes hazardous investment. For it can be worth either the melt value of the gold it contains or a hundred times as much. The same applies to the majority of American gold coins; all depends on their rarity and condition.

A double eagle worth only its melt value would be a badly worn or damaged specimen that no collector would touch. Moving up the scale a double eagle in Fine condition is currently worth 10% to 20% over melt value though the premium fluctuates all the time. Even these coins are treated more or less like bullion. One New York dealer sells two hundred a week to Chinese restaurateurs needing a safe haven for their profits. Another dealer, acting for an investment company, may put a buying order for a thousand double eagles on the Reuter screen and this will be seen

1795. Silver Dollar, Heraldic Eagle, £270.

1795. Silver Dollar. Flowing Hair Type, £1240.

1822. Silver Half Dollar. Capped Bust Type, £110.

1803. Gold Eagle (10 dollars). Capped Bust Type, £3000.

1903. Gold Eagle. 10 Dollars. Coronet Type, £230.

1904. Morgan Dollar. Silver, £1470.

instantly by dealers around the world. This is not unlike the markets for cocoa and copper and differs significantly from the kind that interests the serious collector. He is after coins in Extremely Fine or Uncirculated condition or in the finest grades he can afford. As well as buying a piece of gold he is acquiring an item of numismatic interest. Provided he is not hoodwinked over the coin's condition he stands to make more from his investment than the bullion-oriented buyer.

Coin-collecting in the United States has a long if not specially illustrious history. The few existing collectors in the early 19th century went mainly for rarities such as the 1793 cent and the 1815 half eagle. During the 1850s when dealers began to hold coin auctions, interest spread fast and by the time the *American Journal of Numismatics* was launched in May 1866 there were 3000 collectors. But even in the early days there were problems and the market showed signs of developing into the jungle it is today. The first issue reported '... prices have risen a hundredfold and in some cases almost incalculably and unreasonably. Speculation has been rife. In many instances, we regret to say, dishonesty has exhibited itself in its most glaring and disgusting form.'

Some dealers had secret ties with the Philadelphia Mint and were able to get hold of restrikes, proofs and other issues bearing dates previously unknown to numismatists. Efforts were made to tighten things up, but shenanigans at the Mint continued well into the 20th century. Numismatists had often protested that old dies were not destroyed and though directors of the Mint promised that the abuses would be stopped it was impossible to prevent a few 'fancy

1851. *United States Assay Office of Gold. 50 Dollars, £7800.*

1908. *Gold Eagle. 10 Dollars. Indian Head Type, £300.*

1893. *Silver Half Dollar. Barber or Liberty Head Type, £2000.*

1882. *Gold 3 Dollars, £1200.*

1904. *Quarter Eagle. 2½ Dollars. Coronet Type, £970.*

pieces' being struck while official backs were turned.

There was also bad feeling between dealers about the flattering description of coins offered at their auctions. And plenty of mud was slung at dealers who, by mistake or otherwise, catalogued counterfeit coins as genuine. Condition at this period was important though the market did not move into its obsessional phase until the 1970s and high premiums would not be paid for an uncirculated piece unless of a very early issue.

Coins of certain dates were known to be rare, and so too were coins in the finest condition. But a third criterion of rarity became important in the 1890s with the publication of Augustus G. Heaton's *Treatise on the Coinage of the United States Branch Mints*. Heaton had discovered that in the early days of the Carson City Mint many coins were struck in quite small numbers. His treatise detailed the quantities minted there and at New Orleans, Dahlonega, Charlotte and San Francisco, as well as giving seventeen reasons for collecting mint marks.

The most compelling of these was that certain silver and gold coins – only these bore mint marks – of common date were actually rare and valuable. Countless Americans began to search their change and many turned collector. Premiums paid for rare mint marks began to rise and are now important in the market's price structure.

Today, the 1891 double eagle with the mint mark S for San Francisco just below the eagle is worth $700 in Mint State while a specimen with the CC mint mark for Carson City, of which only 5000 were struck, is worth $5500. Even larger premiums are paid for the major rarities; one of the twenty-four San Francisco dimes

1892. Double Eagle. 20 Dollars, £4000.

minted in 1894 changed hands in 1980 for $145,000; the regular 1894 dime struck in Philadelphia is worth only $210 in Mint State.

Coin-collecting was transformed in the 20th century by B. Max Mehl whose immensely successful *Star Rare Coin Encyclopedia* quoted high prices for rarities such as the 1913 Liberty Head nickel. There were complaints that streetcars were held up while conductors searched their change for rarities.

Over the years the market became increasingly investment conscious. Some buyers still make monthly payments to dealers who have complete discretion in choosing coins which are then sent direct to the buyer's bank. There must be instances where this arrangement works out well; in general though, it is asking for trouble, and investors who have not taken the trouble to learn how coins are valued nor checked on the purchases have come badly unstuck.

The performance of top-quality coins from now on will depend partly on collectors' and investors' willingness to go on paying the current sky-high premiums. To Europeans these have the look of an elaborate dealer-orchestrated hype. A coin graded Mint State 65 according to the ANA system can be worth ten times as much as the same coin in Mint State 60; in Europe the better coin might be worth just twice the lower grade coin.

In a way the premium does make sense. No one thinks a collector odd for aspiring to own the finest work in any other field, and certainly the gap between the prices paid for a great Renoir and one of his everyday sketches has been widening. The premium is not absurd as such; rather it may be unwise to pay it when the physical differences between, say, MS 63 and MS 65 are barely perceptible to the naked eye. And, as the ANA points out, grading is a subjective business and two professionals will often come up with different grades on the same coin.

The outlook for prices to 2000 is mixed. Coins in the lower grades, that is VF 30 and below, may creep up at a few per cent a year. Those above VF 30 and up to AU 50 should do a little better. Those above AU 50 can be expected to be more volatile. A strong stock market and a strong gold price will push prices ahead for all grades but should get prices for AU 50 and above rising faster, maybe above 15% a year. But investors who plan to buy coins in the highest grades should get them graded by the ANA before writing out the cheque.

In March 1986 a group of respected American dealers came up with Professional Coin Grading Service. Each coin submitted is graded by three experts and sealed into a clear hard plastic holder bearing their consensus view on its grade. The extra precision and consistency achieved by this method is significant. Equally important to investors is the agreement of thirty leading American dealers to quote daily bid/ask prices for coins so graded and to buy such coins for cash at the bid price without even seeing the coin. This combination of uncontested grading and liquidity should give the market a boost.

The popular numismatic press has tried to gloss over the market's shake-out of the last five years. The weekly *Coin Dealer Newsletter*, gives a detailed and more objective view of the market.

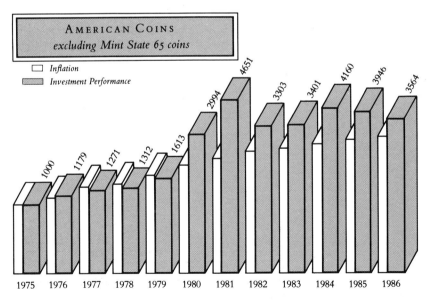

AMERICAN COINS
excluding Mint State 65 coins

☐ Inflation
▨ Investment Performance

1975: 1000 1976: 1179 1977: 1271 1978: 1312 1979: 1613 1980: 2994 1981: 4651 1982: 3303 1983: 3401 1984: 4160 1985: 3946 1986: 3564

Components: A selection of 1 dollar, 5 dollar and 20 dollar gold coins, early half dimes and dollars, proof, commemorative and mint sets. Grades range from Very Fine to Extremely Fine.

US Coin Grading Scale

(Basic categories laid down by the
American Numismatic Association.)

Mint State	The terms Mint State (MS) and Uncirculated (Unc.) are interchangeably used to describe coins showing no trace of wear. Such coins may vary to some degree because of blemishes, toning or slight imperfections as described in the following subdivisions.	About Uncirculated (AU 50)	Has traces of light wear on many of the high points. At least half of the mint lustre is still present.
		Choice Extremely Fine (EF 45)	Light overall wear shows on highest points. All design details are very sharp. Some of the mint lustre is evident.
Perfect Uncirculated (MS 70)	Perfect new condition, showing no trace of wear. The finest quality possible, with no evidence of scratches, handling or contact with other coins. Very few regular issue coins are ever found in this condition.	Extremely Fine (EF 40)	Design is lightly worn throughout, but all features are sharp and well defined. Traces of lustre may show.
		Choice Very Fine (VF 30)	Light even wear on the surface and highest parts of the design. All lettering and major features are sharp.
Choice Uncirculated (MS 65)	An above average Uncirculated coin which may be brilliant or lightly toned and has very few contact marks on the surface or rim. MS-67 or MS-63 indicates a slightly higher or lower grade of preservation.	Very Fine (VF 20)	Shows moderate wear on high points of design. All major details are clear.
		Fine (F 12)	Moderate to considerable even wear. Entire design is bold with overall pleasing appearance.
Uncirculated (MS 60)	Has no trace of wear but may show a number of contact marks, and surface may be spotted or lack some lustre.	Very Good (VG 8)	Well worn with main features clear and bold although rather flat.
		Good (G 4)	Heavily worn with design visible but faint in areas. Many details are flat.
Choice About Uncirculated (AU 55)	Barest evidence of light wear on only the highest points of the design. Most of the mint lustre remains.	Fair (FA 2)	Coin has sufficient design and lettering to be identified. Excessive wear.

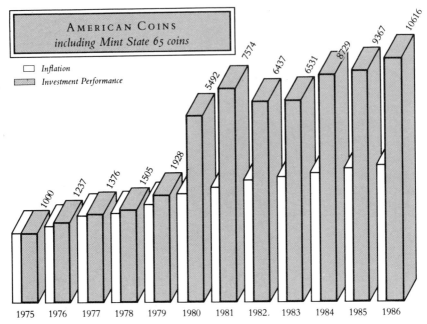

Components: A selection of 1 dollar, 5 dollar and 20 dollar gold coins, early half dimes and dollars, proof, commemorative and mint sets. Grades range from Very Fine to Mint State 65

Further Reading

Chester L. Krause and Clifford Mischler, *Standard Catalog of World Coins* (Wisconsin, 1986)

Martin Jessop Price (ed.), *Coins: an Illustrated Survey 650 BC to the Present Day* (London, 1980)

R. A. G. Carson, *Coins: Ancient, Medieval and Modern* (London, 1970)

G. K. Jenkins, *Greek Coins* (London, 1972)

C. M. Kraay, *Archaic and Classical Greek Coins* (London, 1976)

T. V. Buttrey, *Coinage of the Americas* (New York, 1973)

D. R. Sear, *Greek Coins and Their Values* (London, 1978)

R. P. Mack, *The Coinage of Ancient Britain* (London, 1975)

R. A. G. Carson, *The Coinage of Ancient Britain* (London, 1975)

STAMPS

PRICES FOR stamps of Great Britain are standing at 145% above their 1975 level. That may not seem too bad a performance but as the index shows the stamp market is only now recovering from its worst crisis ever. The trouble began in 1978 when prices for several issues such as the George V Sea Horses and the 1929 £1 Postal Union Congress began to rise unaccountably fast. Having doubled between 1975 and 1978, they doubled again by the end of 1979. As usual, those shadowy scapegoats 'the speculators' were held responsible, but it was a handful of dealers who had been promoting stamps as an investment who were more to blame.

Stamp-investment promotions outside the United Kingdom, often orchestrated by unscrupulous dealers, have a long and colourful history. In the early 1960s the Italian dealer Raybaudi, who had a lucrative contract to market new Vatican issues, began to publish price lists showing the values of earlier Vatican issues climbing fast. Soon prices were going up daily. One philatelist recalls being in Raybaudi's office when a secretary asked what price she should quote a collector for one of the 1934 Vatican Provisionals. Raybaudi glanced at his watch before replying, 'Eighty-five thousand lire – until noon.' Such manipulation can never work for long; the bubble burst days later and Raybaudi was finished.

In the 1970s prices in Britain were hyped by a device already well tried in the United States. At fringe auctions one dealer and an accomplice, usually in collusion with the auctioneer, would bid up the prices of their own stamps to 'establish' new price levels. These would later be used by the dealers as base prices from which to sell other copies of the same stamps and even enabled them to offer generous discounts off the 'going market rate'.

Once the market was primed, genuine bidders appeared at long-established and respected salerooms and helped to drive prices higher still. The progress of the £1 blue-green Sea Horse (George V) in unmounted mint condition was typical of the market. It sold for £12 in 1950, £13 in 1960, £100 in 1970, £250 in 1975, £1000 in 1978 and peaked at £3000 in 1979. The market cracked in early 1980 and by 1982 the price was back to £700. Today the price has climbed slowly back to £800.

But it was not only the collapse in prices that burnt so many fingers. In the scramble to buy, inexperienced investors overlooked all the little nuances of condition that really determine the value of a stamp. They were sold stamps that had been regummed, cleaned, repaired and, in the case of some imperforate issues, had even been given new margins. Those who bought from the stamp-investment companies discovered that they had been sold material no

Block of 18 penny blacks, £150,000.

serious philatelist would allow in his album and had been charged up to five or ten times the true market price. Such people are not easy to protect. Even after recent legislation requiring those setting up as investment advisers or brokers to register, unscrupulous dealers in stamps and other alternative investments remain unfettered in the prices they charge and the forecasts they make. For the more astute investor, an analysis of recent events provides some useful thoughts on how to get it right now.

Having settled for a country in which to specialize, investors must decide on a period. The worst affected period during the market collapse of 1980–3 was the 20th century, traditionally divided into the so-called middle issues from 1901 to the mid-1930s and the later period up to the present day. The 'classics' of Queen Victoria's reign were badly but less seriously affected. The 1867–83 £5 orange on white paper moved from £30 in 1950 to £1200 in 1975 and on to a peak of £3500 in 1979. A post-boom low was reached at £750

in early 1981 and the price has now climbed back to £1500.

For several years before the dramatic rise and fall of 1975–80 interest had been growing in what the trade calls 'entires' – that is, used stamps on their original covers. These often carry several stamps whose cancellations and other marks sometimes make it possible to trace the route taken by the letter right across the world. These are certainly more evocative than stamps in their soaked-off state and look set to develop into the speciality of the thinking collector. Stanley Gibbons's catalogue introduced its 'third column' in 1981, giving the value for a stamp on cover as well as for used and mint copies. The 'on-cover' price is not unusually five times that of the simple used stamp and it seems that such premiums are here to stay. Prices in this area will always be harder to monitor because each item is unique. The handwriting of the sender, the shape, colour and condition of the cover and other details contribute to its attraction, and hence to its value.

1867–83 £5 orange, £1500.

1883–4 5/- rose, £150.

1880–3 4d grey-brown, £50.

1887–92 £1 green 'Jubilee', £800.

1854–7 2d blue, £400.

1902–10 £1 green, £400.

1902–10 2/6, £50.   1902–10 5/-, £80.

1934 10/- indigo, £120.

1913–19 2/6 brown, £35.

1924–6 1½d tête-bêche pair, £125.

1929 Postal Union Congress £1, £250.

1935 Silver Jubilee 2½d Prussian Blue (colour error), £1500.

1939–48 10/- dark blue, £50.

1955–8 De La Rue printing, £1 black, £200.

The most promising strategy for the investor, and the one he is usually least willing to undertake, is to become an expert on one small field of collecting. Dealers have a saying that they make profits out of collectors to recoup the losses they make to philatelists. Most dealers do not know more than two or three fields in any depth, yet they feel obliged to carry stock covering a much wider range. That is how the really knowledgeable collector is able to recognize value where the majority of dealers cannot.

The world of stamps is made up of a thousand specialities each with more recondite subsectors of philatelic knowledge, its own literature and coterie of experts. A treatise was recently published, for example, on the 'Cancellations of Hungarian Post Offices on the First Five Issues of Austrian Stamps, 1850–67 during the Austrian Administration'. It ran to 640 pages and there can be no doubt that its author is well placed to recognize and value the interesting stamps in this field.

Such a study has legitimate philatelic interest in that it throws light on the workings of a particular postal service. Other study collections are merely eccentric, often reflecting a collector's obsession with one stamp. One such collection, offered to a New York dealer some years back, consisted of a Red Cross stamp of which a man had collected 446 corner blocks of eight and 381 corner blocks of four, each block showing on its margin different serial numbers. Catalogue value was around $3000 but in the absence of like-minded eccentrics, market value was perhaps $100.

There are also 'flyspeck philatelists' who will collect copies of a single stamp showing minimal variations in colour and even minute errors caused perhaps by a piece of grit sticking to the printing cylinder.

Buying and Selling

Stanley Gibbons in the UK and Scott in the United States are the catalogues that form the basis of all dealing in the English-speaking world. Although they are mines of philatelic information they are at bottom no more than dealers' price lists. As such they usually show the prices at which the dealers hope to sell and by no means constitute any kind of valuation. Moreover, it is quite common to see dealers offering stamps at 30% to 70% off catalogue prices, suggesting that their buying prices are lower still. Big discounts off catalogue prices do not necessarily mean good value and buyers must be wary about the condition of anything priced as a bargain.

Properly conducted auctions offer the investor the cheapest way into the market. The leading UK auctioneers, Harmers, Robson Lowe (now part of Christie's) and Stanley Gibbons, produce fine catalogues with reasonable statements on condition and with the better lots illustrated. Leaving bids with the auctioneer is a sound way to buy, though this act of faith in the auctioneer to buy as cheaply as possible on your behalf can be misplaced. Collectors and investors who continually find that lots have been knocked down to them at their limit bid usually remove their custom. Most auctioneers stick to a code of practice entitled 'Philatelic Auctioneers Standard Terms and Conditions of Sale' which allows buyers to return a stamp within an agreed time if he can prove it to be a forgery in the opinion of an expert committee.

Fakers have become so ingenious that investors often have valuable stamps 'expertised' before buying. Apart from helping them to sleep peacefully at night it raises the stamp's value when the time comes to sell. In the UK expert committees are formed by the Royal Philatelic So-ciety and the British Philatelic Federation. Each has been known to issue certificates of authenticity for stamps the other has rejected as forgeries. Similar certificates, usually on paper bearing a photograph of the stamp to be 'expertised', are issued by the Philatelic Foundation in New York and by official bodies throughout Europe.

Forgeries and Fakes

There are two kinds of stamp forgery – postal and philatelic. Postal forgeries, once undertaken to defraud the postal authorities, are seldom if ever produced today. Philatelic forgeries were more common and have been so ingeniously produced that they have become a collector's speciality in their own right. The brilliant forger Jean de Sperati operated undisturbed for many years in France where the law allowed reproductions of works of art, including stamps, to be sold provided they were described as such. Sperati produced his reproductions on genuine watermarked stamp paper after first bleaching out the genuine impression from a common stamp and then imposing his own photolithographic impression. When he retired in 1953 the British Philatelic Association bought up all his equipment and records to prevent them falling into more dangerous hands. Robson Lowe, the doyen of British philately, when about to publish a detailed account of every Sperati forgery, was offered £10,000 by a group of French dealers to suppress the section on French 'reproductions' which, Lowe was tempted to conclude, had been sold on as genuine stamps.

Fakes are stamps that have been upgraded for sale to collectors. Stamps can now be regummed, reperforated, have penmarks removed and be supplied with fine all-round margins. Some consider it legitimate to improve the appearance of a stamp by boiling, washing and ironing, and even by treating a sulphuretted stamp with hydrogen, but to use a chemical to change the colour of a stamp is ranked as faking.

Factors Affecting Value

Country of Origin

Every country follows a philatelic policy which determines its status among collectors. Some turned over the responsibility for issuing stamps to philatelic agencies whose object was to maximize revenue for themselves and the issuing country. The rise of these commercial philatelic agencies gathered pace in the 1960s as their success in exploiting thematic collectors grew. Stamp issues became too frequent, too large, and included unacceptably high denominations. Set after set on any theme that was known to interest collectors, from space travel to insects, was churned out. Some of the earliest countries to alienate collectors with their avalanche of commemoratives were Ghana, Tonga and Sierra Leone.

Today there are few countries – including the United States and the United Kingdom – that have not jumped aboard this bandwagon. As a result, the stamp world is more sharply divided than ever into philatelist-collectors and suckers. Though it is possible to find examples of commemoratives that have climbed in value, any hopes of a reasonable investment performance would be wholly misplaced.

Condition

An unofficial grading system similar to that used in the coin world is coming into use. The basic categories that are of interest to serious collectors remain the same.

1 Unmounted mint. The stamp must be in perfect state, as it left the printer. Gum impeccable, perforations intact and no stains, creases or thinnings.

2 Mounted mint. As above, with some minute traces of earlier hingeing or stamp mount.

3 Unused, part original gum. A stamp that has been heavily mounted but retains some of the original gum.

4 Unused, without gum. An unpostmarked copy that has at some time been stuck down, so that in soaking it off its gum has been removed.

5 Fine used. A stamp with the lightest postmark, but otherwise intact.

Argument rages on in philatelic circles over the status of the gum on a stamp. Some insist that it is an essential characteristic; others regard it as quite incidental. Meanwhile, some curators of museum collections have taken to soaking off the gum to prevent it cracking the paper, while others, including the curator of the Smithsonian collection, leave it in place, dooming the stamps, according to some philatelists, to eventual ruin.

All the teeth of the perforation should be present on a perforated stamp and the image should be perfectly centred between the margins. Centring and generous margins are also important in the case of imperforate issues.

Rarity is judged in the case of modern issues by the number of stamps comprising an issue and in relation to the number of collectors of this issuing country. If just one million copies of a commemorative were issued by the United Kingdom, this could prove a good investment because there are many more than a million collectors of Great Britain around the world. If a country with only a modest following were to issue the same number of commemoratives, the price would be unlikely to climb above face value.

All over the world people who might even describe themselves as collectors buy sheets of commemoratives as and when they are issued and store them away expecting to cash in at a profit some years hence. But those who try to sell find to their great indignation that even if they were to be offered face value, inflation would have turned their investment into a loss in real terms, and, worse, they may get only 20% to 30% below face value from a dealer who will sell on to a company looking to reduce the cost of its mailing shots.

The Background

The world's first adhesive postage stamps – the Penny Black and two-penny blue – were issued in 1840. They bore the portrait of the young Queen Victoria and were received with great enthusiasm. As early as 1845 a German magazine told its readers of England's 'very insignificant yet regular postal service' and noted that the new stamps 'with the Queen's heads [sic] look very pretty and the English reveal their strange character by collecting them'.

By the 1860s about a hundred different states and colonies had between them issued 1500 or so stamps and some were already worth a hundred times their face value. Several kings and maharajahs, and even Pope Pius IX, were known to be vying with each other to form the most complete collections. The high social status associated with the hobby helped it to catch on fast.

In 1865 Uruguay became the first country to issue unnecessary stamps and others soon realized that collectors were an easy source of revenue and stamps appeared with values that were too high for postal use. In 1895 the Society for the Suppression of Speculative Stamps was founded in the United States but some dealers refused to join a boycott. They felt it was alien to the spirit of philately to tell people what they should or should not collect and very gradually the stream of commemorative issues grew into the present-day flood causing millions to give up collecting altogether.

Until about 1890 people tended to collect every stamp they could find. But as the goal of completion became harder and eventually impossible to achieve, collectors restricted themselves to one country, one reign or, more recently, one theme.

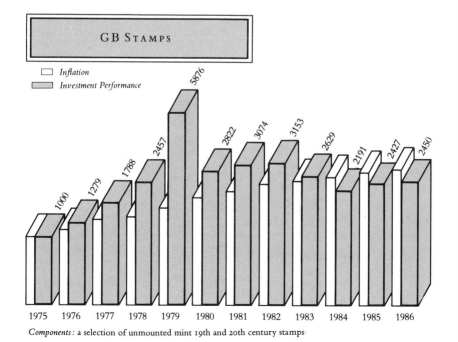

GB Stamps

☐ Inflation
☐ Investment Performance

1000   1279   1788   2457   5876   2822   3074   3153   2629   2191   2427   2450

1975   1976   1977   1978   1979   1980   1981   1982   1983   1984   1985   1986

Components: a selection of unmounted mint 19th and 20th century stamps

Dealers

Argyll Etkin Ltd
55 New Bond Street
London W1
01-499 1781

Cameo Stamp Centre
75 Strand
London WC 2
01-836 0997

Christie's Robson Lowe
47 Duke Street
London W1

David Brandon
77 Strand
London WC2
01-836 2704

Royale Stamp Co.
41 Bedford Street
London WC2

Stanley Gibbons
399 Strand
London WC2

David Field Ltd
41 New Bond Street
London W1
01-499 5252

Auctioneers

Harmers of London Stamp
    Auctioneers Ltd
91 New Bond Street
London W1

Plumridge & Co.
6 Adam Street
London WC2

Useful Addresses

The Royal Philatelic Society
41 Devonshire Place
London W1

British Philatelic Federation
314 Vauxhall Bridge Road
London SW1

Both societies have expert committees
which issue certificates of authenticity
(or otherwise) for stamps or other
philatelic material submitted.

Further Reading

Robson Lowe, *The British Postage
Stamp of the Nineteenth Century*
(London, 1979)

R. M. Willcocks, *England's Postal
History* (London, 1975)

Jiri Novacek, *Guide to Stamp Collecting*
(London, 1985)

R. C. Alcock and F. C. Holland, *The
Postmarks of Great Britain and Northern
Ireland, 1940* (Cheltenham, 1940)

James Mackay, *British Stamps* (London,
1985)

Stanley Gibbons, *Specialised Catalogue
of Great Britain*, 4 vols. (London, 1986)

American Stamps

The index of American stamps is showing a rise of 220% (100% in dollar terms) since 1975. The market peaked in 1981 with a rise of 270% (250% in dollar terms) and continually drifted lower until the beginning of 1985. The same problems have bedevilled stamp-collecting in United States as elsewhere. The growing avalanche of commemoratives has put off many who might otherwise have become collectors. Over four thousand millions copies of the 1931 2 cent commemorating the bicentennial of George Washington's birth were issued and it is hardly surprising that an unmounted mint copy is worth just 2 cents. In all, over 130,000 million commemorative stamps have been issued – the average per stamp coming out at around 160 million.

As in Europe the growth of television during the 1960s also caused a sharp drop in the numbers of schoolboys taking up collecting. Though for many years they swelled the total number of so-called collectors to new records, the fall-off seems to have mattered not at all. For, paradoxically, there are believed to be more serious collectors now than ever before. As in other fields of American collecting, a scholarly interest in the subject is evident at the expensive end of the market. The fall in prices from 1981 to the end of 1984 was bad enough but even the minor recovery of 1985 petered out in early 1986 and prices drifted lower. Market men do not doubt that a turnaround will come in time and when it does 19th century issues should do best. Among these the famous Postmaster Provisionals are tipped to perform strongly.

Soon after the penny postage was introduced in Britain, Americans began to clamour for a change in the extortionate rates they were charged. A single sheet of paper carried over four hundred miles cost 25 cents – equivalent to $1.60 today. If you wrote two sheets and used an envelope, it counted as three and cost thrice as much. The government acted in 1845, but during the two years to March 1847 when the postmaster general was authorized to issue stamps, postmasters in several cities had 5 and 10 cent stamps prepared and sold them to the public at a slight premium to cover costs. These stamps have, as two English philatelists L. N. and M. Williams wrote, 'in addition to the glamour surrounding them the spice of rarity and value that enables them to capture the imagination of philistine and collector alike'.

The first was issued by Robert H. Morris in New York on 12 July 1845. It was a 5 cent black bearing the head of George Washington taken from a contemporary banknote. To prevent counterfeits Morris countersigned each stamp RHM but later delegated the job to his brother-in-law Alonzo Castle Monzon. Used copies signed ACM are worth $350 today against $2250 for those bearing Morris's initials. Prices have underperformed the American index since 1975 but now look set to catch up.

Equally evocative are the Confederate Provisionals issued in the early days of the Civil War. Each of the thirteen rebel states provides a colourful story but that of Memphis, Tennessee, is typical. The Confederate Government took over postal affairs in the South as of 1 June 1861, but did not issue stamps until October. A Memphis newspaper reported that since Tennessee had seceded the previous Saturday it must expect an edict

1869 90c Abraham Lincoln, £12,000.

1908–10 Imperforate block 5c George Washington, £120.

1857 90c George Washington, £1000.

1845 Postmaster's Provisional (initials A.C.M.), £250.

1898 Trans-Mississippi Exposition, Omaha, $1, £800; $2, £1100.

1893 Columbian Exposition, $3, £700; $4, £1200; $5, £1500.

1845–6 St Louis, Missouri, 10c Postmaster's Provisional, £2000.

1933 Zeppelin set, £850.

from 'the despot enthroned at Washington' commanding the withdrawal of mail facilities. Sure enough Washington ordered the post office at Memphis to close. The Memphis postmaster replied that his honour, interest and inclination forbade compliance with these orders. He could not hand over as ordered 'every letter written by fathers, brothers, sisters, wives and children of our brave volunteers', for to do so would make him a traitor to his state and to the South. By the 19th he had issued the first Provisionals. The 2 cent blue adhesive is one of the crudest makeshift stamps ever issued. But that matters little. The stamps call up feelings of deep personal involvement at a time of crisis for the South and that is what really gives them a value. The 2 cent blue now ranges in price from

$80 for a mint copy to $900 used and up to $7500 for the same stamp on cover.

Though there are plenty of counterfeits and reprints – stamps printed at a later date from the original plate – for the collector to contend with, a different trap is set for the unwary today. A mint stamp is stuck on to a forged or original cover and cancelled. The hardest part of the operation is to make the cancellation look right but the rewards are high when it is successful.

A record price for a Confederate Provisional of $160,000 was paid in 1985 for a pair of Livingston, Alabama, 5 cents on cover at Christie's Robson Lowe in New York. On its last auction appearance in 1967 it sold for $19,000, suggesting an annual growth of 12% over the period. But Provisionals make up just one sector of a vast field that takes in special subjects such as patriotic covers from the Civil War period and potato tax stamps of 1935/6.

But whatever a collector's speciality it is well known that the value of his collection can be raised if it has won awards at philatelic exhibitions. Mug-hunting has therefore become a serious business. Entries for the competitions are judged on well-established points such as philatelic knowledge, original research, precise description, pleasing layout and, of course, the quality of the stamps themselves. One collector who had often shown some fine German material but was never awarded a higher medal than a bronze asked a New York dealer to help him improve the descriptions and layout. At the next exhibition the gold medal was duly won and the dealer found himself smothered in kisses by the delighted collector. And with reason, for the market value of his entry had just risen by 30%.

The American stamp market is no more or less rife with malpractices than any other. There will always be shady dealers and gullible collectors, and rip-off stories will always be picked up by the media. For all that, investors who pay and receive true market prices should find United States stamps, other than commemoratives, a sound investment.

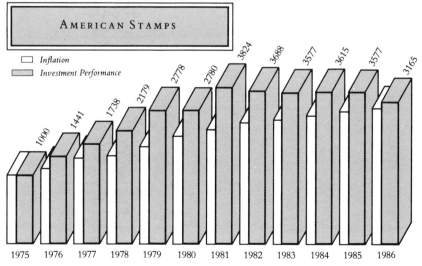

AMERICAN STAMPS

☐ Inflation
▨ Investment Performance

1000   1441   1738   2179   2778   2780   3824   3688   3577   3615   3577   3165

1975   1976   1977   1978   1979   1980   1981   1982   1983   1984   1985   1986

Components: a selection of fine used to very fine mint 19th and 20th century stamps

Further Reading

Lester G. Brookman, *United States Stamps of the Nineteenth Century*, 3 vols. (New York, 1947)

M. Johl, *United States Postage Stamps: 1902–1922* (New York, 1937)

Delf Norona, ed., *The Cyclopaedia of United States Postmarks and Postal History* (Moundsville, 1935)

Scott's Specialised Catalog of the United States (New York, 1986)

WINE

FOR OVER ten years claret, port and champagne have proved exceptionally good investments. The growing strength of the dollar against sterling over the 1980–5 period made wine for sale in London seem cheap to American buyers and their activity in the auction rooms has helped to produce remarkable rises in sterling terms.

While the sterling-dollar exchange rate will continue to affect London prices, the widespread swing towards wine consumption, often at the expense of spirits, will increase the demand for fine wines. For the great wines, pressure of demand has become intense. Some correction in the present steeply rising trend is already evident in 1986 prices, though in the longer term an annual growth of 15% or more should be maintained.

Claret

The vintage claret index – made up of twenty-five top wines of the Bordeaux region – now stands 710% above its 1975 level. The wines in the index are of the 1961, 1966 and 1970 vintages and are mostly from the Médoc (see page 220). To the annoyance of wine buffs, news of their remarkable performance as investments has spread and much of the buying is now done by people who have no intention of drinking the wines they acquire.

The rapid rate of growth has recently attracted publicity though, as the table below shows, claret prices have been climbing fast for some time.

Period	Annual Growth %
1950–5	7.1
1955–60	5.4
1960–5	14.9
1965–70	13.1
1970–5	19.2
1975–80	25.8
1980–5	20.7

Like any other wine-growing nation the French praise their wines to the heavens. In doing so, however, every serious wine-drinker would have to agree that they were justified. Their vineyards have probably been tended more lovingly than any land on earth, and in return they produce some of the wonders of the gastronomic world.

The French, who have a passion for classifying every kind of produce from artichokes to oysters, dealt with the wines of the Médoc in 1855. Sixty wines were given the rank of great classed growth – *grand cru classé* – and were arranged in five sections known as first growths, second growths and so on. Thereafter came several hundred so-called bourgeois growths, still good wines by any standard but lacking the distinction of the top sixty.

Almost exactly the same vineyards are to be found in each class today as in 1855, and this proves how near to impossible it is to upgrade the conditions that nature has provided. Apart from the composition of the soil, the microclimate is vitally important to the culture of the vines. When wine buffs claim to know just where in a particular valley a wine has been produced, this need not be dismissed as affectation. The palate can be taught to discern little nuances of taste just as the eye can be trained to look for the subtler points of a painting. Vines situated fifty yards from each other can produce fundamentally different wines. The soil and subsoil may have changed over that distance, as well as the exposure to sun, wind and rain.

At one time or another vines have been planted in nearly every corner of France in the hope of producing wines to match the great names of Bordeaux. Many regions are of course famous for different kinds of wine – Burgundy, Champagne and Moselle for instance – and drinkable wines can be produced in many areas. But, for all its mystique, wine is just one

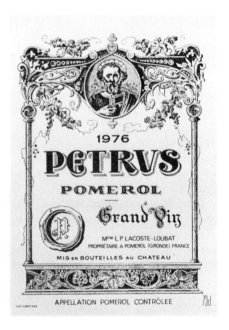

216

more agricultural commodity and current overproduction in France makes viticulture economically unattractive at the moment, unless, of course, it is possible to find that magic combination of soil and climate enabling wine to be produced that can be sold at premium prices. No such sites have been found for well over a hundred years and it is reasonable to assume that none will be found in the future.

For investment purposes then, one important hurdle has been cleared. There is no real danger of any vineyards coming into production that could compete with those currently producing the classic wines. Not only is the area of production effectively fixed, so too is the quantity of wine per acre that may be sold under its regional name.

The complicated *appellation contrôlée* system allows on average a maximum of 2250 bottles of wine per acre to be made in the Bordeaux area. The limit can be raised or lowered in years when both quality and quantity are exceptional. For the great classed growths, reputation is so important that in poor years, such as 1963 and 1965, many châteaux will sell no wine under their own label, preferring to let it go under the title of *Bordeaux supérieur*. The greatest châteaux are usually able to make a tolerably good wine even in bad years, but these are of little interest to connoisseurs and their record as investments has been mediocre.

Much has been written about speculation in wine, yet only once has there been a sharp fluctuation in the market and even then 'the speculators', those handy scapegoats, were not really to blame. Rivalry between vineyards owned by two Rothschild cousins had been simmering since 1855 when Château Mouton-Roths-child was classed as a second growth while Château Lafite was ranked a first growth. Baron Philippe de Rothschild, the owner of Château Mouton-Rothschild, had tried, unsuccessfully in 1971 to stop the spiralling in wine prices by offering his previous year's vintage at an artificially low price. In 1972 he changed tactics, reckoning that by offering his second growth wine at a higher price than the first growth Château Lafite, and using the market's acceptance of this differential, he could prove the superiority of his own wine. After waiting a few days Baron Philippe capped Lafite's opening price of 110,000 francs a tonneau (about £7 a bottle) by 10,000 francs. The ploy worked and Mouton-Rothschild was given first growth status in 1974.

Price differentials between the classed growths had been established for well over a hundred years, so it was not long before the *vignerons* of Bordeaux were claiming, 'If Mouton-Rothschild is worth X, my wine must be worth at least Y', and prices for wines of all qualities began to lift off. The bubble burst in 1973 when owners of first growths tried to charge the same or more for their 1972 wines even though they were worse than the 1971 wines.

Prices in the auction room rose across the board during 1972 but many fell by 30% or more the following year. A strong recovery in 1974 was followed by a dip in 1975. Since then the market has enjoyed steady growth.

There are three main reasons why wine prices have risen and these hold good for the future. First, fine wines improve as they age, and naturally become worth more as they taste better. The improvement comes about because wine contains living organisms whose behaviour determines its life

cycle. Precisely when a wine will reach its peak will depend on how it has been made. The tendency nowadays is for even the greatest wines to be made in such a way that they reach their best within ten or fifteen years rather than in the twenty or thirty years which was required by the demands of vinification used in the 1950s. No one pretends that the resulting wines are better for having a shorter period of development; it is simply that the costs of financing wine stocks, whether borne by growers, merchants or consumers, are now so high that no one can afford to wait while the 'long haul' wines inch their way towards maturity.

Fine wines will hold their peak, once reached, for many years. The market, however, does not discriminate between those that have reached their peak and those on their way

towards it, since the rates of appreciation are about the same for both.

The second reason for expecting fine wine prices to continue their climb is that the wine-drinking universe itself is expanding. Although some of the cheaper brands which serve as an introduction to new wine-drinkers might be expected to put them off wine for life, the number of wine-drinkers grows year by year. Sooner or later most will taste a great wine and are not likely to forget the experience. From that moment, all of them may be classed as potential buyers of fine wine. Some become actual, if irregular, buyers and thereby drive up demand for the limited supplies.

Thirdly, wine growers are just as exposed to inflation as others in the agriculture business. Insofar as demand permits, they will push for higher prices for each new vintage.

Such price increases as they are able to secure are bound to affect the price structure of the whole market including that for older wines. Existing wine stocks are therefore more or less direct beneficiaries of inflation.

For all these reasons the investment outlook for fine claret could hardly be better. It should be remembered, however, that one or two estates can have a disastrous vintage even when an outstanding year is proclaimed for Bordeaux wines generally. With that proviso, investors would do well to concentrate on the five first-growth châteaux, the thirteen second growths and three exceptional châteaux outside the Médoc area. These are Château Cheval Blanc and Château Ausone in St Emilion, and Château Pétrus in Pomerol. This last is the current glamour stock of the claret market, a case of the 1961 vintage having fetched a record £8800 for

a case of a dozen bottles in 1984, making the cost of a single glass £150.

An investor can buy wine at any stage of its development. Auctions provide an efficient two-way market in physical wines of any age. The expenses of an in-and-out investment including selling commission, buyer's premium and taxes fall in the 20% to 25% range. Between them, Christie's and Sotheby's now hold regular sales in London, Geneva, Amsterdam and Chicago. Prices more or less conform to an international pattern and opportunities for arbitrage are few. Just as traders in antiquities squatting in the dusty markets of the Middle East can be seen clutching the latest priced catalogues from Christie's antiquities auctions for reference, so the latest wine prices move quickly along the international grapevine.

But investors get their first chance to buy Bordeaux wines six months or so after the grapes have been picked. UK wine merchants offered the 1985 vintage in the spring of 1986. The wine is offered *en primeur*, which means that at the time of offer the wines are maturing in barrels at the château. The investor receives a piece of paper establishing his title to however many cases of a certain wine when it is shipped in two or three years' time.

Investor-drinkers in Britain evolved a trading cycle many years ago which enables them, after their initial outlay, to drink fine wines for nothing. They simply buy *en primeur* from their wine merchant and leave the wines in store with him. Five or so years later they take their profit on half of their holdings by selling at auction, keep the other half for drinking and reinvest the proceeds of sale in younger wines.

Within the overall upward trend for claret prices there is sometimes a seasonal dip in the early months of the year, largely as a result of the Christmas and New Year festivities. Quite apart from timing, seasoned wine investors resort to a variety of tactics. A case of six magnums tends to fetch quite a bit more at auction than twelve ordinary-sized bottles (75 centilitres) of the same wine, mainly because wine is reckoned to mature better in the larger bottle. Many investors therefore buy magnums in the first place. Furthermore, investors tempted to consume part of their holdings will think longer before drawing the cork on a £200 magnum than a £100 bottle.

Market forces also dictate that when the price of a wine reaches £500–£750 a case, single bottles of the same wine will fetch proportionately more, sometimes as much as 25%. It may therefore pay investors to pitch straight into cases of very expensive wine which they can split up for sale later. It is also clear that wine buffs prefer, and often pay a little more for, wines in their original wooden cases. Investors should therefore buy and keep their wines in these cases.

Only those with long experience of tasting young wines are able to forecast with any accuracy the eventual style and quality of a young and potentially great wine. Moreover, wines do not always develop as expected. The 1975 clarets, for instance, are taking longer to reach their peak than was originally anticipated and this has held back their market value. Investors in immature wine should therefore monitor the progress of their holdings in the wine press.

The asterisked vintages were exceptional in nearly all Bordeaux districts. In the other years very fine wines were also made. Investors should consult works listed under Further Reading for detailed reports on the individual châteaux and districts within the Bordeaux region.

Leading Investment Clarets

First Growths

Ch. Lafite
Ch. Latour
Ch. Margaux
Ch. Mouton-Rothschild
Ch. Haut-Brion

Second growths

Ch. Brane Cantenac
Ch. Lascombes
Ch. Léoville Barton
Ch. Léoville-Poyferré
Ch. Pichon-Longueville-Baron
Ch. Pichon-Lalande
Ch. Rauzan-Gassies
Ch. Ducru-Beaucaillou
Ch. Cos d'Estournel
Ch. Montrose
Ch. Gruaud-Larose
Ch. Rausan-Ségla

Selected third, fourth and fifth growths

Ch. Palmer
Ch. Giscours
Ch. La Lagune
Ch. Talbot
Ch. Beychevelle
Ch. Lynch-Bages
Ch. Cantemerle

From outside the Médoc

Ch. Ausône
Ch. Cheval Blanc
Ch. Pétrus

Top Bordeaux Vintages

*1961	1979
1962	1981
*1966	*1982
*1970	1983
*1975	1985
1978	

*Exceptional years

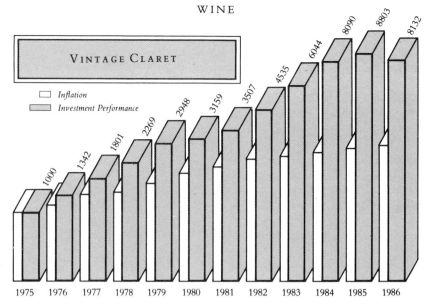

VINTAGE CLARET

□ Inflation
▨ Investment Performance

1000 1342 1801 2269 2948 3159 3507 4535 6044 8090 8803 8132

1975 1976 1977 1978 1979 1980 1981 1982 1983 1984 1985 1986

Components: all first and second growths, and Châteaux Palmer, Giscours, La Lagune, Talbot, Beychevelle, Lynch Bages, Cantemerle, Ausone, Cheval Blanc and Pétrus of the 1961, 1966 and 1970 vintages

Champagne

Any wine that improves over the long term, such as claret and port, seems a natural choice for investment. Vintage champagne, which hardly improves at all and may even deteriorate after a certain age, would therefore seem quite unsuitable. Yet supplies of vintage champagne are limited and demand is rising. Furthermore, wine drinkers more or less expect champagne to follow the market trend of claret and port.

An index of twenty-five vintage champagnes from among the dozen best-known firms or *grandes marques* – Moët & Chandon, Mumm, Krug, Piper-Heidsieck, Perrier-Jouët, Taittinger, Louis Roederer, Laurent Perrier, Lanson, Veuve Clicquot, Bollinger and Pol Roger – and based on a number of vintage years of the 1950s and 1960s, is showing a rise of 470% since 1975.

Prices per case of a dozen 75-centilitre bottles range from £200 up to £1000 for a case of Dom Pérignon 1955 (made by Moët & Chandon).

Many pleasant sparkling white wines are now made by the *méthode champenoise* in California, Italy, Spain and even in France. Yet the reputation of real French champagne seems unassailable.

The Champagne region lies ninety miles east of Paris and comprises some 15,000 vineyards, some no larger than a tennis court. Though these rarely change hands, the going rate is now about £30,000 an acre. Every year the *vignerons* sell their produce to the 120 different champagne houses who blend and market the wine. The dozen leading firms account for 80% of all champagne made and investors will find their wines more marketable.

US investors should not be tempted by the fancy packaging of 'de luxe' champagnes often retailed at twice or more the going rate for regular nonvintage champagne. Connoisseurs have seldom found these to justify any premium at all and regard them as clever marketing gimmicks.

The special status of French champagne among sophisticated drinkers is not based on gimmicks, though nobody finds it easy to explain exactly how it has been earned. Any alcohol consumed to excess will make a person drunk. But drinking patterns vary as widely as the effects the drinks produce. Some drinkers go for the quick knockout with a burst of cocktails around the happy hour, knowing that the quality of life will take a dive soon afterwards. By contrast, any poll of seasoned drinkers will confirm the unique ability of French champagne to raise the spirits, hold them in a state of mild euphoria and return them to earth without penalty a few hours later.

Whatever the effect, the making of champagne comes close to a miracle. It is a blend of wines from up to fifty different vineyards, many of which, tasted on their own, are far from pleasant. It is the exceptional skill of the blender that turns these unpromising ingredients into a drink that is far greater than the sum of its parts.

The wine is made principally from the white Chardonnay and the black Pinot Noir and Pinot Meunier grapes, the juice being drained off before the skins have time to colour the wine. Not only is champagne a blend of grape-varieties and vineyards, it is also a blend of different years. Wine is kept in reserve from earlier years so that whatever the following harvest may bring the big champagne houses will be able to produce the style of champagne for which they are well known year after year.

Wine made from different years will be a non-vintage champagne and must not be sold for a year after it has been bottled. In practice the leading houses keep their non-vintage wines in bottle for at least three years before shipment.

In certain years when weather conditions have been perfect and a maker can get hold of all the wines he needs to create a memorable blend, he will declare a vintage year, sometimes as early as six months after the harvest. Grapes harvested in that year only will go to make up the wine, giving the vintage its own special character. This is appreciated by knowledgeable drinkers who consider the 20% premium paid for such wines to be worthwhile. French law requires vintage wines to be kept in bottle three years before being sold, but again the leading houses invariably hold them longer.

The sparkle of champagne is the result of the second fermentation, encouraged by adding a little yeast and cane sugar, which takes place inside the bottle. During this time bottles are stacked upside down and turned regularly to allow the floating particles to deposit themselves in the neck of the bottle.

When the maker considers the fermentation has gone on long enough he carries out the procedures known as *dégorgement* and *dosage*. The wine in the neck of the bottle is frozen, the cork removed and the deposit ejected. The bottle is then replenished with a dose of cane sugar dissolved in mature champagne and a new cork forced in. The size of the dose varies between 0.1% and 10% depending on the preference of each market. Very sweet champagne, usually marked *doux* or *riche* on the label, is nowadays served mainly with desserts but was once the favourite champagne of Tsarist Russia. The taste for very dry champagne, marked *brut*, dry, or *nature*, originated in England but is now widespread. Intermediate tastes are catered for, but for investment *brut* is the right choice.

About 20% of all champagne produced in the last ten years has been designated 'vintage' and investment interest in these wines is growing – even though it is clear that once the *dégorgement* has removed the substances that enable the wine to develop, no significant improvement can occur. Investing in vintage champagne is therefore largely irrational; the case rests on its cachet, rarity and the supposition that the price trend of recent years will be maintained.

No champagne house would recommend keeping its vintage wines for more than ten years; indeed the longer the bottles are kept the more likely they are to have become undrinkable. A case of champagne dating from the 1930s would now be unlikely to yield more than six good bottles. Investing in the older vintages is therefore a high-risk activity and some holders decide it is safer to sell it than open it. A drinkable bottle would in any case have become a very different wine to what its makers intended – a thin, golden yellow, barely effervescent drink, closer to a liqueur than a wine. Yet the curiosity value, cachet and even the taste are enjoyed by a small coterie of champagne buffs.

The United States now consumes about 25% of all French champagne exported. Demand for vintage champagne in the United States has not been strong to date, though the picture could well change as more and more Americans become wine buffs. Whereas in Europe the word champagne can only be used to describe wines originating from one small area of northeastern France, in the United States the seller of any sparkling white wine, however unpalatable, may, and often does, call his product champagne. Americans have therefore been under the impression that champagne was a generic term for all sparkling white wines, from

which the French variety stood out as the most expensive.

Although the quantity of champagne produced in any one year can vary from 80 million bottles (1978) to 300 million (1983), the champagne houses are keen to maintain the rare and special image of vintage champagne. There is consequently no danger of the market being swamped. The *code du vin* allows the champagne houses to declare as vintage up to 80% of the wine made in any one year; in practice the amount declared is often in the region of 10%.

Vintages are declared four or five years after the year in which the grapes are picked. The excellent 1983 *vendange* was also the largest on record, so even if vintages are declared in 1988–9 the wines will not be as rare as many of the earlier years recommended for investment.

Evidence is mounting of substantial quantities of champagne being held by shippers as well as by private individuals for investment. Prices are almost certain to rise in line with wines such as claret and port which actually improve with age. All the same, investors should remember that the argument for buying vintage champagne is by no means rational and they should take account of the risks.

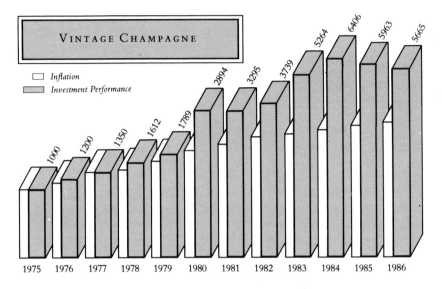

VINTAGE CHAMPAGNE

□ Inflation
▨ Investment Performance

1000 1200 1350 1612 1789 2894 3295 3739 5264 6406 5963 5665

1975 1976 1977 1978 1979 1980 1981 1982 1983 1984 1985 1986

Components: Bollinger 1959, 1961, 1962, 1964, 1966, 1969; Veuve Clicquot 1961, 1964, 1966; Dom Pérignon 1955, 1959, 1961, 1964; Charles Heidsieck 1959, 1962, 1964, 1966; Krug 1955, 1959, 1961, 1962, 1964, 1966; Moët & Chandon 1962, 1966; Louis Roederer 1961, 1966, 1969

Vintage Port

Vintage port has risen by 600% since 1975, putting it in line with fine claret and champagne. The annual growth rate of 19% owes nothing to buying by the Americans who are only just discovering the glories of vintage port.

Port is a wine fortified with grape brandy that was 'invented' by the English in Portugal three hundred years ago. Some 100 litres of brandy are added to every 450 litres of wine, partly to arrest the fermentation so that some of the sugar in the grape-juice is not converted into alcohol, and partly to boost the alcoholic content. Sometimes when the wine

shippers of Oporto know they have made an exceptional wine they 'declare a vintage', and the wines made in those years are the ones the English have made it their business to drink. Twenty-eight vintage years have been declared so far this century, sometimes by only two shippers, sometimes by twenty or more. Vintage ports can take twenty years or more to reach their peak of maturity, so the English have always tended to buy port young and watch it grow in quality and value over long periods. In this way port became the archetypal investment wine.

The vintage port index is made up

of the 1945, 1955, 1960, 1963 and 1970 wines shipped by the ten leading firms in Oporto. These are Cockburn, Croft, Dow, Fonseca, Graham, Martinez, Quinto do Noval, Sandeman, Taylor and Warre. Britain took the largest quantity of these wines though small shipments were made to most Western countries.

In the United States some liquor stores keep vintage port for the benefit of customers who know what's what, but it can be hard to find. For in some parts of the United States port is still thought of as a wino's drink – a cut above methylated spirits perhaps, but a drink with an unsavoury image all the same. Californian and other imitations of Portuguese non-vintage port tended to have a grapey raisin flavour and were a pale shadow of the real thing. Since the 1970s there have been promising developments in Californian port though it presents no serious threat to the original Portuguese wine.

The trade has seen consumption in Britain fall from 50 million litres in the 1920s (and from 28 million in the 1793) to just 7 million today. Fortunately the French market has taken up the slack. Exports to France last year reached 23 million litres – nearly double the figure since 1975. Most of this is drunk as an apéritif and treated much like Dubonnet, Vermouth and so on. A good deal of it gets used in the kitchen. Surprisingly, the French show no interest in vintage port. The 1984 import figure was 12,000 litres, a total that could be explained by a single order from the British Embassy in Paris.

The case for investing in vintage port rests on its unassailable position in the UK market and the prospect of rising demand in the United States. But only vintage port is worth considering, for it is the finest 2% of all port made, blended from wines of outstanding quality.

The vines that produce this remarkable wine are grown on the harsh but beautiful mountainsides of the Douro valley. The grapes are gathered and in some cases trodden by peasants. The purists rightly maintain that squeezing the grapes by machine brings too much acid out of the stalks. Modern vinification methods are being phased in but nothing will speed the maturing process. The vintage wines will be bottled after two years in wooden cask but should be left another twenty before being drunk.

Non-vintage or wood ports are blends of different years and are also matured in wooden casks. They make a superb drink but improve no further once they are bottled and are therefore unsuitable for investment. Most are either tawny, ruby or white. Tawny is a rich mahogany colour; ruby is a blend of rich, fruity wines, while white is made from white grapes and is golden in colour. A drier version of this, to be served chilled as an apéritif, was introduced after the war. The age of these wood ports varies from three to twenty years, but because the process of blending young wines with old has gone on for so long, some may contain wines that are over a century old.

Vintage port by contrast is bottled together with all the colouring matter which forms into a crust inside the bottle and makes it essential to decant before drinking. Connoisseurs rhapsodise over these wines, but on the whole are content to drink them in small quantities. At £50 or more a bottle the decision may be forced on them though the strength and sweetness play a part.

In Portugal today, the port trade is still dominated by English firms, three of which – Croft, Taylor and Warre – have been in business there since the 17th century. But there can be no doubt that the English shippers – sometimes known as the portocracy – were slow to develop new markets earlier this century. For many of them, the idea of advertising was almost too vulgar to contemplate. When Sandeman broke ranks in 1928 and used the famous silhouette of a Portuguese Don in cape and wide-brimmed hat to promote their wines,

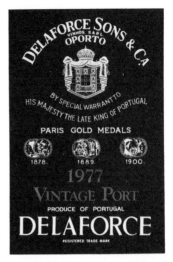

there were bitter feelings and snide remarks about 'grocer's port'. But it was no coincidence that Sandeman rapidly outgrew its rivals.

The Second World War interrupted shipments of port to Britain and the enormous market of the 1920s and 1930s, when the favourite drink of millions of women pub-goers was a port and lemonade, was lost forever. After the war, cocktail and sherry parties became fashionable, while 'British' wines, made with imported grapes and grape juice, which escaped the heavy duty paid on port, put further pressure on the market.

The ideal investment scenario for vintage port would include strongly rising demand for non-vintage port in the UK, for, in theory, every drinker of non-vintage port could one day trade up if he had the means. Yet the static demand for non-vintage port has left the top of the market unaffected. Furthermore, since the recovery of the pound from its all time low of $1.05 in early 1985, port prices have held up well, suggesting that the increases of recent years did not depend on Americans buying 'cheaply' while the pound was weak.

Apart from the plateaux of 1981–2 and 1985–6, the price trend has risen smoothly. The independent strength of the London market underwrites a forecast of 15% annual growth for the foreseeable future.

The Background

The English link with Portuguese wine goes back to the twelfth century when some crusaders *en route* for the Holy Land put into Oporto for supplies. After softening them up with wine, the Bishop appealed to their piety and greed, asking them to help drive the heathen Moors from Lisbon. In return for the 'spoils of the city' – in other words, permission to loot – the English agreed to stay.

But it was the recurring Anglo-French wars that gave port its real opening. Apart from beer, claret had been the Englishman's favourite drink ever since Gascony (including Bordeaux) came under English rule in the twelfth century. But supplies were often interrupted. In a sequence of tit-for-tat sanctions Charles II of England finally banned the import of French wine. But a treaty had only recently been signed in 1654 allowing the English to trade freely with Portugal and her colonies. Apart from the trading opportunities this opened up in wine, it gave the English the chance to buy slaves in West Africa and sugar from Brazil.

The English residents seized their chance. Wine known as 'red Portugal' had already been supplied to the Navy as a 'beverage for sailors' but had not been highly rated in England. English families began to establish themselves in Oporto at the end of the seventeenth century and created a colony which, though never part of the British Empire, was accorded special rights and privileges. They planted vineyards along the banks of the Douro which produced fuller and bigger wines. Small quantities of brandy began to be added to stabilize the wine for the sea-journey to England and by the early years of the eighteenth century business in Oporto was booming.

The lowliest Portuguese farmers sold their wines for good prices in Oporto and 'bought cloaths of the richest brocades of France and strutted with them in the streets like so many Peacocks'. But if the poor farmers did well, the Jesuits made a killing. They owned the best vineyards, were more skilful at making the wine and sold it for higher prices in England where it was known as 'priest port'.

The English in Oporto also prospered. Ships trading with America would put into Oporto and barter a black slave for a pipe of port (about 550 litres). But in Portugal as elsewhere the English were slow to fraternize with the natives and rarely learned the language. They had some cause for reserve, for the Portuguese were fanatically religious at the time and had on several occasions kidnapped English Protestant children in order to bring them up as Catholics and so save their souls. After strong protests, the English community was dumbfounded to find that a new Decree of 1706 forbade the kidnapping of children under seven but regarded any older children, who would then be free to choose their religion, as fair game.

Back home in England, hostility towards the French had grown to the point where to drink claret at all was considered unpatriotic, and from this time the loyal toast was always drunk in port. The Methuen Treaty of 1703 allowed Portuguese wines into England at one third less duty than was levied on French wines, and port became even more a part of English life.

Dr Johnson was proud of being a 'three bottle a day man', though what he drank was not the port we know today. It was a drier wine, probably closer to Burgundy in taste and was drunk during the meal – in Dr Johnson's case, no doubt, before and after as well.

Yet even two hundred years ago port's image was presenting problems. Prime Minister William Pitt suffered acutely from gout, and this affliction was put down to his heavy intake of port. No medical evidence for such a link has ever been found, yet this regrettable effect of gout is something every English schoolboy has always 'known' and the myth persists today.

Leading Vintages since 1945

1945	A great and classic year. Big and powerful rivalling 1912.	1967	Plenty of breeding and style.
1947	A fine and delicate vintage.	1970	A superb year.
1950	Good sound vintage.	1977	Exceptional vintage – the best of the 1970s.
1955	One of the greatest of the century.	1980	Fine, well balanced and promising.
1960	Sound and well balanced.	1982	A good year with excellent potential.
1963	A truly great vintage, full-bodied with tremendous colour and freshness.		

Further Reading

Michael Broadbent, *Great Vintage Wine Book* (London, 1982)

Hugh Johnson, *The World Atlas of Wine* (London, 1971)

Patrick Forbes, *Champagne* (London, 1967)

Jeffrey Benson and Alastair Mackenzie, *Sauternes* (London, 1979).

Serena Sutcliffe (ed.), *André Simon's Wines of the World* (London, 1981)

Wyndham Fletcher, *Port. An Introduction to its History and Delights* (London, 1978)

Jeffrey Benson and Alastair Mackenzie, *The Wines of Saint-Emilion and Pomerol* (London, 1983)

Wine Merchants

Corney & Barrow Ltd
118 Moorgate
London EC2
01-638 3125

Hedges & Butler Ltd
153 Regent Street
London W1
01-734 4444

La Vigneronne
105 Old Brompton Road
London SW7
01-589 6113

Findlater, Mackie & Todd
Findlater House
Wigmore Street
London W1
01-935 9264

Adnams
The Crown
High Street
Southwold
Suffolk
0502 724222

Lay & Wheeler Ltd
6 Culver Street West
Colchester
Essex
0206 67261

Justerini & Brooks Ltd
61 St James's Street
London SW1
01-493 8721

Saccone & Speed
32 Sackville Street
London W1
01-734 2061

Laytons Ltd
20 Midland Road
London NW1
01-388 5081

Christopher & Co Ltd
4 Ormond Yard
London SW1
01-930 5557

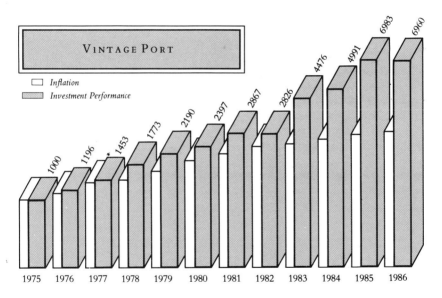

VINTAGE PORT

☐ Inflation
▨ Investment Performance

1000 1196 1453 1773 2190 2397 2867 2826 4476 4991 6983 6960

1975 1976 1977 1978 1979 1980 1981 1982 1983 1984 1985 1986

Components: Cockburn, Croft, Dow, Fonseca, Graham, Martinez, Quinto do Noval, Sandeman, Taylor and Warre of the following vintages (when shipped): 1945, 1955, 1960, 1963 and 1970

BOOKS

FOR MOST people, books are a means of communication, a source of pleasure, and perhaps even of enlightenment. For book-collectors on the other hand they stand for something even more important. They are tangible evidence of human thoughts, ideas and achievements, a physical counterpart of creativity which they feel a strong urge to possess.

As well as being concerned with the text, collectors of books are attracted to their binding, illustration and printing. But even when a book has virtually no physical appeal – as, for example, the first edition of Emily Bronte's *Wuthering Heights* – they willingly pay a thousand pounds for it even though the text may be available in paperback.

Though literacy seems unremarkable today, it is worth remembering that the ability to communicate by making marks on paper is taken in some primitive societies for black magic. In 1877 Henry Morton Stanley was nearly killed by Congolese tribesmen after he had been caught 'making medicine on paper'. They demanded his notebook be burnt. As it happened he gave them his precious edition of Shakespeare to burn – for they could not tell the difference – and he was soon back in their favour.

The Congolese tribesmen were on to something important. They recognized, albeit unconsciously, as people have before and since, that words and ideas are powerful and even dangerous. The fear of them and attempts to destroy them recur throughout history. In the 16th century the Spaniards all but annihilated the written culture of the Mayan people of Central America. And by burning so-called degenerate literature in the 1930s the Nazis were only engaged in an extreme form of suppression and censorship that is widely practised today.

The result of this widespread reverence for the printed word is that a huge international market in rare books flourishes today, divided into as many sectors as there are spheres of human interest. The principal fields of collecting have hardly changed over the years. Fifteenth-century printed books, known as incunabula (that is, things from the cradle, or early days of printing) are a scholarly taste. Prices range from around £200 for minor, incomplete or damaged works to perhaps several million pounds for a copy of the Gutenberg Bible – the first book ever printed dating from 1455. Printing spread fast through Europe – by 1500 twenty thousand editions had been published – and collectors mostly go for the works that were printed in their own towns or countries. Prices for incunabula have risen steadily over the years though this is unlikely to become a fast-growing market.

English literature is a mainstream subject for collectors though fine editions of Chaucer and Shakespeare are unobtainable or unaffordable and works by lesser figures of the period, mainly of interest to academics, have been dull performers in the market. Of the 17th century writers, Milton is in greatest demand though some of his later works are not expensive. Prices for the lesser Restoration poets have dropped.

The first period of English literature that is easy to collect is the 18th century. Postgraduate students in need of neglected writers on which to base their doctoral theses have unearthed interesting material though prices for even the big names have been static for years. *Pamela* by Samuel Richardson is considered the first novel in the English language and fetches up to £5000. Richardson, a printer, was working on a volume of letters for use by those who could not write and is presumed to have been drafting number 139 – from a Father to a Daughter in Service, on hearing of her Master's attempting her Virtue – when it occurred to him that a series of fictional letters home from a girl in service with a lecherous squire would make an amusing read. The subject matter was well judged for nearly every potential reader employed servants. In the end the virtuous Pamela is married to the supposedly reformed Squire B. The seminal work in its genre, *Pamela* is the highest priced of Richardson's novels – *Clarissa* and *Sir Charles Grandison* still selling for a few hundred pounds. Most of the first editions by Henry Fielding, Laurence Sterne and Tobias Smollett also sell in the low hundreds.

Prices for poetry of the first half of the 18th century have been climbing, as often happens, following the publication of an exhaustive bibliography of the subject. Reference works for most sectors already exist and give buyers this necessary reassurance in what are often bibliographically complex fields.

The 19th century was being worked over by collectors well before it had run its course. Among the novelists, Dickens and Thackeray are the popular choice with new collectors though prices have barely stirred in ten years. The popular fiction of the mid-19th century – usually published in three volumes and known as three-deckers – has not climbed far either and the greatest potential probably lies in modern first editions. The craze for these entered a new phase in the 1890s when, according to the *Literary Review*, 'it reached the extremest form of childishness ... every little volume of drivelling verse becomes a more or less hazardous speculation and the book market itself a stock exchange in miniature'.

Science and Medicine is a favourite field which takes in many of the landmarks in the history of the human race. First editions of works by Vesalius, Copernicus, Harvey, Darwin, Freud and other household names now command great sums. A sector closely related to Science and Medicine, known as the History of Ideas, includes philosophers and economic and political theorists such as John Locke, Adam Smith, John Stuart Mill and Karl Marx, and has been supported over the years by institutional buying – mainly universities – but is vulnerable to cuts in funds available for such purposes.

Medical books have an almost ghoulish fascination. From the comparative safety of the 1980s the operations performed several hundred years ago on compliant and credulous patients look horrific. Surgeons of the period were often floundering in the dark or simply repeating the senseless and sadistic 'treatments' sanctioned by long usage.

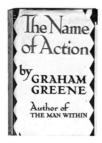

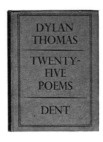

Just occasionally a breakthrough would be made and its first publication would create a stir in medical circles. Now, centuries later, the records of these discoveries are coveted by collectors and prices for the great watershed publications have soared. Vesalius' *De Humani Corporis Fabrica*, published in Basel in 1543, started a revolution by asserting the need for independent observations in anatomy and clinical medicine. An exceptional first edition recently sold for £44,000.

One glance at Braunschweig's *The Noble Experience of the Vertuous Handy Wark of Surgeri*, published in its first English edition in 1525, makes the reader especially grateful not to have been born in the 16th century. Nevertheless, it is an important treatise and a good copy can fetch over £10,000.

There are many more accessible titles in the field. Edward Jenner's *An Inquiry into the causes and Effects of Variolae Vaccinae ... or Cowpox* (London, 1798), dealing with his method of vaccination, can still be bought for around £3000. In the same price-range comes William Withering's *An Account of the Fox-glove* (1785), which marks the beginning of the use of digitalis in cases of cardiac failure.

Even further down the scale come the vast majority of antiquarian medical books, most of them costing a few hundred pounds. A copy of Laennec's *De l'Auscultation* of 1819, which describes the first use of a stethoscope (originally a roll of stiff paper held to the patient's chest), may be bought for well under £1000. Edward Tyson's *Orang-Outang ... or the Anatomie of a Pygmie*, the first work to compare the anatomy of man and monkeys, is available for under £500 while Florence Nightingale's *Notes on Nursing* may be bought for around £100. Prices for medical books are picking up after the recession of 1979–82 but should only resume a modest rate of growth.

Travel and Natural History and colour-plate books of plants, birds and animals have generally been a strong market though prices reflect collectors' obvious and well-established preferences. Roses are more appealing, for instance, than herbs, and parrots are more appealing than spiders. The recent surge of interest in contemporary travel writers such as Bruce Chatwin, Dervla Murphy and Jan Morris has prompted several publishers to reprint the texts of famous early travellers. The effect of these reprints on the market for early editions will be negligible, just as the ready availability of other classics in paperback makes no impression on demand for their first editions. Besides, the appeal of many of the great topographical publications was based on lavish illustrations and these are not being reproduced.

The great masterpiece of natural history publishing remains John James Audubon's *Birds of America* which appeared from 1827 to 1838. Most of the original folios have been broken up and the 435 individual plates have become blue chips of the art-investment world. The latest price for a full set stands at $1.7 million. When sold individually, the plates range in price from $65,000 for the Wild Turkey down to $25,000 for the Virginian Partridge and down again to $900 for the Marsh Wren. The original aquatints are of double elephant folio size. Later lithographic editions have been printed and investors must be careful to establish what kind of print they are buying.

There was a time when 'breakers' were looked down on as the hyenas of the art market. They would take damaged or incomplete colour-plate books and sell off the prints individually. It seemed a sound idea since collectors are a fastidious lot and have little time for works in poor condition. It may be regrettable to split up a perfect set of Audubon's Birds or any complete set, yet the drive for profit is strong and for as long as dealers can make more from individual sales, the breakers will not be stopped. Eventually, when very few complete sets are left these may become more valuable than the sum of their separated parts.

Whereas during the 19th century American and British literature had shared a slightly prim elegance, there developed in the United States over the course of the 20th century a specifically American style. The racy new idiom that was born had a sharp edge, pace, wit, colour and depth which make its practitioners most collectable today.

But there are two distinct markets for modern American first editions. The larger, accounting for 90% of turnover, is concerned with medium- and low-quality books bought by collectors for under £250. Apart from a few high spots there has been little growth in this market since 1975. The other 10% is accounted for by wealthy and often eccentric book-lovers who pay astonishing prices for copies of the same books provided they are in sparkling new condition. The overall rise for books in this category has not been less than 300% and prices could keep climbing. The willingness to pay thousands of pounds for the privilege of owning first editions calls for some explanation anyway, but can a market based on such apparently irrational premises really be stable?

There can be good reasons for buying a first edition, and these would presumably include cases where the text in all subsequent editions was changed or incomplete, or where the printing, binding or some other physical characteristic was exceptionally fine. But collectors of modern first editions do not offer such explanations. For them a first edition brings to life a moment in the history of human communication and the mysterious thrill which that provides is reason enough.

One key question faces anyone considering first editions for investment. Will collectors buy fast enough to keep pace with the avalanche of print threatening to engulf us all? Over 75,000 new titles are published in the English language every year.

Even if the average number printed were just one thousand, that would mean a thousand million more first editions by the end of the century. Of course few titles in the trade and technical sector will be of interest to collectors. Yet, surprisingly, many non-fiction subjects, including the literature of television, computers, space travel, economics, chemistry and so on are now seriously collected.

In the literary field the flood may even be abating a little as publishers find they cannot break even on works by minor novelists. Of the hundreds of novelists who still get published very few will be in print in ten years' time and fewer still in fifty. One of the attractions of the literary field is that collectors can exercise their own taste and judgement. They can buy first editions inexpensively as they come out and if they spot the big prizewinners of the future and keep the books themselves in pristine condition they may make some useful profits.

Investors should be careful not to fall prey to the pseudo first-edition industry now flourishing in the United States. The idea is to create small limited editions where the ordinary first edition of an established author would be too large to arouse any real interest among collectors. If a new novel by John Updike were published today the first printing might be as high as 50,000. In such a case the publishers will do well, but they know they can also create a rare edition that will appeal to collectors.

This may be limited to one or two hundred copies and priced at around $75. If the marketing is handled right the books will go to a premium right away – similar to what happens on the stock market when an issue is oversubscribed.

Small publishing houses uncon-nected with the author's main publisher will sometimes pester the author for a minor work that they can turn into a limited edition. Although the resulting works are supposed to be fine press items over whose production extra special care is taken, the quality is sometimes mediocre. In these cases publishers are able to play on the obsession many collectors display for completeness. In the stamp world, albums are sometimes pre-printed with squares ready to receive the stamps of a particular set. Collectors hate to see blank spaces gaping at them from the page and usually acquire the missing stamps when the opportunity arises. Similarly, book-collectors tend to build collections of one or more authors. They always aim at a complete collection and therefore constitute a ready-made market for these editions. Completeness is the unconscious goal of all collecting even though in most fields it is unattainable.

The book market has become increasingly dominated by the question of condition. Any collector will naturally prefer a copy of a book in fine, clean condition to one in such poor shape that the dealers ironically describe it as a 'reading copy only'. Nevertheless, the premium collectors pay for superb copies has risen to a point of absurdity. It has also, in the case of 20th century first editions, inaugurated the cult of the dust-jacket. Premiums of 1000% and over have been paid for copies of a book with its wrapper in near-perfect condition, thus valuing the wrapper at ten times the book inside it. Some dealers are predicting a decline in this obsessional behaviour on the grounds that copies in the very best condition with dust-jacket are seen less often in the market. If the material isn't there to collect, so the reasoning goes, people will lose interest in it and prices will fall.

The two areas of 20th century American literature to have attracted most collectors over the last ten years are the 'Greats', including Ernest Hemingway, Scott Fitzgerald, William Faulkner and John Steinbeck, and 'escapist' literature. Although more collectors appear to be going for the 'Greats', this does not strangely enough seem to have been accompanied by any overall increase in prices in the mainstream of the market. William Faulkner is regarded as a barometer of the market. At least fifty collectable Faulkner works are sold at auction every year, but prices have declined by 20% since 1975. Over the same period Hemingway prices have crept up 20%. John Steinbeck has marked time. Scott Fitzgerald has performed best with a jump of perhaps 100% even in the middle-quality range. Whenever a book is made into a film or television series, prices for the first editions move up. Prices of *The Great Gatsby* and *Tender is the Night* have thus risen strongly.

Anyone looking for performance rather than pleasure from first editions should beware books priced below £20. Ninety-five per cent of such books are likely to remain static for many years. The other 5% in that price-range may be on the way up, but you need flair or clairvoyant powers to pick the right titles.

'Escapist' literature has been a growth field for many years. This includes science fiction, detective stories and fantasies ranging from Edgar Rice Burrough's *Tarzan of the Apes* to Anne McCaffrey's dragon stories of the 1970s; and from the British sector, Tolkien's *Lord of the Rings* and Richard Adams's *Watership Down*.

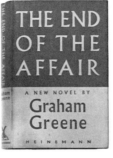

The masters of the detective story such as Raymond Chandler and Dashiell Hammett are bought by less literary collectors. The cult of the dust-jacket makes more sense in this sector than others. Most of the books in this class that were not originally published as paperbacks had lurid covers that now seem to encapsulate the image of hardboiled America of the 1940s and 1950s. Gaudy and lascivious ladies in transparent lingerie smoking cigarettes or fending off gun-toting private eyes adorn the wrappers. Nobody rates the art on these covers very highly, indeed art can seldom have been cruder. All the same it calls up the memory of a racy, tough and simple America to which many look back with growing affection.

Other big names in the field whose first editions are sought high and low are Ellery Queen, James T. Farrell, Ross Macdonald, John D. MacDonald and Mickey Spillane. There are no guarantees though that these names will appear in the charts in twenty years' time. Back in the 1930s most collectors of American fiction owned works by Booth Tarkington and Joseph Hergesheimer whose names are scarcely remembered today.

Price movements in the rare book market are particularly hard to monitor, partly because the same editions of a rare book do not pass through the market with any regularity and because, when they do, they are seldom in similar enough condition to draw meaningful conclusions from the prices they fetch.

Nevertheless, prices for a broad range of 20th century English first editions appearing in the catalogues of Bertram Rota Ltd – the leading London dealer in the field – have risen by 300% since 1975 and this may be taken as a rough measure of the change in the market over that period. The writers in the sample are a mixed bag including Samuel Beckett, Joseph Conrad, T. S. Eliot, Ian Fleming, Robert Graves, Graham Greene, James Joyce and Bernard Shaw. The variation in literary stature may be striking, yet all, for the time being at least, are highly collectable.

New stars are appearing in the firmament all the time. Among the writers whose first editions are keenly sought after are Martin Amis, Julian Barnes, William Boyd, Salman Rushdie, Graham Swift and D. M. Thomas. Prices for most are for the time being in the £10 to £50 range. The up-and-coming names in the poetry sector are Seamus Heaney, Andrew Motion, Geoffrey Hill and James Fenton. Of these, Heaney commands prices of up to £250 but most of the rest can still be bought for less than £50.

As for Nobel prizewinners, all were thought illustrious in their day, yet the list contains several writers whose literary reputations have fallen, among them Galsworthy and Pearl Buck. To their admirers, recent winners such as Isaac Bashevis Singer and Elias Canetti seem unassailable, yet they could well be downgraded by the next generation.

The literary world operates like a team of coroners that is continually revising its verdicts, which means a change in literary status and, indirectly, in market price. Since fashion is so fickle it may in the end require more luck than judgement to pick out the rising stars of the next century.

There is, however, a price-cycle, well known to dealers, through which most authors move. Their reputations grow during their lifetime and admiration for their work reaches a peak soon after they have died. Flattering obituaries draw collectors into the market who had hardly known their work, and the resulting boom can last five years or more. That, say the cynics, is the time to sell your holding of that author, for there may follow a period of stagnation or even falling prices that can last twenty years.

With modern first editions, associative interest is particularly important. A presentation copy, inscribed and signed, can be extremely valuable, especially if the recipient was famous. Some authors signed their work quite freely: others were loath to do so and that extra rarity enhances the value of the few they did sign. T. S. Eliot signed quite freely but usually made it clear that it was a solicited signature by writing 'inscribed for X' before it. A sharp-witted collector once handed Eliot a book of his own verse in a New York bookstore in the 1950s and when Eliot asked to whom it should be inscribed the collector replied, 'Just put, "To Allen Ginsberg".' Eliot did as he was asked and there came into being a wholly spurious but valuable presentation copy.

One problem investors need not worry about is forgery. To forge a book from scratch presents fiendish problems. Every detail from the paper, ink and type to the endpapers and binding needs to be imitated accurately enough to pass laboratory tests. Even if such an exercise were feasible it would hardly be a paying proposition. That is why in the book world the forger's activities have been confined to doctoring books in poor condition, replacing missing leaves and so on.

Even so, buyers should take the basic precautions. Specialist bibliographies covering most modern editions are available and these allow the prospective purchaser to collate the book – that is, to verify that the right number of leaves, plates and so on are present.

Further Reading

Alan G. Thomas, *Great Books and Book Collectors* (London, 1975)

Eric Quayle, *The Collector's Book of Books* (London, 1971)

Jean Peters (ed.), *Collectable Books: Some New Paths* (New York, 1979)

Grant Uden, *Understanding Book Collecting* (London, 1982)

William Rees-Mogg, *How to Buy Rare Books* (London, 1985)

Dealers

E. P. Goldschmidt & Co
64 Drayton Gardens
London SW10
01-737 2266
Early, illustrated and scientific books.

Pickering & Chatto Ltd
17 Pall Mall
London SW1
01-930 2515
English Literature, Science and Medicine, History of Ideas.

Bertram Rota Ltd
30 Long Acre
London WC2
01-836 0723
Modern first editions, private press books, literature.

Maggs Bros. Ltd
50 Berkeley Square
London W1
01-493 7160
Rare books and manuscripts of all periods.

Bernard Quaritch Ltd
5–8 Lower John Street
Golden Square
London W1
01-734 2983
Rare books and manuscripts of all periods.

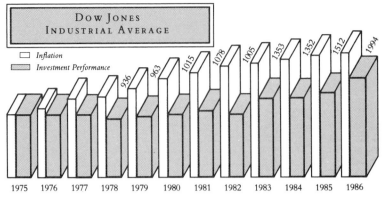

DOW JONES INDUSTRIAL AVERAGE

☐ Inflation
▨ Investment Performance

936 963 1015 1078 1005 1353 1352 1512 1994

1975 1976 1977 1978 1979 1980 1981 1982 1983 1984 1985 1986

Base. 1973–7 = 1000

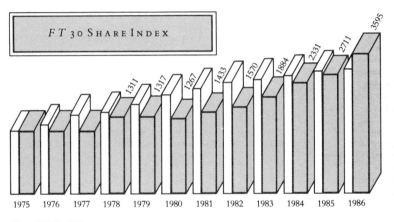

F T 30 SHARE INDEX

1311 1317 1267 1433 1570 1884 2331 2711 3505

1975 1976 1977 1978 1979 1980 1981 1982 1983 1984 1985 1986

Base. 1973–7 = 1000

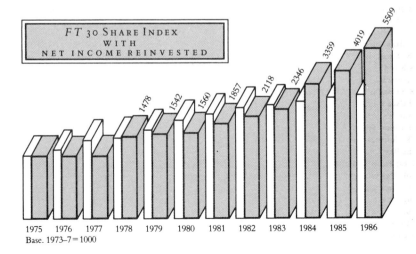

F T 30 SHARE INDEX
WITH
NET INCOME REINVESTED

1478 1542 1560 1857 2118 2346 3359 4019 5509

1975 1976 1977 1978 1979 1980 1981 1982 1983 1984 1985 1986
Base. 1973–7 = 1000

INVESTMENT PERFORMANCE TABLE

Sector	1975	1976	1977	1978	1979	1980	1981	1982	1983	1984	1985	1986
American Coins	1000	1237	1376	1505	1928	5492	7574	6437	6531	8729	9367	10616
Vintage Claret	1000	1342	1801	2269	2948	3159	3507	4535	6044	8090	8803	8132
American Impressionists	1000	1080	1150	1531	1511	2109	3515	4854	4880	5595	6707	7210
Vintage Port	1000	1196	1453	1773	2190	2397	2867	2826	4476	4991	6983	6960
18th Century English Painting: Portraits	1000	1085	1190	2015	1687	1511	3148	3150	3573	4863	5644	6208
Vintage Champagne	1000	1200	1350	1612	1789	2894	3295	3739	5264	6406	5963	5665
Georgian Furniture	1000	1300	1815	2062	1856	2062	2095	2332	3032	4093	5582	5582
FT 30 Share Index (net income reinvested)	1000	*	*	1478	1542	1560	1857	2118	2346	3359	4019	5509
English Watercolours	1000	1057	1118	1368	1493	1992	2798	3052	3528	4113	4849	5455
English Sporting Painting	1000	1066	1137	1194	1456	1773	2362	2291	2926	4012	4867	5354
American Painting (1910–40)	1000	1072	1150	1200	1294	1862	2899	2742	4202	4000	4681	5149
Meissen	1000	1127	1258	1427	1617	2050	2598	3112	3727	3951	4185	4708
French Impressionists	1000	1025	1054	1148	1600	1682	1832	1948	2374	3724	4272	4699
19th Century American Painting	1000	1130	1270	1535	1330	1670	2726	3639	3524	3725	4347	4564
Chinese Porcelain	1000	1003	1189	1720	3078	4012	4158	3846	3982	4319	4400	4359
20th Century English Painting	1000	1087	1181	1036	1495	1834	1991	2012	2446	2595	3781	4254
Old Master Prints	1000	1349	1535	2139	2141	2928	2374	2791	3260	3505	4206	4206
Regency Silver	1000	1221	1566	1585	2055	2968	2831	2806	2995	3573	4109	4109
German Expressionist Prints	1000	1349	1535	1702	1531	2021	1967	2158	2683	3402	4082	4082
17th Century Dutch and Flemish Painting	1000	1109	1199	1493	1934	2287	2035	1955	2025	2390	3248	3735
Victorian Furniture	1000	1150	1600	1900	2241	2486	2624	2800	3083	3374	3711	3711
German Expressionists	1000	1344	1805	1129	1913	1289	2827	2330	2481	3369	3286	2697
Victorian Painting	1000	1110	1230	1782	2236	2113	2031	2169	2481	2723	3316	3647
The New York School	1000	955	911	1040	1013	1048	1479	1396	2442	3070	3646	3646
The School of Paris	1000	945	880	1218	1050	1351	1404	1598	1675	2463	3357	3609
FT 30 Share Index	1000	*	*	1311	1317	1267	1433	1570	1884	2331	2711	3595
American Coins (excluding MS 65 Coins)	1000	1179	1271	1312	1613	2994	4651	3303	3401	4160	3946	3564
Modern Master Prints	1000	1349	1535	1581	1660	1882	1723	1821	2232	3287	3451	3451
The Surrealists	1000	1018	1038	1113	944	1238	1351	1224	1295	1739	3198	3438
18th and 19th Century American Silver	1000	1263	1345	1272	1676	1429	1531	1966	2352	2899	3426	3426
18th Century English Silver	1000	1060	1175	1271	1294	1838	2298	2315	2397	2925	3364	3364
Chelsea Porcelain	1000	1389	1398	1485	1662	1839	2061	2438	2613	2908	3053	3358
American Stamps	1000	1441	1738	2179	2778	2780	3824	3688	3577	3615	3577	3165
Victorian Silver	1000	1260	1432	1527	1675	1859	2875	2946	2996	2844	3123	3123
UK Consumer Price Index	1000	1165	1350	1462	1658	1956	2188	2377	2486	2610	2769	2885
The Barbizon School	1000	894	800	1291	1166	2328	2150	1953	1671	2331	3002	2700
Great Britain Stamps	1000	1279	1788	2457	5876	2822	3074	3153	2629	2191	2427	2450
Gold Price Index	1000	*	996	1305	2062	4145	3103	2533	2857	2432	2140	2293
Dow Jones Industrial Ave	1000	*	*	936	963	1015	1078	1005	1353	1352	1512	1994
English Coins	1000	1072	1149	1314	1504	1879	1781	1687	1680	1673	1673	1548
Ancient Greek and Roman Coins	1000	1055	1118	1233	1233	1416	1378	1328	1462	1355	1355	1355
Diamonds	1000	994	1171	1722	2762	4807	2845	1722	1565	1405	1253	1220

INDEX

Numbers in italics refer to illustrations